Take Me Home

Take Me Home

Protecting America's Vulnerable

Children and Families

Jill Duerr Berrick

OXFORD

UNIVERSITY PRESS

2009

OXFORD
UNIVERSITY PRESS

Oxford University Press, Inc., publishes works that further
Oxford University'sobjective of excellence
in research, scholarship, and education.

Oxford New York
Auckland Cape Town Dar es Salaam Hong Kong Karachi
Kuala Lumpur Madrid Melbourne Mexico City Nairobi
New Delhi Shanghai Taipei Toronto

With offices in
Argentina Austria Brazil Chile Czech Republic France Greece
Guatemala Hungary Italy Japan Poland Portugal Singapore
South Korea Switzerland Thailand Turkey Ukraine Vietnam

Copyright © 2009 Oxford University Press, Inc.

Published by Oxford University Press, Inc.
198 Madison Avenue, New York, New York 10016
www.oup.com

Oxford is a registered trademark of Oxford University Press

Library of Congress Cataloging-in-Publication Data
Berrick, Jill Duerr.
Take me home : protecting America's vulnerable children and families /
Jill Duerr Berrick.
p. cm.
Includes bibliographical references and index.
ISBN 978-0-19-532262-0 1. Foster home care—United States. 2. Foster children—
United States. 3. Child welfare—United States. I. Title.
HV881.B47 2008
362.73'30973—dc22

2008002540

9 8 7 6 5 4 3 2 1

Printed in the United States of America
on acid-free paper

To Keilah and Elijah and the promise of a better future for vulnerable children.

Acknowledgments

This book has been under construction for several years. Inspiration for many of the ideas was sparked by my colleagues participating in California's Child Welfare Redesign process and the Blue Ribbon Commission on Children in Foster Care. I thank all of the members of both of these esteemed groups for their thoughtful contributions to my own intellectual, professional, and personal growth.

Funding for the qualitative interviews was provided by the Stuart Foundations. Thanks go to Pat Reynolds-Harris, Program Officer at the foundation, for her commitment to understanding the lived experiences of families touched by child welfare.

I am grateful for the dedication of several graduate student assistants including Denicia Cormier, Ken Eisinger, Jennifer Garcia, Victoria Garcia, and Chelsea Neel, and to the always cheerful assistance of Loretta Morales. And a special thanks to Susan Stone and Gillian Lester for our productive and restorative writers' retreats.

I offer thanks to my husband for his patience with the process. I am blessed by the emotional and intellectual landscape of our lives. Importantly, our deep exchanges about child welfare policy past, present, and future have given me confidence to raise provocative questions, even if they land uncomfortably against the tide of conventional thought.

And finally, I extend my heartfelt gratitude to the women who spoke with me so honestly about their intensely personal lives. I hope that, in some small measure, their stories can inspire a lively debate and a positive resolution about how to best care for America's vulnerable children and families.

Contents

TAKE ME HOME

1

Securing a Safe Home for Children:
A New National Priority

"I knew my baby needed things, but he just wasn't a priority. He was not a priority."

Across the nation, children are in desperate trouble. The child welfare system, designed to protect and secure children's safety, is ill -prepared for the task. To make matters worse, the clamor for reform heard most urgently in child welfare circles is not likely to affect the well-being of the half-million children for whom Child Protective Services agencies are responsible.[1]

In state after state, children known to child welfare agencies die at the hands of their parents or caregivers,[2] abuse and neglect is investigated by authorities but untreated,[3] large numbers of children are removed from their homes to foster care, and many spend their childhoods separated from their birth families but never achieving permanence with others.[4] The crisis in foster care is so profound that no state has yet passed its federally mandated Child and Family Service Review;[5] two-thirds of states have seen class-action lawsuits to force their systems to change,[6] and unless dramatic reform occurs quickly, financial penalties will begin to accrue to states[7] and many more childhoods will be lost to a bureaucracy poorly equipped to manage the complexity of troubled families' lives.

The problems besetting child welfare systems are so profound and so seemingly limitless that reasonable people often disagree on the priorities for change, the pace of change, and the direction for change. As a result, the array of new initiatives in the field is dizzying. New reforms chase old reforms so quickly that line workers are often bewildered about which philosophy and plan of action prevails when working with individual families.

In the middle of the seeming cacophony of voices among advocates and professionals, policymakers are largely silent on promoting child welfare reform. Their reluctance to set a new course for child welfare stems in part from the complexity of the families. Children and families involved in child welfare have long-standing problems in multiple domains: many are drug-addicted or criminally involved; domestic violence is prevalent, many children have behavior problems, parents and children have health and mental health issues, and the vast majority of families are living under conditions of significant poverty.[8] When so many family issues are competing for center stage, lawmakers can be overwhelmed and many turn their attention elsewhere. Wading into the waters of intimate family relations is tricky policy business; in child welfare, public policy tensions inevitably emerge between the competing rights of parents and the needs of children. Thus, vilified by Democrats and Republicans alike, child welfare is uncomfortably ignored by politicians who shy away from the thorny and contentious problems that social workers address every day.

If policymakers are indisposed to tackle child welfare reform, they receive little encouragement to do otherwise from a sometimes indifferent and often ignorant public. Children in foster care make up about 1% of any state's child population.[9] Such a marginalized group is easy to overlook, and when the headlines that *do* bring child welfare into the public eye speak only to the tragedies of social worker error, unrecognized safety hazards, or bureaucratic bungling, public perceptions of hopeless family dysfunction and organizational failure tend to thrive.

Amid this struggling system – with a public policy milieu that is hesitant to promote leadership and a societal backdrop that is largely mute on the topic of child welfare – children and parents walk along a relatively lonely path as they wend their way through the "system" called child welfare. These are the families that try to cope with the mundane aspects of their everyday lives. Their stories are infrequently told in the clamor for policy reform.

Yet their story is important to tell if we are going to get it right; if we are going to improve the lives of our most vulnerable children. Take Amanda, for example.[10] We can not begin to appreciate the problems in child welfare unless we understand something about women like Amanda and the parenting they offer their children. Because parenting is an experience so many American adults share and it is a task many adults view as challenging under average conditions, to imagine raising young children while also battling the grip of poverty, homelessness, illiteracy, and drugs is almost incomprehensible. Most Americans do not know women like Amanda, but as she tells the story of her children's early years, we not only gain insight into the private struggles of individual families but also recognize the urgency of child welfare reform.

Amanda's Story

Amanda was raised in foster care. Shortly after emancipating as an adolescent, Amanda found herself pregnant and on the streets. While Amanda shuttled in and out of jail, baby Jaclyn lived with Amanda's drug-addicted sister or sometimes with a family friend. Amanda's parents had died years earlier, and there were no other family connections in her life. According to Amanda:

> I don't have parents. I don't have aunts, uncles. I don't have anyone. I had a sister, who was on drugs, who had about four kids, who had been taken this place, that place, this place.

Jaclyn moved around between friends' and relatives' homes for about 5 years. Then, Amanda gave birth to Jamar. As Amanda recounts it, the early months of Jamar's life were difficult:

> I came back out of jail, I had the baby, and I got the baby home from the hospital, but he had positive tox for cocaine.[11] When I brought him home, I was—everyone in the house was using—I didn't have nothing prepared for him. Nothing. As far as clothes, diapers, milk, nothing. And there was my addiction. I knew my baby needed things, but he just wasn't a priority. He was not a priority.
>
> I was stuck in the house. And the only drugs I could get was if I had money, or if I hustled and brought it in.[12] So there were nights of smoking dope. Jaclyn changing the diaper—a five-year-old—and until the disease progressed for all of us and the father was smoking drugs out on the street all day, and he'd bring me just a little bit. And I'd be tweakin' and want more. And I began to leave the children when they were sleepin' in the middle of the night.

Amanda and Jamar's father argued bitterly and Jaclyn regularly watched them assault one another. When a social worker showed up following a report of child abuse, Amanda and Jamar's father were in the middle of one of their fights.

And he threw a pair of scissors and they stuck in my head and I was standing there bleeding. And my daughter saw this happen. The social worker came, and we had to have another appointment.

The social worker returned the following day and Amanda and her children were gone. Amanda regularly left her 5-year-old in charge of the infant while she prostituted, exchanged sex for drugs, checked out while she was using drugs, or left the house for several hours at a time. She and her children moved from place to place, finally landing in a rundown SRO[13] where most of the residents were using. Months later, social workers returned, following a hotel desk clerk's child maltreatment report.

I didn't have a hustle, and I had my kids and a welfare check, and when that welfare check was gone, that food stamps was gone, that was it for me. And so I began to let guys come over when the kids was sleeping, when he (Jamar's father) wasn't there. And then they wanted sex, and that wasn't working for me. Cause now Jamar is walkin' and he's lookin in the bathroom, and I'm trying to date this guy and I was havin' a really hard time, and my sister lived there, and she had a little boy and another little girl and sometimes I'd watch her kids for drugs and she would never really watch mine. And I'd drag them up and down with me. And I was just in a lot of pain and I was really addicted at this point.

So, the father was my biggest source of drugs, so I had to go find the father in order to continue getting high, and this particular time I asked my sister, who was on drugs, to watch my kids. And she said yes, so I gave her $10 and I bought her a drink, because I thought that was what to do. My mentality was just – do what you got to do. Just survival. It was not clear at all. So I asked my sister to watch my kids and I walked and bought some Pampers, and I walked to where the father's mother lived and found him to get some drugs. But that wasn't enough, so now I got to walk back to the hotel and I ran into his friends and they had a car and they had a whole bunch of drugs and now I want to go get a room next door to where I live at the hotel, and we get there and two ambulances are outside and my kids are in each ambulance, and the police are there and they tell me to get into the police car and they went to Children's Hospital to have the kids evaluated. And they put a police hold on the children and took me to jail.

Once placed in foster care, Amanda's children were hardly protected from harm. Jaclyn went to live with her father for a time. When he went to jail, Jaclyn moved in with one of Amanda's friends.[14] Still later, Jaclyn was removed from the friend's home and placed with her half-brother, Jamar, in kinship foster care with a paternal relative. Amanda returned to the streets where she found herself pregnant once again. When Jelani was born, he was placed directly into kinship foster care with his siblings.[15] Jelani was born with drugs in his system and Amanda had no money, no place to live, and no viable means of social or economic support. The children were moved back and forth among various paternal relatives, all of whom were using drugs and some of whom physically abused Jamar. Amanda complained, but nothing changed until Jamar landed in the hospital with several broken bones. Social workers finally moved him out of his kinship foster home and into a regular foster home. Jaclyn remained with her relatives for several more years until she, too, was removed to a foster home. Jelani remained in the grandmother's care under a legal guardianship arrangement for the duration of his childhood.

In foster care, Jamar never stayed in one place for long. By the time he was age 10, he had lived in eight different foster homes. Some of the moves were instigated by social workers who learned of his or other children's maltreatment in care. Other moves were requested by foster parents who were unable to manage his increasingly difficult behavior.[16] When Jamar was age 10, Amanda took a hard look at her life and made a change. Jamar reunified with his mother at the age of 11, a decade after he was placed in care.

> So they let me have him, and when I got him, the kid was crazy! He was crazy. He would sleep with knives. … The school called me almost every day. And Jamar had like 12 or 13 suspensions in one school year.

By the time he returned to Amanda, Jamar was a very disturbed little boy.

Reconsidering Child Welfare's Mission

Amanda's story speaks volumes about the overwhelming problems of the child welfare system – a system that is unable to solve intense family problems relating to drug addiction, domestic violence, and criminal behavior. A system that removes children from their homes only to see them languish in a state of impermanence without the promise of a stable family. A system that promotes extended family relationships to such an extent that it ignores children's health and well-being and makes a mockery of the government's role as an intermediary in vulnerable children's lives. A system that separates children from maltreating parents, too often placing them with caregivers who are either unprepared and ill supported for the work or who do not even meet the minimum qualifications to provide adequate care.

Last year there were over a half-million children living away from their parents in the foster care system. These are the children for whom we have an enormous responsibility. These are the children that government has been given the authority to protect.

But child welfare has lost its focus. Rather than targeting these children and their families as those for whom we are essentially responsible, the field has drifted. Rather than maintaining clarity about the fundamental mission of child welfare, the field has lost its way. As a result, children suffer.

Maybe it is because family reunification, foster care, and permanency work are so hard to do. One professional recently bemoaned the seemingly intractable problems of foster care and simply declared, "I give up. I don't think we'll ever provide good foster care. It's just too hard to fix."[17] Predictably, in these and other such discussions, the spotlight shines on those children walking in the door of the system. Prevent children from coming into foster care, and the whole system can die away, becoming a relic of the past. Indeed, the passion for prevention is strong, and the advocates' message is powerful: We can save families. We can prevent child abuse. Every child can live in a "safe, stable, permanent home, nurtured by healthy families and strong communities."[18]

Attractive as this vision may be, it is utopian and it is naïve. As detailed in Chapter 2, this book shows that our efforts to prevent child abuse currently bear little fruit. Try as we may to develop new strategies designed to prevent child abuse, our knowledge base in this area is still in its infancy. We know very little about how to help troubled parents love and protect their children or, in short, how to help maltreating parents make their children a priority.

This book does not argue that government efforts to help families should be abandoned. Indeed, Chapter 2 distinguishes between *family support*, *child maltreatment prevention*, and *family preservation services* and argues that while we should shy away from family preservation, we should expand empirically based family support models and develop research-tested programs to prevent child maltreatment.

The benefits of universal family support strategies largely accrue to children—not parents—and those benefits can be seen in the areas of improved educational success, health outcomes, and—to a more limited extent—children's delinquency and later use of public assistance. Family support programs can improve relationships between some parents and children, but they do not appear to alter the risk of maltreatment, and they do not prevent entry into foster care. As such, family support programs are not effective *child welfare* interventions. They are helpful tools in promoting child and family well-being for those families that are unlikely to ever come to the attention of the child welfare system. As such, they should be expanded and an infrastructure to support their availability for a wide range of families should be developed across the U.S. All families should be offered an opportunity to raise their children well, with adequate income, safe communities, and strong schools. But we cannot use current child welfare funding or other human resources to establish that infrastructure at a time when the fundamental child welfare system is in such disarray.

If child welfare cannot provide universal supports to all families, can it support higher risk parents to care for their children well? The evidence from the existing literature indicates that targeted programs designed to prevent child maltreatment have enjoyed very limited success. Although many programs are theoretically sound, reviews of studies across several different kinds of programs indicate that the effects of these programs are very small—if they have effects at all. In general, we are still a long way from knowing what works to prevent parents from harming their children.

And finally, family preservation efforts targeted toward families at risk of losing their children to foster care are not effective strategies. Although new models may be developed at some point in the future, today's programs are not sufficiently robust to keep children safe at home.

Child welfare advocates' enthusiasm for a large prevention agenda—which includes family support, child maltreatment prevention, and family preservation—is not only misdirected but also has a subversive effect. The prevention agenda distracts us from our fundamental mission: the real work of child welfare is about protecting children when they are harmed by their parents and enhancing such children's life opportunities beyond what they would have experienced had they stayed home.

This book attempts to reaffirm the fundamental mission of child welfare, rebalancing our priorities away from family support, child maltreatment prevention, and family preservation. Instead, the book examines the centerpiece of child welfare: reunification, permanency, and foster care.

When children can no longer live at home and must be separated from their parents, child welfare agencies have an obligation to support parents' efforts at reunification. Time lines to reunify have narrowed considerably since the federal government passed the Adoption and Safe Families Act,[19] but time should not be parents only opportunity for reunification. Services, we hope, should also aid parents in their efforts to care for their children effectively. While the research legacy in the field of family preservation is extensive, research on reunification services is limited. Chapter 3 calls for a renewed emphasis on reunification research. If we learn that concentrated services can be helpful, these efforts should be aggressively pursued during each child's first year in foster care. Parents should be afforded reasonable opportunities to reunite with their children, and children should be offered a "last best chance" to go home.[20]

Aggressive efforts to reunite children with their parents must be paired with clear expectations about alternative permanency arrangements should reunification efforts fail. The research literature suggests the considerable benefits that accrue to the majority of children who are adopted; thus efforts to secure safe and loving adoptive families should be pursued forcefully. But in our efforts to identify alternative families for children, birth parents are often left behind. The field has typically embraced an either/or approach to children's lives: you either belong to one family *or* you belong to another. In the murky world of family relations, however, many children outside of child welfare live in blended families where they negotiate relationships with parents, stepparents, half-siblings, and others. Chapter 4 suggests that open and semiopen adoption can allow parents some degree of contact or knowledge about their child's well-being, making this system of intrusive government intervention more humane for the families involved.

And while permanency through adoption may be an appropriate choice for many children, the large proportion of children living in kinship foster care may need an alternative permanency arrangement. Increasingly, states are turning to legal guardianship to secure children's permanency with kin. But our efforts to pursue permanency with kin have developed with great haste and little forethought. Kinship guardianship offers a unique blend of state-sponsored care within the context of family relations. As such, it should continue with an understanding about the kin caregivers' unique capacities and limitations and with respect for their interests in securing a child's position within the family. Guardianship should also proceed with a judicious appreciation for the sometimes long-standing and ongoing relationship between kin and birth parents. Chapter 5 suggests that maintaining a role for the state in guardianship arrangements with kin will make more credible child welfare's responsibility for protecting children.

While we pursue every effort to move children out of foster care and to secure safe, lifetime families for these children, we can not ignore the fact that in any given year, over 300,000 children will enter foster care, and every one of them will deserve a safe, comforting, and caring environment for the days, weeks, or even years of their stay.[21] Too often, the quality of foster care is poor. Too often, children receive mistreatment or even maltreatment while living in care. Chapter 6 argues that at the very least, the well-being of children in foster care should improve beyond what they would have experienced had they remained at home.

Child welfare can not be all things to all people. It can not bear responsibility for changing communities, altering drug policies, improving economic conditions, correcting school systems, or housing families. In fact, claiming these as part of the child welfare agenda diverts precious resources—time, money, commitment, human capacity, and creativity—from Jaclyn, Jamar, Jelani, and the hundreds of thousands of children who deserve so much more.

Maybe someday we'll get it right. Maybe someday we will have devised a child welfare system that honestly and actively helps parents bring their children home. Maybe someday we can feel proud of the children who have moved to permanent families instead of shamed by the thousands lingering in care. Maybe someday we can showcase our quality foster care programs that give children a chance to repair, to grow, and thrive. Maybe then we can turn our attention to the next great challenge and tackle a new population of children and families—those "at-risk" of entering foster care. But until then, child welfare efforts should be focused and unified, giving children a safe place to call home.

2

Prevention:
Unrealized Potential, Unrecognized Faults

*"I didn't have no income and everything, and then
it got hard."*

It's those nasty headlines that grab our attention. "Manslaughter charge in Newark neglect case."[1] "Richmond mother arrested in murder, torture of son,"[2] "Mom who drowned kids takes stand."[3] We shake our heads, baffled at the inhumanity of some parents. We murmur to ourselves, incredulous at the child welfare agency's inattention to needy families. Not surprisingly, tragedies such as these often spawn investigations, commissions, and blue-ribbon panels, most of which call for efforts to redouble prevention efforts, identify troubled families sooner, and offer multiple services to match the unique needs of individual families.

The call for prevention is strong. When California administrators completed their 3-year "redesign" of child welfare services, their report suggested that "prevention of child abuse and support of families is not only good practice, but also a cost-effective strategy to protect and nurture children and maximize the quality of life for California residents."[4] Similarly, in a recent restructuring of New Jersey's child welfare system, their plan "targets many of the problems that are precursors to child abuse and neglect, including substance abuse, inadequate housing, domestic violence, and the lack of community-based social services, and commits the state to working to prevent abuse and neglect before they happen."[5]

Child maltreatment is a significant problem in the United States. In 2005, child welfare agencies received over 3 million reports of child abuse or neglect on over 6 million children. Of these, almost 900,000 children were identified as victims of child abuse or neglect. The youngest children in the United States were at greatest risk; infants and toddlers were more likely to be identified as victims of maltreatment than any other age group at a rate of 16.5 per 1,000.[6]

Child maltreatment also seems to be on the rise.[7] Every decade or so, the federal government sponsors a national study to determine the underlying extent of maltreatment in the population. (These studies differ from examinations of official child abuse reporting, as they are designed to detect maltreatment that may or may not come to the attention of child welfare agencies.) In the last National Incidence Study (NIS-3), released in 1996, maltreatment rates had almost doubled since the previous study (1986). The number of children who were seriously injured as a result of maltreatment had almost quadrupled.[8]

The National Incidence Studies and the official child maltreatment reporting studies differ somewhat in identifying the scope of the problem, but both sources of data tell a similar story about the nature of maltreatment. The problem of child maltreatment is not just an issue of physical or sexual abuse. The majority of reports for maltreatment concern child neglect—a particularly pernicious form of maltreatment both for its effects on children and its intractability to treatment.[9] In 2005, over 60% of child maltreatment reports nationwide were for child neglect—problems relating to parents' incapacity to provide for children's basic necessities, including care and supervision.[10]

Child abuse and neglect do not affect families equally. Children from single-parent families are more likely to be maltreated, as are children from large families and those from low-income families. According to the NIS-3, children in families with incomes below $15,000 per year are 22 times more likely to be maltreated than children living in families with incomes above $30,000. Importantly, there are no differences in maltreatment rates based upon the race or ethnicity of the child.[11]

Given the scope of maltreatment in the United States and the sobering fact that tens of thousands of children enter foster care each year, our quest for prevention is inevitable. We believe that children should have reasonable opportunities to live with their birth parents and that parents should be given a fair shake in raising their children outside of government control and intervention.[12] We also know that the opportunities for all families are not the same. The odds of raising children well in low-income, economically distressed communities are long,[13] as the structural conditions of our society significantly disadvantage some parents; these are the adults who often need extra supports. We all have a vested interest in children's healthy upbringing, as no one wants to see children maltreated. And certainly there is no appetite for placing children in foster care away from their parents if such an outcome can be prevented.

At its essence, prevention makes sense. If we can affordably prevent parents from maltreating their children, these costs are likely to fall far short of the costs associated with foster or group care. And practically, we know that it is challenging to locate and support substitute caregivers who can rival the care of a loving parent. When birth parents can do their job reasonably well, children should be offered the chance to stay home.

Unfortunately, many families in the United States struggle mightily to care for their children. Although some families' difficulties are quite simple to overcome, the vast majority of families coming to the attention of child welfare services have multiple vulnerabilities in several domains, including the material, physical, psychological, and environmental. Looking at a given family experiencing parenting challenges, many could readily identify their problems and could probably suggest some of the services that might help. Where reasonable people may disagree is on how much families need and whether any of it makes a substantial difference.

Identifying Need: The Easy Part

Bill, Kate, and their children were deeply involved with the child welfare system for a little over a year. A brief introduction to them and to their personal circumstances can shed light on the challenges of identifying and serving struggling families and to the significant difficulties associated with helping parents change patterns of behavior that put their children's well-being at risk. With their large family, their challenge with drug addiction, an attenuated support network, unemployment, and history of intimate partner violence, Bill and Kate share many similarities with other parents coming to the attention of the child welfare system. Their family's difficulties can be quickly identified, but whether services would have prevented their children's placement in foster care is a subject of great debate.

Bill and Kate were high school sweethearts. They married soon after graduation and had their first child, and then another shortly thereafter. Bill picked up jobs here and there, but Kate stayed home with the kids, as Bill had very traditional views about family. He felt strongly about his role as the family's supporter and protector; Kate was supposed to raise their children, but Kate did not know much about child-rearing and felt very uncomfortable seeking advice. Bill was so defensive about outsiders' influences that he tried to keep his family from public view, scorning doctors and other professionals who might meddle in their affairs.

The family grew rapidly and finances were tight. Jobs were hard to find and tempers were short. Within a little more than a decade, the family included five children, most of whom were frequently irritable and difficult to care for. Bill and Kate's relationship to one another and to their children began to fray. Their youngest children, Bobbi and Jasmine, were particularly hard to manage. Jasmine was born with a significant hearing impairment that went undiagnosed when she was born. Bill and Kate shunned doctors, so Jasmine never received the medical checkups that might have revealed her problem. Although language should have emerged by the time she was 2 years old, Jasmine could not hear the world around her. Her speech was delayed and her rage was uncontrolled because she could not communicate her needs effectively.

In addition to Jasmine's hearing problem, both Bobbi and Jasmine had very severe vision impairments. These were also undiagnosed at birth and, without access to medical care, there was no opportunity to detect them during early childhood. The children's vision affected not only their physical abilities and confidence in moving about the world but also the early lessons of infancy that rely on reading others' faces and responding to caregivers' smiles and murmurs; such lessons were largely lost to both of these youngsters. Their developing social skills were thus altered, and they became difficult to manage throughout early childhood.

Kate somehow knew the limits of her parenting, so she often sent one or more of her children to live with her parents for long stretches of time. Her own life with Bill grew increasingly violent, and when Bill turned to drugs, it became more dangerous still. Kate began using drugs shortly after Bill did, and their circumstances deteriorated rapidly. Bill stopped working altogether and their only income source was welfare. Groceries were in short supply, as the food stamps never stretched to the end of the month. Even the children's clothes were a problem, since the family moved from apartment to motel to the grandparents' house to shelters, losing personal belongings with each transition.

After Bill went to prison on drug charges, Kate and the children shuttled from place to place. Kate's recollections convey the enormous transience she and her children experienced for about 2 years:

I finally ran into a friend of mine and she let me stay there rent free. I didn't have no income and everything and so I stayed there after my brother took my son (Kent) in for a minute.[14] And then it got hard for him and he knew where I was, and he said, "You know, do you think you could take your son because I lost my job and it's kind of hard for me," 'cause he was sleeping out of his car. So he gave me my son back and I applied for AFDC (welfare) and then it kind of got a little rough there because (my friend) was using. And I didn't want my son around that environment and there were all these people in and out, and I was trying to not use. … So eventually I told my brother, "Hey look, if you want to go in, we can go in together and get a room and that way we all have a place to lay our heads at night." So we did that for awhile, and then my husband got out [of prison] so he got his own place and back on his feet. And then he was out for about 10 months. And then eventually, like we were making only about $500 … and it was kind of hard there. So we went to a shelter, me and my son. So that's kind of where we went wrong, too. I had this pride and thought shelters aren't for me and I had to swallow my pride 'cause it's like I have nowhere else to go.

Kate's parents did what they could, but even they were reluctant to interfere too much. Then, shortly before Kate's sixth child, Tiffany, was born, Kate's parents were killed in a car accident. All of the children were returned to Kate,[15] and the family's only source of positive support vanished. In Kate's grief, her dependence on drugs intensified. She let her children, ages 1 to 10, fend for themselves as she scoured the streets for drugs and money. When Tiffany was born testing positive for cocaine, medical personnel and one of Kate's brothers called Child Protective Services (CPS). The social worker who looked into the circumstances of their family removed all of the children and placed them in foster care.

A close examination of Bill and Kate's family suggests that they desperately needed help well before their children were placed in care. But their story also raises questions about which professionals or community members should have detected their problems. It also leads to questions about the nature of the services they might have received, whether services would have been accepted voluntarily, and how effective they would have been in stemming such a broad array of problems.[16]

Although three of Kate's children had significant health concerns,[17] they had little or no contact with health professionals who might have responded to their needs. Kent's developmental delay ensured additional attention from school personnel, but Beth and Isabel were typical children who drew no special notice from their teachers. Jasmine and Bobbi were not yet in school, so they had no contact with a community of professionals who were also mandated to report suspected child maltreatment or who might have reached out to the family. Of course school personnel should have investigated the children's erratic attendance, and they may have done so, but if a child abuse report was filed early on, Kate is unaware of it. Her transience would have made it difficult to conduct an investigation, and there is no guarantee that social workers would even have found this family.

If their family problems had been known to community professionals, it is possible that services might have helped, but access to and engagement in services does not necessarily translate into changed circumstances. A nurse/home visitor (discussed in more detail below) might have knocked on their door, but given Bill's distrust of community professionals, the nurse likely would have been turned away. Surely Bill and Kate both needed to engage in substance abuse treatment. In fact, some might argue that substance abuse was the family's essential problem. Their daily focus on getting, using, and finding more drugs kept them entirely distracted from their children's needs. And when Bill was in prison, Kate was willing to forgo housing, food, clothes, and nurturance for her children in order to feed her addiction. In spite of her need for treatment, the literature on engagement suggests that many parents with substance abuse problems do not utilize drug-treatment services.[18] Among those who engage in treatment, a large proportion drop out before treatment completion,[19] and the effects of treatment on their ability to actually reduce or discontinue substance abuse are modest at best.[20]

Bill and Kate were extremely poor. Although they had sporadic income from employment, their welfare checks still kept them well below the federal poverty level. Because the younger children were undiagnosed, they were not receiving SSI, to which they were entitled (another source of income that would have improved their financial circumstances measurably). While additional income would have helped, there is little from the literature to suggest that increased income alone would have solved the family's problems. The research literature points to a strong association between family poverty and child maltreatment. And some child welfare critics have argued that poverty alone is a substantial determinant of child welfare involvement.[21] But the long-standing known association between poverty and maltreatment has troubled researchers for many years; poverty, of course, could not be the sole or main determinant of maltreatment, as the vast majority of low-income parents do *not* maltreat their children. Something else, in addition to poverty, had to explain the connection. Relatively recent evidence from one large-scale study indicates that certain characteristics distinguish some low-income parents from others. Parental characteristics including their involvement with drugs, domestic violence, and a recent history of arrest all increase the risk of child welfare involvement for children in low-income families[22]—characteristics which, in the case of Bill and Kate, were present on all fronts. Improving Bill and Kate's financial circumstances might have helped, but it is doubtful that increased income alone would have sufficed to protect their children.

The family might also have benefited from more stable employment. Employment could have lifted their income and regularized daily family routines; it therefore might have—as some have argued—contributed to a stronger sense of self-esteem.[23] But employment would not serve as a panacea for this family's problems. Most families moving from welfare to work rarely see their incomes rise substantially.[24] Besides, Bill was in prison and Kate had a household full of children, all of whom would have needed day care if she worked outside the home.

Finally, Kate clearly needed stable housing, but her lifestyle, including her substance abuse, interfered with her capacity to maintain a home for her children.

From Identified Need to Service Provision

Anyone examining the circumstances of this family could identify some of their multiple needs—from drug treatment, to intervention and treatment for intimate partner violence, to housing, to medical assistance, to basic parent education. The child welfare agency had no contact with this family until their problems were so severe that all six of the children were removed to foster care. Some have argued that a service design such as this is akin to a team of lifeguards racing into a turbulent river just in time to save the children from certain drowning. The service design is costly, it ignores the plight of the children struggling as they float downstream, and it attends to people whose needs are acute rather than addressing more modest concerns early on.[25]

Although most critics of child welfare agree that a better system would target children further upstream, the form and construction of the rafts, lifeboats, bridges, and barges that might be offered have been hotly debated. How far "upstream" must we go to prevent foster care placement? And what kind of raft would be effective in keeping families afloat?

The banner of "prevention" is large and encompasses an assortment of strategies designed to serve a wide range of families under a large variety of circumstances. Three categories of prevention falling beneath this banner may be helpful to delineate some of these differences. At one end of the spectrum are *family support* services, designed to enhance child well-being within the context of healthy families. These programs have elsewhere been referred to as primary prevention programs[26] or universal programs.[27] Next along the continuum are *child maltreatment prevention* approaches offered to targeted families showing risk factors associated with child abuse or neglect. Other common terms to differentiate this approach include "secondary" or "selective" prevention programs. "Tertiary" or "indicated" prevention efforts generally are those strategies targeting families where maltreatment has already occurred. For purposes of this discussion, *family preservation services* are described as a form of tertiary service designed for children at risk for imminent placement into foster care.

Prevention Approach	Goal
Family support Primary prevention	Enhanced child well-being and general parenting improvement
Maltreatment prevention Secondary prevention	Prevention of child abuse and neglect
Family preservation Tertiary prevention	Prevention of foster care placement

The Family Preservation Approach

For years, intensive family preservation services have been used by child welfare agencies to target children at imminent risk of foster care placement. These services, initially supported with private foundation funding,[28] flourished throughout the 1980s and 1990s and continue in many jurisdictions today. The model includes intensive social work support with weekly and sometimes daily contact, 24-hour crisis availability, assistance with concrete supports (e.g., bedding, furniture, help paying bills), and a flexible array of services customized to each family's unique needs. Programs are normally limited to several weeks or months, and few last longer than a year. The intensity of services, coupled with material and psychological supports are designed to shore up the family, improve parent-child relationships, reduce maltreatment, and alleviate the need for out-of-home care.

Although initial research suggested the promise of this type of intervention,[29] later studies cast serious doubt on its efficacy. In fact, in a field with a very thin evidence base overall, the one area of child welfare where we now have robust empirical findings based upon rigorous, large-scale research is in the area of family preservation. The largest of these studies was conducted by faculty at the University of Chicago. In that study, several thousand families across the state of Illinois who were identified as at "imminent risk" of foster care placement were assigned, at random, into one of two groups. The experimental group received intensive family preservation services and the control group received typical child welfare services. Following these families for 3 years, researchers discovered that the rates of child placement were relatively low for *both* groups. Children receiving the intensive family preservation services were no less likely than children receiving traditional services to be placed in care; among children remaining with their birth families (the majority of cases), family preservation services did nothing to reduce the likelihood of subsequent maltreatment—both experimental and control group children were equally likely to be maltreated again by their parents.[30]

The field of child welfare has struggled with these findings for some years—perhaps the goal of preventing removal was misplaced; perhaps improvement in parent–child relationships should suffice; or parent satisfaction with services should be an adequate indicator of success.[31] In these and other areas, findings from several studies were equivocal. Intensive family preservation services sometimes offer some benefits for some families. But if we are concerned about stemming the tide of children entering foster care, if we want to fish children out of the river just a bit sooner – indeed, whether family preservation services can change the trajectory of families such as Bill and Kate's, the data are plain: family preservation services are not enough to eliminate or reduce the need for out-of-home care.

Slowly the field has accepted the evidence. Today, few advocates argue in favor of family preservation services on a large scale.[32] Because the evidence is weak on the effects of family preservation for averting foster care placement, other efforts have been developed to move upstream, to catch children further up the river, and to target services to families that are at risk for child maltreatment but not so troubled as to be candidates for imminent placement in foster care.

Child Maltreatment Prevention

Efforts to target families showing risk factors associated with maltreatment have been ongoing for decades. The nature of such programs ranges substantially. Some are therapy-based, some rely on modeling and social learning, some target the associated risk factors more than the maltreatment per se. Studies examining the effects of these programs now number in the scores. The studies, of course, range in quality from simple preexperimental designs to rigorously controlled randomized experiments. Several research reviews have been conducted in recent years to summarize the findings from these various studies. The reviews indicate that there are sometimes program effects, but importantly, such effects are very small. In Geeraert and associates' meta-analysis of 19 studies and in MacLeod and Nelson's meta-analysis of over 50 programs, positive results were found, but the overall effect size on reducing maltreatment averaged only about 0.20 in both reviews—which is considered small by conventional standards.[33]

Considering again our river analogy, intensive family preservation services may target families too far down the river, and child maltreatment prevention services may not accurately target the families at risk or may not yet have identified the intervention that can most effectively respond to maltreatment. One could argue, therefore, that if we were to move upstream to families facing fewer or less severe risks, family problems might be better addressed, and we could stop maltreatment before it occurred. By definition, fewer children would need foster care services.

What Do We Know About Family Support Efforts?

Reviews of the research literature on family support services suggest the promise of these programs for helping vulnerable children and parents. Some programs appear to improve parenting practices, enhance parenting attitudes, support parent-child attachments, and encourage greater reliance on social support networks.[34] These comprehensive reviews suggest that not all programs are effective but that certain program components may lead to better effects. For example, longer-term programs may be more effective than programs of short duration.[35] Intensity is also important in that families may need weekly or even semiweekly contact in order to change long-standing behavioral patterns and adopt new parenting practices.[36] Professionals may be more effective in supporting parents' change process than paraprofessionals. And timing is critical. Family support interventions offered to families directly before or at birth provide an important window of opportunity when parents may be most amenable to program engagement and behavioral change.[37]

A vast array of programs exist that fall under the wide umbrella term *family support*. They range from nurse home visiting programs for postpartum women to early childhood education to Big Brothers, Big Sisters of America.[38] Some focus on children's needs in the areas of health, education, or development; others hope to bolster parents' economic well-being, their parenting skills, or social support. Most programs for parents, whether targeted specifically to an at-risk child welfare population or to another group, intend to influence the broad behaviors of positive parenting and good citizenship, which include reduced maltreatment, fewer arrests, greater connectivity to the labor market, and less alcohol and/or drug consumption. Many of these programs have been studied, although the weak research designs employed in most tell us little about their outcomes for children and families. But a literature is certainly developing that relies on stronger research designs, building confidence in our knowledge about programs that may have benefits for families.[39] These benefits are important. If parenting can be improved, children will no doubt be better off. And theoretically, if parenting can be improved, children are more likely to experience a safe childhood, free from maltreatment. Yet the difference between less-than-optimal parenting and child maltreatment is great. While an array of family support programs offer significant opportunities to improve parenting, none have shown consistent effects on reducing maltreatment or, importantly, on preventing foster care placement.

We now have extensive research on home-based programs; for example – family support initiatives offered to mothers and children that take place in living rooms and kitchens across the country. In general, the evidence on "home visiting" for improving parenting has been positive.[40] The most extensively and rigorously studied of these programs is the Nurse Family Partnership Program, which includes nurse home visiting to vulnerable women prior to and following the birth of a child.[41] Long-term examination of this program suggests important effects for mothers, including fewer subsequent births, reduced smoking, improved parenting, fewer total months of public aid receipt, less drug and alcohol use, and fewer arrests.[42] A review of several home visiting models indicates, however, that effects on child maltreatment are largely nonexistent or unknown.[43] In the one study that found effects on maltreatment outcomes, 4% of children participating in an intensive home visiting program were reported and verified for maltreatment within the first 2 years of life; among the control group, 19% of children were similarly reported. Two years following the intervention (when the children were 4 years old), the differences between groups had disappeared. Fifteen years later, the differences reemerged, with children from home-visited families less likely to be reported for maltreatment throughout childhood; but the differences were small.[44] The findings are not only somewhat counterintuitive but they have not been replicated in other studies, including different populations in different geographic regions of the country.[45] Overall, however, findings from the Nurse Family Partnership program are exciting, as they suggest important effects for families in multiple domains over long periods of time. Yet effects on child maltreatment are equivocal. Home visiting does not offer a sufficiently sturdy lifeboat to protect children from the turbulent waters of child maltreatment.

In addition to home visiting, some family support programs are specifically targeted to young children. These programs can be categorized as "center-based" and include intensive early childhood education paired with services to parents.[46] Evidence from these programs shows that high-quality care can have important effects on children and that these effects may be greatest for vulnerable children in low-income families.[47] For children participating in high-quality child care, program effects include greater educational achievement – such as improved grades, reduced rates of special education utilization, and greater high school completion and college attendance – as well as reduced juvenile delinquency.[48] Effects are strongest when children receive high-quality care characterized by consistency, sensitivity, and a stimulating environment.[49] Taking these program characteristics to scale has been challenging, however. Implementation of the Chicago Parent Child Centers has shown that quality *can* be maintained, and strong outcomes for children can be assured when such a program is implemented in a large urban context.[50] But outcomes associated with Head Start's national implementation have not been as encouraging. In the most recent national study of Head Start, for example, impacts on 3- and 4-year-olds were limited in the areas of children's academic gains, and they were negligible or nonexistent in children's social development.[51] Effects on parents have been less pronounced across most programs, probably because parents are not the principal focus of intervention. Nonetheless, center-based programs have shown effects on mothers' educational attainment and employment in the labor market.[52] Effects on parenting practices have been more limited.[53] Of the many studies examining the effects of child care on parenting practices, only one indicated that rates of child maltreatment might be lower for children participating in high-quality care than for those with no exposure to care or exposure to preschool care of variable quality.[54] In that study, however, only a small minority of children were ever reported for maltreatment, suggesting that their initial risk was low, and findings from this study have not been replicated elsewhere.[55]

Efforts to reach families even earlier in the family life cycle show promise. Studies of the Early Head Start program, including blended interventions in center-based settings and the home, indicate that young children up to age 3 can benefit from program participation in terms of their cognitive and linguistic development. Program impacts on parents may be important as well. Early Head Start participation may promote more emotionally supportive parenting, more cognitively stimulating parenting, and less harsh parenting. Importantly, however, program effects do not appear among the most at-risk parents—those most likely to potentially maltreat their children.[56] As one approach to help support families in their care of children, exposure to high-quality child care may be significant. To pronounce child care services as a promising practice for reducing child maltreatment, however, would be a mistake. To date, the data are not compelling.

Other programs specifically targeted to improving parenting practices among vulnerable families show promising effects.[57] One of these, the *Incredible Years*, has been lauded as an evidence-based family support program, having the potential to catch families upstream. The program is offered to parents of children with behavior problems and includes a parent training program comprising videos, group discussion, and modeling techniques. The program is designed to improve children's behavior and increase parents' effectiveness in parenting their challenging children. The program has been widely studied and appears to reduce harsh disciplinary practices, improve parent–child interactions, and increase parents' involvement in their children's schooling;

the effects are relatively consistent across studies.[58] Although the benefits of this program show its value, the program has not been studied with a high-risk, maltreating population.[59] Other parent training programs targeted to high-risk parents largely have shown ineffective results with regard to reducing child maltreatment.[60] Parent training thus may be one component in the arsenal of family support programs designed to improve parenting, but it can not yet be considered sufficient to protect children from maltreatment.

One of the problems with the literature on family support is that it is extremely varied.[61] For example, although the home visiting program developed by David Olds shows significant and lasting effects, other programs based upon a similar model, or taken up to a large scale, have shown less robust findings.[62] The same can be said for large-scale implementation of early childhood programs.[63] Although some family support programs may help children and families in some domains, family support programs usually have shown little if any effect on reducing child maltreatment, reducing recurrence of maltreatment,[64] or even on moderating the risk factors that place families at risk for maltreatment (e.g., maternal depression, maternal substance abuse, domestic violence, etc.).[65] Among the programs that *have* shown effects, the vast majority influence disciplinary practices that narrowly correlate to child physical abuse.[66] Child sexual abuse[67] and child neglect—which account for one-half or more of all child maltreatment reports and entries to foster care[68]—continue to be especially resistant to effective prevention approaches.

Reexamining the Role of Family Support in Child Welfare Services

What we learn from the evidence on prevention services is sobering. Family preservation services have not yet been devised to protect the most vulnerable children from foster care placement, and child maltreatment prevention efforts have had exceedingly small, if any, effects. Evidence from the family support literature suggests that the programs are incredibly varied; that program effects—where they exist—are generally modest, and that effects are just as likely in the educational, criminal, substance abuse, and employment arenas as they are in the parent-child domain. Further, although family support provides durable effects in multiple domains, we know almost nothing about family support as an approach for preventing maltreatment or entry to foster care.

Does this mean that we throw up our hands and abandon efforts to support families? Absolutely not. But it does suggest, first, that we must engage in much more high-quality research to find out how to prevent child maltreatment. Studies must either target families at risk for maltreatment or have the capacity to separate out these families from large samples in order to gauge program effects. A variety of family support strategies should also be tested so that we do not fall prey to the notion that a single promising practice is a magic antidote for the field. As these studies are conducted, greater efforts to translate developing knowledge into the field will be especially important. Ineffective programs represent a terrible waste of scarce resources. The value of each dollar spent on effective services is thus magnified compared with the many dollars currently spent on ineffective approaches.

Second, the data suggest that family support efforts should not fall on the shoulders of child welfare agencies. Indeed, based upon the literature, family support programs are *least* likely to affect child maltreatment and *most* likely to affect children and families in other social and educational domains. To think that child welfare should carry the burden—both financially and intellectually—for developing, disseminating, and funding the machinery of family support is ludicrous. Instead, education, health, criminal justice, and cash assistance programs—bureaucratic structures that are far more richly funded than child welfare[69]—should be the leaders in future efforts to develop and strengthen family support programs. These service systems have the most to gain, in the long term, from the effects of family support programs.

Family support services *should be* widely available to vulnerable families across the United States—especially if they are refined and carried out with consistency and high quality when they are taken to scale. The evidence on program effects is sufficiently compelling to suggest that many families could benefit from these services quite substantially. Nurse home visiting programs for new moms, high-quality early childhood education, and other new approaches not yet devised and tested should be made available to help vulnerable families parent their children with warmth, affection, and concern for their physical, emotional, and academic well-being. The question is not whether family support services should be offered. Indeed, they should be dramatically expanded if they are implemented with care. The point is that child welfare should not be the responsible agency for their development or dissemination, since their effects on maltreatment and foster care placement have not yet been shown.

Such a notion will not be warmly embraced by the field. Family support work is considered by many to be more enjoyable than family reunification or foster care services. Therefore if the field of child welfare insists upon providing prevention-oriented services, then it should only do so with new, dedicated funding that is true to its purpose – a purpose quite different from the one the field carries today.

Current funding under the Promoting Safe and Stable Families Amendments of 2001 (P.L. 107–281) is broad-based and can be used for a variety of purposes, most of which relate to maltreatment prevention, child protection, and permanency. For example, the law allows for

coordination of services offered under the program; *preventing child maltreatment among at-risk families through supportive family services* (emphasis added); assuring children's safety within the home; *preserving intact families where children have been maltreated, when problems can be addressed effectively* (emphasis added); addressing problems of families whose children have been placed in foster care so that reunification may occur in a safe and stable manner; and supporting adoptive families by providing necessary support services for them to make a lifetime commitment to their children.[70]

Typically, funding to support the basic activities of the protective child welfare system is too limited, and Safe and Stable Families funding is used to enhance protective services for families. Therefore, current funding cannot be used to develop a wholly new family support branch of the child welfare system. Redirection of such resources only amounts to a divestment of resources for America's most vulnerable children. If child welfare systems are to carry the mantle of family support to a broad base of the population, they will require new and substantial funding in order to carry out that purpose effectively.

And what is that purpose? Child welfare agencies must be honest with the public about the targeted benefits associated with family support services: to improve parenting practices and parent–child interaction.[71] The term *family support* could then peel off the veneer of maltreatment prevention and be true to its goal: to improve the quality of parenting and support general child well-being. Such an agenda would be a departure from traditional child welfare services as it would target neither child protection nor the prevention of child maltreatment. Children would be better nurtured, they would live in more cognitively stimulating and affectively satisfying environments, and their life trajectories would likely be enhanced. Children would not, however, be safer.

They would not be protected from maltreatment. They would not be prevented from entering foster care.

The distinction is important. As long as the field of child welfare is committed to using family support and family preservation services as a mechanism to prevent maltreatment and entry into foster care, it will be using valuable system resources to little or no effect. While we must fund and develop new research enterprises than can determine *how* to prevent maltreatment, the dollars typically spent on ineffective prevention services should be redirected to the children already under the supervision of child welfare agencies and the courts.

Returning to our analogy of the river, the evidence on family support programs suggests that a few rafts can probably be devised to keep some children and families afloat. But the large majority of children at risk of maltreatment will be missed and will eventually drift downriver into turbulent waters. As unpalatable as it may seem, until we can devise a new strategy that is effective in preventing child maltreatment, we can not abandon the current cadre of lifeguards, ready to catch children, downriver. The fundamental mission of child welfare is downstream, where children must be served, where the child welfare system accepts its greatest responsibility, and where the public is holding it accountable. Some families, like Bill and Kate, live in desperate circumstances. These families need opportunities to come ashore, to raise their children, to take them home.

Today, Bill, Kate, and their six children *are* home. Bill and Kate have been clean and sober for well over 3 years and they regularly acknowledge and celebrate their success. Bill and two of the children receive Temporary Assistance for Needy Families (TANF)[72] and the other children are all on SSI. Kate has completed a training program and is looking for work. Tiffany—who was born completely deaf—is enrolled in a special preschool for deaf children, and Kate and Bill are taking a course in sign language. The older children are progressing in school, each with an established plan to receive specialized educational services. The family has enjoyed stable housing for over two years, and Bill and Kate's relationship has strengthened through their family's adversity. Although their experience with the child welfare system was painful—they were separated from their children for about a year[73]—involvement with child welfare offered their inspiration for change. Both Bill and Kate credit CPS with saving their family:

> Kate: The only thing to me that I got out of it, I'm glad that [CPS was] there. I'm glad that they pushed us from the drugs. We needed to,

otherwise we could have been dead and our kids would have been elsewhere. But I am thankful for that and thankful that we got our head back on our shoulder and got an opportunity to get housing where we can get back on our feet. And I'm glad that they were there for that. I'm not going back to that lifestyle. My children mean a lot to me and I've already hurt them by being in the foster care system. We can't go back in time and change that so we move on from here and get family therapy to get an understanding of what they went through.

Bill: When we first started this, you know, I told my wife that [CPS was] wrong for what they did. And now I really feel like, taking a look back, if it wasn't for them we wouldn't be where we are right now. And both of us are going on three years clean pretty soon. You know, I'm more happier than I've ever been.

3

Reunification:

One Pathway Home

"I just feel light. I got all my kids back."

Lawyers are milling about in the hall outside the courtroom, catching their clients for a few minutes' conversation before their case is called. Inside, the courtroom is almost empty. The judge and a handful of court staff discuss a case; two lawyers sit in a corner conferring. Tracy is tired but shows her excitement to me. The mother of nine children (two since deceased), she's seen all of them but one enter foster care. Today, the last of them is coming home.

Judge Tamis calls the case. Tracy stands. The judge asks about her housing, transportation, and school for the children. Tracy is taciturn. By objective measures, Tracy is doing well and there is no reason the court hearing would not proceed favorably. But Tracy is wary of the judge, of the lawyers, and of all that they represent in the system; rather than comfortably reveal all of the details of her life, she is defensive, eyes cast down, reserved.

After some discussion, the judge congratulates Tracy and confirms that her son is returning home. She then closes the case. Tracy turns to leave, but then speaks up. Looking directly at the judge, she stammers: "May I say something? I don't want to ask something that might be inappropriate, but I'm wondering if I can take a picture with the judge who returned all my kids to me?"

The federal framework for child welfare services rests upon the notion of providing "reasonable efforts"—both to prevent children from entering foster care and to expeditiously reunify children following placement. Much has been written about the "reasonable efforts" provision in federal law, but Congress pointedly omitted an articulation of the nature and range of services that should be provided.[1] The clause has been criticized largely for allowing birth parents opportunities well beyond reason to reunify with their children. In the 1990s these debates found a place among congressional leaders who argued against exaggerating parents' rights at the expense of their children's needs:

> The foster care system is keeping children in foster care for too long, ... Abusive parents are, today ... given a second chance, a third chance, a fourth chance, a fifth chance, and on and on. ... while they try to get their act together ... their poor little children are shuttled from foster home to foster home.[2]

In 1997, Congress's discomfort with excessive efforts on behalf of parents was translated into a narrowing of parents' opportunities to reunify with their children, limiting the availability of "reasonable efforts" to 12 from 18 months. In exceptional circumstances, services need not be provided at all.[3]

Legislators' concerns about the amount of time parents were given to reunify were indeed valid. National data from 2005 suggest that the mean length of stay for children in out-of-home care was 27 months (the median length of stay was 15 months), while approximately 17% of children who left care in 2005 had been in care 3 years or more.[4] Parents were given ample time—well beyond the federal guidelines—to change their behavior and meet their case plan goals; how much of the change process was facilitated by the efforts of child welfare service providers is less clear.

Parents' stories about the path to reunification suggests a lonely experience that speaks largely to issues of compliance and less to changes in real-life circumstances.[5] The large majority of parents are given case plans that include parent education, drug treatment, and sometimes therapy – services that may match some of their needs but may also be less directly related to their parenting experience. Waiting lists for services are long, and parents are often asked to locate agencies on their own. If the literature on case plan goals and services is thin, knowledge of parents' internal change process is even thinner.[6] We know little about the triggers that motivate parents to change and still less about the factors that maintain new behavioral patterns. What we do know is that the family problems that often bring children to the attention of child welfare services are usually severe, with patterns entrenched.

Tracy and Her Children: No Happy Beginnings

Tracy never had a simple childhood. Her father abandoned the family when she was very young, leaving Tracy and her six siblings in the care of their schizophrenic mother. Their mother was in and out of mental institutions, providing only marginal or intermittent care; by the time Tracy was 13, she was pregnant and ready to leave home. At 14, Peter was born.

> And I started selling drugs because welfare was giving me money. But that wasn't no money. That was nothing. And I would see my neighbors and they was out there selling and I said, "Shit. I'd always seen them counting hundreds and everything and I said, "Shit, that's what I need." And I said, "I don't have to leave my house." I'd go right outside and sit on my porch because the traffic was already there, you know what I mean?

At age 18, Tracy gave birth to Oliver. Tracy was depressed, overwhelmed, and isolated. She had no positive role models, and her prospects for education, employment, and healthy relationships were bleak. She began drinking heavily and using drugs.

> I see everybody else doing it and they seemed like they were so cool. And then when some people were stressed out and sad it was a way of depressing stuff and making it go away. And it did that for me too. So I didn't have to deal with the pain of not having a mother, I didn't have to deal with the pain of not having a father. I didn't have to deal with a whole lot of stuff. It was an easy way out. And I see that now, that's what it was; it was a way out for me.

A year later, her third child, Tamika, was born, and a year after that, Germaine. When Tracy turned 21, she was sent to prison on drug charges. She called her sister Fay, who took home Peter and Tamika. Oliver's father whisked him away and moved; Tracy never heard from him and never saw her son again. Germaine's father took her home, giving Tracy access to her daughter only sporadically over the years.

Prison hardly rehabilitated Tracy. A year following her release she was still using, and her sister Fay and mother were using too. Peter and Tamika lived where they could, sometimes with Tracy and sometimes with their aunt Fay, depending on which adult was living in a motel or apartment between periods of homelessness. When Tamika was 4 years old, Tracy left her for the afternoon with Fay and her mother.

Fay lived around the corner with my mom. And come to find out when I came back, my daughter, she didn't look good and her eyes was rolled in the back of her head and I took her to the hospital and they said she had got a hold of barbiturates and had rock cocaine. I was worried about my baby and nurses and people didn't want to let me see her. They had a police hold. So that's when they told me they found the cocaine and the barbiturates and found out the barbiturates came from my mom. ... But I knew where it came from. It came from my sister. ... So they took her from me. At that point I just went downhill, just totally downhill. There was, what the hell? It was like, "fuck you," and that's how it was. I just felt like that's my baby. I've been robbed. I just felt robbed.

Social workers removed Tamika to foster care. They also tried to determine whether other children were living with Tracy or with Fay. Tracy hid Peter, claiming that she had no other children, and after the Child Protective Services (CPS) workers' initial investigation, Peter continued to live alternately at his mother's and his aunt's homes.

At age 24, Tracy gave birth to Shawna, but sadly Shawna died of sudden infant death syndrome (SIDS) a few weeks later.[7] A year later, Amber was born, testing positive for drugs. Although CPS workers conducted an investigation, they did not remove any of the children. Tracy, however, sent Peter and Amber to live with her sister Fay, and a short while later Fay called CPS to report Tracy for child neglect. The children were formally placed in foster care under a kinship arrangement with their aunt Fay.[8]

So I felt betrayed by my sister when I found out 'cause I went to her for help 'cause I didn't want my kids in foster care and she put them in there... in order to get that thousand and some dollars a month.[9]

By now, Tamika was in traditional foster care, and Peter and Amber were in kinship foster care. Tracy's access to Tamika was limited. She visited her daughter at the foster home, the park, or other neutral locations, but visits were relatively brief and somewhat irregular. Tracy's experience of parenting Peter and Amber, however, did not change. She had daily access to her son and daughter and she regularly took them home for days and weeks at a time without the knowledge of her child welfare worker.

At age 27, Tracy had her seventh child. Tyson was also born with drugs in his system. Although Tracy had an open child welfare case, had three children living in out-of-home care, and was actively using, social workers did not place Tyson in care. The case was closed after an initial investigation and Tracy returned home from the hospital to parent her infant son.

Tyson stayed with me every step of the way. He never went nowhere. Tyson was right there under my wing, we wasn't going nowhere. We let him go nowhere. He was stuck to me like glue.

The period called "family reunification"—an 18-month phase[10] where services are provided to the parent—was discontinued and her children remained in foster care under a long-term-care arrangement. The court held review hearings every 6 months and Tracy attended during some of these, trying to make a plea for her children's return. However, she had made no progress on her case plan, so she was routinely denied the opportunity to bring her children home.

And this is what turned me out. If I'm such a bad mom, why did you let me—Why, when I tried to get Amber back, they wouldn't let me have her. … Yeah, if I'm such a bad damn mom, why didn't you come take Tyson? Even though sometimes people had called. [CPS] say they got a call twice. They came twice to where I lived, but they never did anything. They came and they looked, they said, somebody said I didn't have food or some bullshit. I think they were just trying to see if I was taking care of him. Personally this is what I believe, but they came and said nothing. You can come in, you can look, and they seen the house was clean and I had food and Tyson was dressed and Tyson was going to school and whatever and they left. And then they came again another time and they did the same thing and they left. But here it is 5 years this child has been with me and if I'm such a bad parent, why didn't you take him? And this is how I felt. Why didn't you take him? Why did you let him live with me 5 years?

When Tyson was 1 year old, Tracy gave birth to Raymond, who also tested positive for drugs. Social workers conducted an investigation and removed Raymond to Fay's home but left Tyson in Tracy's care.[11] As if her children had not experienced sufficient injustices in their young lives, tragically, at the age of 9, Tamika died in an accident during a family vacation with her foster parents.

At the age of 32, Tracy gave birth to Asia. Again this baby was born with drugs in her system and social workers removed her to Fay's home. Now 5 years old, Tyson was also removed to Fay's home, where he lived with his siblings, Peter, Amber, Raymond, and the newborn, Asia.

*So I brought [Tyson] to court with me. [The social worker] looked at him
and because he had a scar that I could not tell her where it came from,
they said it was consistent with marks from a switch and child abuse....
So that was their basis. What kills me is that their basis for taking Tyson
wasn't because I was using [drugs] or because I had Asia high. They said
it's because some marks that he had on his body that looked like I abused
him, whipped him with a switch. Come on now. I would have felt better if
you said you took him because Mom is using and she had the baby while
she was high so apparently she must be getting high with him. I would
have felt—I mean I could have dealt with that. It would have been true,
but then come up with some falsified stuff to make shit up from old
wounds that you see that my son couldn't even tell you where they came
from. ... Tyson told that lady I didn't hit him. Tyson was crying and
screaming, told that lady, "You lie, you said I was going to go home with
my mommy." He was hollering and screaming, "My mommy didn't hit
me, my mommy—You just trying to make me say my mommy hit me."
And he's been caught up in that system ever since because I was high
when I had his sister. But for bullshit, for made up shit.*

With Asia and Tyson's entry to care, Tracy was given a new plan for
reunification. The clock was rewound, and another 12-month service
plan was put in place with requirements that Tracy enter drug treatment
– that she show a "commitment to recovery" and to visit with her children regularly. Tracy called a local drug treatment program and enrolled.
Her participation, however, had no effect on her addiction.

*The first three months I just was really in denial. I was like, "fuck it, I'm
just going to sit here until I can get my kids back." That's all it was for
me. "I'm just sitting here and I'm going along with they shit just so I can
get my kids back." I had no desire to change, no desire to really do shit but
get my kids back.*

The children continued to live with her sister, and Tracy finally took
notice of the kind of care they received. In particular, the children started
complaining about Fay's boyfriend—how he would berate and threaten
them, how they felt unsafe. It took a couple of months of soul searching,
long talks with her drug counselor and with peers in her program, but
Tracy finally decided that she had had enough: she had had enough of
the drugs, and she was tired of watching her children suffer in Fay's
care. Tracy insisted that her social worker move her children. Amber and
Raymond were sent to a traditional foster home, where they lived

together. Tyson was moved to a separate foster home. Asia moved with Tracy into a new residential drug treatment program, and for Tracy, everything changed:

> *Asia was my turning point. I don't know. When they took Asia it was different because not only did they take Asia, they took Tyson. Tyson had been with me those whole five years of his little life, almost six. And we did everything together. That was my buddy. He was not only my child, he was my friend. You know, he was, in a way he was like my—how do you say?—my co-, my codependent in a way. And when they took her, you know, it hurted. But when they took him, it literally was like they killing me. All he knew was me. I was his world, you know, and I just had to fight.*
>
> *And I sat there and I prayed and I talked to God about it and I realized I didn't have the wrong motives. My motives was I wanted what was best for my kids. Because like when they were in [Fay's] home it was like they wasn't in foster care anyway. This is my sister. I could go get my kids whenever the hell I wanted. I could come over whenever I wanted. She would bring them and drop them off to me whenever I wanted. They'd spend weeks with me at a time. Even though during all this time I'm not supposed to be nowhere near them.... But that motivated me because my kids were with strangers. They weren't convenient anymore. They weren't with my sister. Even though me and my sister had these issues, they were with family and they were all together.*
>
> *Now all my kids were separated except for Amber and Raymond. They always managed to stay together no matter where. Now all my kids were separated, they were with strangers.*

Kids in Care: Waiting for a Change

One might guess that Tracy's recovery began when her most cherished child was taken from her care. Or perhaps it was the pain of seeing her children separated from one another, or maybe it was the children's transition away from family and into strangers' homes. Perhaps it was a combination of all three, but there's no question that her inspiration to change came late; very late for her children. Tamika entered foster care in 1992. A full 10 years later, Tracy took a hard look at her life and pledged a change.

Tracy reunified with her children largely from sheer determination. Formal reunification services for the older children had been terminated years previously, but with Asia and Tyson's entry to foster care, a reunification plan was once again put in place. Tracy was required to attend parent education, engage in drug treatment, submit to random drug testing, and find stable housing. When asked about the services she was offered, however, Tracy frowned, then looked quizzical:

> I never really got any services from them. The only service I got from them was going to see the shrink... They helped me be able to get back and forth to see my kids, like... they paid for my Greyhound ticket, you know, and then they gave me bus passes.
>
> I mean I can understand it if the system would work with you more, could give you the benefit of the doubt and sometimes give you what you need, like extra services that the system don't provide for. Or if they could work with you. But they're like, "oh, no, you're on your own." But they all the time they holler that they want you to get yourself together so you get your kids back and they holler and they point their gun butts.

One by one, Tracy's children returned home. First Asia, then Raymond and Amber. Peter had long since emancipated from care after turning 18. Initially he visited, then he too moved home. Tyson returned 2 years later, following 13 placements in care—first with kin, then in foster care, still later in group care, and finally residing for over a year in residential treatment.

Tracy proudly displays her certificates of completion from her drug treatment programs, her parent education classes, and her special class for "Parenting a Child with ADHD." A year after reunifying with all of her children, Germaine, raised by her father since early childhood, found herself in foster care after her father gave her a brutal beating. Tracy showed up in court, ready to accept Germaine into her home, and was surprised to receive a new reunification plan, replete with requirements for parent education and a how-to class on parenting a child with ADHD. Although she laughs as she recounts her tale, she is nevertheless incredulous that she must once again engage in services, and intimates the futility of the services that were recommended.

> They want me to take classes for ADHD, which I'm not going to do 'cause I already [did] that!!... But they wanted me to take another parenting class.... Which I already did that.... Yes, here it is. Here's my case plan. And so I brought them my proof of my parenting certificate and other stuff, you know, but I just think these people are crazy. How many times do they want me to do this!?

When Tracy was working to reunify with Asia, Raymond, Amber, and Tyson, she needed to learn how to engage in positive parenting experiences; she needed a coach to help her learn techniques for managing her children's now challenging behaviors; she needed support in responding to their needs in their new dyadic, intimate, day-to-day relationship. Tracy also needed concrete help establishing a home for her children. She needed an apartment in a new community, away from the familiar triggers she associated with the drug use of her past. She needed furniture, phone service, kitchen paraphernalia, bedding, clothes – Tracy needed all of these and had none. She needed an enriched child care program for her youngest and after-school services for the others. She needed reliable transportation. When Tracy was trying to reunify with Germaine, she needed another bed, sheets, and blankets. What Tracy needed was income to clothe and feed a very large family. What she got was another generic parenting class.

Reunification: When and for Whom?

What do we know about the reunification process? Does anything "work" in fixing families? Or is the process entirely idiosyncratic and reliant on parents' willingness to acknowledge family problems and set about changing parenting practices entirely on their own? Remarkably, federal, state, and local governments combined spend over $20 billion annually on the child welfare system.[12] A large proportion of that effort is focused on helping parents and children reunite. Tens of thousands of social workers are engaged with families across the country in efforts to promote reunification between parents and children. But at the end of the day, we know almost nothing about what services help parents bring their children home.

Research in the past decade has informed the reunification discussion considerably, as it has highlighted the characteristics of parents and children that are associated with reunification, but neither social workers, child welfare administrators, nor policymakers can do much to alter the characteristics of families that present to the child welfare system. What the child welfare industry *can* control are the services it provides to families to improve the odds of a safe reunification. Today, the knowledge to build such an effective industry is only in its infancy.

Parents involved with the child welfare system typically struggle with an array of entrenched problems including mental health issues, homelessness or housing instability, criminal activity, and domestic violence. The role of drug abuse is also key, as a large majority of children entering out-of-home care are touched by issues of substance abuse.[13] Further still, the time line for recovery from drug abuse often well exceeds the reunification time line available to parents under federal law[14] and collides squarely with children's developmental and affective needs for stability, security, and permanence.[15]

In spite of these significant challenges, about half of families reunify.[16] The large majority of those reunifications (about two-thirds) occur relatively shortly after a child enters care.[17] With each year a child remains in care, however, the likelihood that he or she will return to her parents declines markedly.[18] Although some parents, such as Tracy, reunify long after their children enter care, such a pattern is less typical.[19]

Not all children have equal odds of reunifying. Children entering care as infants or teenagers are less likely to go home than children of other ages.[20] Children of color[21] are also less likely to return home.[22] Children who have suffered from neglect[23] and those with behavioral or emotional problems are less likely to reunify.[24]

The characteristics and personal circumstances of parents also play a role in children's reunification patterns. Parents with substance abuse problems are less likely to see their children returned to them,[25] and low-income parents, parents suffering from material hardships,[26] parents with mental health problems,[27] and parents experiencing recent episodes of homelessness are less likely to reunify.[28] Not surprisingly, parents whose children were previously removed to foster care are less likely to see their children return home,[29] as are parents who infrequently visit their children while in care.[30] Parents who make progress in resolving family problems in multiple domains are more likely to reunify with their children.[31]

Since about half of children return to their parents, one could view reunification as one of the successes of the child welfare system. But many reunifications fail. Estimates vary, but several studies indicate that upwards of 30% of children who reunify eventually return to foster care, yielding a net reunification rate of about 35%.[32] Some reunifications could be predicted with better decision making. According to one study, the most significant factor associated with reunification among drug-involved parents was parents' compliance with drug treatment—even though a substantial proportion of these compliant clients continued to use drugs and many had not changed their parenting behaviors substantially.[33] Another study found that among mothers reunifying with their infants, a significant proportion still struggled with issues of drug abuse, criminality, and housing instability at the point of reunification[34]—all factors contributing significantly to family fragility.

Some reunification decisions, therefore, are inappropriate. Others may seem appropriate at the time, but certain family characteristics may suggest greater vulnerability to re-entry. For example, including infants and young children,[35] children from low-income [eligible for Temporary Assistance for Needy Families, or TANF) families, and children with health problems[36] are more likely to re-enter care. And some studies point to ethnicity as a factor: some studies have found that African-American children are more likely to re-enter care,[37] and another suggests that Hispanic children are the least likely to re-enter.[38] Other factors that appear to increase the chance of re-entry include having had previous child welfare referrals or multiple placements while in care, child neglect, the criminal history of the parent, social isolation, poor parenting skills, parental mental illness, negative relationships, and housing instability.[39] Re-entry is also most likely to occur for children who have been in care for the shortest periods of time.[40]

One conclusion to draw from the literature is that stable reunification[41] is largely a matter of family characteristics and circumstances. A crude assessment would indicate that stable reunification is most likely among Caucasian, latency-aged children with few behavioral or emotional difficulties. Parents who have not had previous contact with the child welfare system, who physically abuse their children (rather than neglect them), who are drug-free, and whose family income provides a buffer against extreme hardship are also somewhat protected from their child's future re-entry to care. But that is a crude assessment. Other families obviously reunify, and other factors probably play a role. At the heart of a safe and lasting reunification is an improved home environment for the child, including changes in parents' behavior. We know little about the role of parents' motivation to change, however. And we also know surprisingly little about the role of child welfare services in supporting parents' efforts to change.

Reunification Services for Troubled Families

Prior to P.L. 96–272—the Adoption Assistance and Child Welfare Act of 1980—there were no federal requirements to provide "reasonable efforts" to reunify. These requirements were imposed in part owing to research findings from studies conducted in the late 1970s, which suggested that if parents had case plans with specified goals, regular contact with child welfare workers, and support for visitation, they were more likely to see their children return home.[42] So indeed, some services matter.

But the question remains: Can we do better? If we currently net a 35% reunification rate using a fairly generic reunification model of case planning, social worker contact, and visitation, could we increase the proportion of safe reunifications using a different array of services and supports? If some families were offered more intensive or more thoughtfully customized services, would they see their children return home faster than the 10 years it took Tracy to achieve reunification?

Some studies have been conducted to address this question, but their number is remarkably small.[43] One of the earlier studies conducted by Fein and Staff targeted families in New England. Child welfare workers referred families who—the workers determined—were not likely to reunify.[44] Services were provided for approximately 6 months, with the provision for aftercare services following reunification for up to 18 months. Staff worked together in teams of two, with small caseloads. At the end of the study, 38% of families—all of whom had been selected because they were *not* likely to reunify—had indeed reunified; factoring in later re-entries, the project resulted in a net reunification rate of 28%. There was no comparison group in this study, so the results only beg for replication using a stronger research design.

A study conducted in Utah included provision of a 90-day intensive Family Reunification Services program[45]—similar to the intensive family preservation service programs described in the previous chapter. Families were randomly assigned to a treatment condition, where they received specialized attention, or a control condition, where conventional child welfare services were provided. Targeting was broadly defined to include children in placement longer than 30 days whose reunification was not imminent. The program was designed to move children home quickly. Most services were provided *following* family reunification rather than *during* the process of reunification.

About half of the children in the control condition reunified with their parents—a rate similar to that of most studies of reunification with conventional services. In contrast, 97% of children in the experimental condition reunified. Taking into account the proportion of children who later re-entered care, the net reunification rate for children receiving the Family Reunification Services program was 70%, compared with 47% for children receiving conventional services.[46]

And in Illinois, intensive reunification services were targeted to children who had relatively good prospects for reunification.[47] Service duration was about 6 months. Although reunification rates for children in the specialized program were about 40% better than reunification rates for children receiving conventional services,[48] the overall reunification rates for targeted children still hovered around 50%, and re-entry rates were high.[49]

Given the substantial proportion of child welfare families with substance abuse problems, some service models have targeted the interplay between these cooccurring issues. One of the more rigorously designed studies of family treatment drug courts suggests that parents who were voluntarily offered frequent court hearings, rapid entry to drug treatment, regular drug testing, other ancillary services, and close judicial and child welfare supervision had better reunification rates than similarly situated families receiving conventional child welfare services. The reunification rate for children whose parents participated in drug court was 45%, compared with 34% for children whose parents received conventional services.[50]

Combined, the study results are provocative. Findings from the Illinois project suggest that intensive services provided to all children eligible for reunification may be of no more value than conventional reunification services.[51] Findings from Utah indicate that intensive post-reunification services—targeted to more functional families—may be an effective tool for reducing re-entry to care.[52] The New England study[53] points to the marginal value of specialized services targeted toward those least likely to reunify as a "last best chance" prior to alternative permanency planning. And the inclusion of timely drug treatment services and close judicial oversight may also play a role in supporting reunification outcomes. Importantly, this handful of studies represents the state of the evidence on the role of child welfare services in promoting reunification for children in foster care. In short, we know that about half of children in foster care reunify and about 35% maintain reunification safely; we know almost nothing about the importance of child welfare services in promoting safe and stable reunification. We must know more. One might question why we would further study intensive reunification services if they bear distinct similarities to the family preservation programs—discussed in the previous chapter—that have not reduced entries to foster care. The reason is threefold: first, one might posit that the motivational forces driving a parent to change her behavior and circumstances are different when her children are no longer with her than they are when there is only a threat of removal. Second, we know that many families reunify. If many do so without the benefit of agency supports, then still others might be able to experience success with additional assistance. And third, the legal and ethical implications of separating children from their parents for years—if not a lifetime—demand that we better understand whether and under what conditions government supports can help families repair and reunite.[54]

The evidence collected since passage of the Adoption and Safe Families Act suggests that reunification may be on the decline.[55] This may be due to a renewed emphasis on adoption since passage of the law, but it also may be related to a watered-down notion of what reasonable efforts entails. Current reunification services are often so modest that they are unlikely to have significant effects. When reunification services look like those that Tracy received, it is surprising that reunification is so common. Generic, didactic parenting classes that cover childhood topics from infancy to adolescence are not effective. Generic parenting training is not likely to have much effect on parents' daily interactions with their children.[56] Two-hour weekly visitations arranged in the local mall will scarcely help parents practice new parenting skills that are responsive to children's needs.[57] And a list of phone numbers that identifies local drug treatment centers can hardly be called a service at all. The federal standard of "reasonable efforts" to reunify families is certainly appropriate. But the definition of reasonable efforts should turn on an evidence base that can point to those efforts that are effective versus those that are ineffective. The current framework of knowledge about effective reunification services is remarkably thin. New, rigorous research on concentrated reunification services could help pave the way toward safer reunifications for families. Findings from these studies could also provide clearer expectations for child welfare agencies to follow the "reasonable efforts" provisions of the law.

Permanency for Kids: Alternative Planning for Their Sake

Parents need a fair chance to get their kids back. If parents can change their behaviors and provide safe homes for their children, they should be given honest opportunities to do so—opportunities that rely on services proven to stimulate change within a limited period of time. But children can not wait forever; when they do wait, the effects can be disastrous.

After reunification, all of Tracy's children had difficulties managing their behavior and received regular therapeutic and educational services. Tyson's problems, in particular, were severe. By the time he returned to Tracy, Tyson had significant mental health problems that were treated with multiple medications. He received treatment to manage his aggressive, out-of-control behavior, and he needed to be carefully supervised around his siblings and peers. He needed extensive psychological and educational supports and was likely to continue receiving these services for many years.[58] The entire service delivery system responded too late for Tyson. Whether his emotional problems were rooted in his first 5 years of life, during which he was neglected by his mother, or his next 4 years in multiple kin and foster care placements of marginal or inadequate quality, Tyson was forced to keep waiting for his mother to change. When she finally did, it was far too late.

Reunification is neither the only nor necessarily the best outcome for all children. With a net reunification rate of approximately 35%, a full two-thirds of children *do not* return to their parents. They, too, deserve lifetime families with caring adults. Among children who do not go home, many will be placed with kin and will stay with them, either through adoption, guardianship (discussed in more detail in Chapter 5), or long-term foster care. For children in non-kin care, however, adoption may be a viable plan for securing legal and emotional permanency should reunification fail. The younger children are when they are considered for adoption, the more likely it is that adoption will occur.[59]

But for the large majority of children in out-of-home care, efforts toward alternative permanency do not begin until reunification services to parents have been terminated, generally after several months. These delayed permanency decisions can extend a child's stay in foster care by years while new foster placements are identified, adoptive home studies are undertaken, and proceedings for termination of parental rights begin. Sequential planning such as this has been standard practice in child welfare for decades.

In the 1970s and 1980s, new program models were developed to place children in "preadoptive" homes prior to a permanency decision. Parents received conventional reunification services, but in the event that reunification efforts failed, children's adoptions could proceed expeditiously.[60] The model, referred to as "concurrent planning," attempted to remedy the delays inherent in sequential planning, giving equal due to parents' rights to reasonable services and children's rights to permanent families.

Concurrent planning was approved as an appropriate child welfare activity under the Adoption and Safe Families Act. As a philosophical framework guiding practice, concurrent planning appears to have gained currency in child welfare agencies across the country.[61] Effective *"concurrent doing"* in large-scale public agencies, however, has been elusive to date.[62] If conventional concurrent planning has been difficult to implement, alternatives may be necessary to forward a permanency agenda.

Pathways to Permanence: Balancing the Needs of Parents and Children

Developing new models of permanence for families – models that are even-handed for parents and appropriate for children – means formulating policy guidelines that (1) are *time-sensitive;* (2) respond to parents' needs for *real services;* (3) impose *reasonable expectations* on case workers, foster parents, and judges, and (4) are *permanency-oriented* from the first days of care. What follows is a description of a new approach toward reunification and permanency that theoretically maximizes the principles listed above. This model, of course, would need further testing to assess its true value.

Developing a New Approach to Reasonable Efforts

Data on child welfare trends over the past 15 years show that reunification is most likely in the first 6 months of care and that the probability of reunification drops significantly thereafter.[63] Public policy should be data-sensitive when feasible; to the extent that time limits are necessary in child welfare, 6 months should hold meaning for decision making regarding permanency for children.

In a new model of child welfare policy, all eligible parents would be offered 6 months of conventional services upon entry to care, designed to advance reunification (Figure 3.1).[64] The large majority of families who are going to reunify will do so with these typical supports. At the 6-month court review, another 6 months of conventional services would be offered to families using kin-and-kith care[65] and to those families in non-kin placements where there is a good probability of reunification by

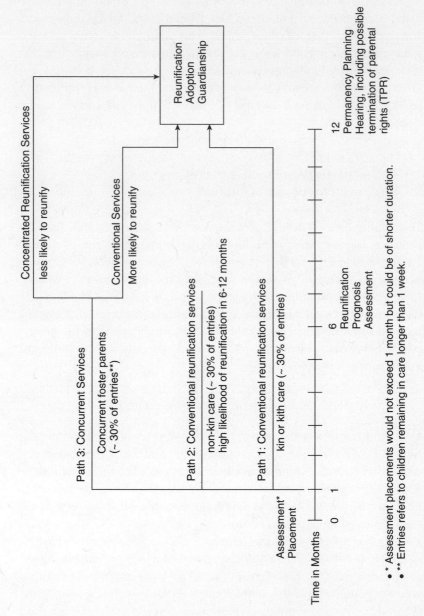

FIGURE 3.1 In a new child welfare policy model, families may take one of several paths through the system.

- * Assessment placements would not exceed 1 month but could be of shorter duration.
- ** Entries refers to children remaining in care longer than 1 week.

1 year. Prognosis assessments to determine which families are most likely to reunify would be made using existing data (such as those described previously on the characteristics of children, parents, and their cases), and new research[66] combined with good clinical judgment.

The other families, whose prognosis for reunification is dim at 6 months, would be offered Concentrated Reunification Services (CRS) in a concurrent planning framework, where each family would be assigned two staff. CRS and concurrent planning would *not* be offered to all families entering care but only to those families still in care after 6 months who were unlikely to reunify—possibly up to one-half of the entry caseload. One staff member would be focused intently on the special needs of parents (the other staff member is described in greater detail below). Caseloads would be small, interaction between workers and parents would be frequent, and family needs would be adequately assessed and addressed quickly. Services would be "concentrated," meaning that they would be intensive, saturated, and customized. But importantly, they would be short-term, lasting no more than 6 months. At 12 months, in concert with federal law, judges would make permanency decisions so that children and parents would know their future relationship unambiguously.

Such an approach should be rigorously tested with realistic expectations about the potential results. That is, the CRS model likely would not produce large increases in rates of reunification.[67] Because it is targeted specifically to those children least likely to return home, modest reunification rates might be expected. Under optimal conditions, it might boost total reunification rates from about 50% up to 75% or so. Taking into account re-entries to care, the net reunification rate would probably be closer to 50% instead of the current 35%.[68] More parents would reunify with their children. More parents would feel as though they had been given a fair chance by the state. More children would go home, and they would do so within a reasonable period of time.[69]

Such an approach would be a significant departure from current practice and would respond to two of the principles listed above: It would be *time-sensitive*, so that children would not be allowed to languish in care while social workers tried to deal with their ambivalence and discomfort, and it would give clear time-oriented messages to parents about the need for change. Second, it would provide *real services* to parents that were both responsive to their individualized needs and that showed the government's honest interest in assisting troubled families.

Concentrated services for parents, without an attendant responsibility to children, does nothing more than take us back to a time when reasonable efforts were misconstrued to mean exceptional efforts at all costs.[70] Focusing solely on parents leads to errors concerning children's safety and ignorance about children's need for permanency and well-being. Therefore the only way to optimize parents' opportunities to reunify *at the same time* that children's needs for permanency are addressed is to develop a concurrent practice model that begins within 1 month of entry to care (see Figure 3.1).

Under a new model of child welfare practice, children's needs would be assessed and appropriate concurrent foster parents matched to meet those needs during each child's first month in care. The model assumes that kin and kith are located and utilized whenever safe and appropriate and that, otherwise, social services agencies draw from a sufficient pool of available, appropriate concurrent foster parents for non-kin placements (discussed in greater detail in Chapter 6). Concurrent foster parents would be supported to work with parents directly as part of the intervention team in order to help encourage the parents' change process. Working together on behalf of children's interests, these alliances would be designed so that they could be sustained over time as children grow and develop. Importantly, once a child were placed in a concurrent foster home, caregivers would make a commitment to raise the child either temporarily or permanently, depending on the life course of the case.[71]

At 6 months, following the reunification prognosis assessment, some families would be assigned to the CRS program described previously. Where one caseworker is appointed to attend to the parent's needs for 6 months, the other caseworker would help the child and concurrent foster parent move toward alternative permanency. The two-worker model has the effect of shining a bright light on the child's need for permanency and pushing reunification workers to make honest assessments about parents' actual changed behavior, rather than their hoped for change.

Concurrent practice that is effective must be much more than a series of guiding principles or a set of new requirements for already overburdened child welfare workers. At a minimum it should reflect the "essential elements" outlined by Frame and associates, which include a philosophy of concurrent planning that saturates the agency, structures and protocols to support the practice, and sufficient resources (including reunification services), an ample pool of concurrent foster parents, and workload standards that promote good practice.[72]

Realizing concurrent practice is no small task in public child welfare agencies. It requires attending to the intense emotional needs of parents, children, and caregivers. Child welfare workers must be alert to parents' needs to bring their children home, children's needs for their parents' love and affection or that of alternative parents who will love them forever. In spite of the challenges associated with concurrent practice, development of such a model addresses the third principle listed previously: it suggests an approach that is *reasonable* for all parties involved.

An individual public child welfare worker can not do all of the work associated with concurrent practice. A single social worker can not reasonably assist parents in the reunification process while helping children forge new relationships with permanent families. Most importantly, in fulfilling both roles, a single worker can not see children's needs for permanency clearly when juxtaposed with parents' emotional wells of pain; thus decision making at critical junctures may be impaired. Most parents are similar to those described in this volume—they love their children deeply, even if they have failed in their role as nurturing caregivers—and their plea for more time, even if progress has been small, can be sufficiently compelling to delay permanency decisions. When child welfare workers are more responsive to parents' emotional needs than to children's future well-being, they can not communicate clear information to judges, which either leaves the door open for judicial continuances or allows judges to fill the vacuum, making decisions that are not fully informed.[73]

Judges, of course, are in the unenviable position of making the ultimate decisions about parents' and children's fates. They determine when and if children will go home; when and if parents will maintain legal ties to their children. Decisions of this magnitude are so profound—easily rivaling the liberty interests involved in criminal proceedings—that judges should demand full and complete information about the cases before them. They too should feel confident that parents have been afforded significant opportunities to change their personal circumstances through their involvement with evidence-based reunification services. Knowing that reasonable efforts have been made and information pertaining to both parents and their children is complete, judicial decision making would be more timely and fair for all parties involved.

Finally, foster parents involved in the kind of concurrent practice described here would participate in a system of care that is reasonable rather than extraordinary. Foster parents carry a deep emotional burden when they raise foster children. Falling in love is dangerous business, yet this is what the child welfare system asks of strangers every day: "Fall in love with our kids, but be prepared to give them up at a moment's notice." Caregivers enter into relationships with children that they hope will endure. Although the work also involves relationship building with birth parents and the development of caregiving networks surrounding children, the hope of concurrent caregivers is a lifetime legal and emotional relationship with a child. Therefore, in developing concurrent practice, it should be recognized that caregivers assume a high degree of risk during the first 5 months of placement, prior to the reunification prognosis assessment.[74] That is, they risk losing the child to reunification with the parent. In a new model of concurrent practice, many children would return to their birth parents during the first 5 months. Therefore, for these concurrent foster parents, opportunities for adoption would be faint, but the hope for sustained contact and support for the child could be ongoing. Following the 6-month review, however, the risk of losing the child to reunification would diminish considerably—particularly for those families with a slim prognosis for reunification.

At 12 months, a permanency planning decision would be made, and concurrent foster parents would no longer reside in that period of lengthy ambiguity that characterizes the current child welfare system. With more clarity about the nature of the legal and emotional risk they are likely to sustain, the duration of that risk, and knowledge about a solid endpoint to their waiting, more families would be drawn to concurrent foster care as an avenue to starting or expanding their families. With a larger pool of potential concurrent foster parents, child welfare agencies could better consider aspects of quality care (discussed in greater detail in Chapter 6) that, today, are often ignored.

A new model of concurrent practice would be responsive to the fourth principle listed above. It would put *permanency* at the forefront of the child welfare system. The Adoption and Safe Families Act specified that safety would guide child welfare decision making throughout the life of each case. The call for a permanency focus does not diminish the role of safety in child welfare. Instead, it is meant to suggest only that permanency must frame all decision making from the very first days of care. When that focus is misplaced, days and months are lost while children wait.

Articulating Permanency as a Profamily Agenda

The research literature on family preservation services is richly varied and comprehensive, including examinations of multiple models of service provision and a range of outcomes for children and families. The field's enthusiasm for preventive services has been long-standing, and efforts to study these initiatives so thoroughly should be applauded. But the fact that we count only a small handful of studies on the effects of reunification services is a testament to the field's ambivalence about birth parents, parents' capacity to change, and reunification itself.

The field holds great promise for the struggling families who have not yet experienced child removal. Although these are families challenged on multiple fronts, many of whom have maltreated their children, there remains a steadfast faith that adults can change, patterns of behavior can be broken, and parents can learn to prioritize their children's needs over their own. We have less faith in the parents who have seen their children removed to foster care. But in reality, how deep is this divide? Do parents transform from difficult to intransigent at the point of removal? Obviously this is not the case, since about one-third of parents reunify safely and stably. Therefore, until we know what motivates parents to change; until we know about the configuration of services that can help parents care for their children safely, this dual view, which separates the field, should be set aside. Instead, we must make greater investments in the fundamental mission of child welfare: to protect children within the context of their families. To do so means redoubling our efforts to identify effective strategies that can promote safe reunification. Given a "last best chance," more parents will safely reunify with their children. For those parents who are unable to use these services effectively, concurrent practice will ensure that their children can move on swiftly to families that are ready to take them home.

Parents like Tracy can change. Today, Tracy lives in a four-bedroom subsidized home caring for her six children. Her parenting is not perfect. Her daily challenges are still severe. But she is largely making it without the need for extra support.

> I don't feel like there's anything [CPS] can give me now because I feel like I've already got everything. That's one thing that everybody will tell you about me, I am very resourceful nowadays.... I have a lot of resources, because I had to did and learn stuff on my own. They didn't help me like they were supposed to so I had to find out for me.

Tracy is enrolled in community college and works part-time. Someday, she hopes to help other women who have been involved with the child welfare system. In her view, her story is one about hope and renewal. According to Tracy:

For the most part, this is a good "the end."

Tracy's journey was, indeed, remarkable, but for her children, the story is mixed. Indeed, they have returned to their mother, but the path home was lengthy and dangerous. Neither court reports nor conversations with Tracy suggest that workers ever discussed alternative permanency possibilities for any of her children. Foster care was always offered as a series of temporary arrangements, even after her children had been in care for several years. Amber and Raymond spent most of their childhood in foster care, first with a relative whose care was substandard and then in two more foster homes before they returned to their mother. Tyson spent almost 5 years in foster care. Whether his present, serious mental health problems are a result of inadequate parenting or inadequate foster parenting, Tyson was failed by both his mother and the system. As a result, he will probably suffer deeply for years to come.

Children can not watch their childhoods pass while they wait for their parents to change. But neither can they be denied an opportunity to go home, even when their parents' care has been identified as grossly inadequate. Children's well-being hangs on the stable, loving care they receive from the family that surrounds them. Thus, balancing their needs for healthy development in the context of family with parents' needs to raise their own children represents the critical tension underlying all of child welfare. Understanding how child welfare services can help pave the way toward safe reunifications, giving clear signals to parents about the expectations and time lines for change, and concurrently giving children an early and durable experience of permanency will help to balance these competing strains. Then children's stories may better match those of parents like Tracy, with a "the end" that is equally positive.

4
After Adoption:
Keeping a Connection to Home

"They took them, and that was the end."

Some children do not return home following a stay in foster care. These children may live with kin long-term. Others may be adopted. In 2005, a total of 51,500 children in the United States were adopted from foster care[1]; over 100,000 children were still waiting for adoption.[2] Adoption has long been seen as a second-best alternative when reunification proves impossible. It represents a legally binding, lifelong relationship between a child and his or her new set of parents, and it assumes an emotional tie matching that of a birth parent and child. Under adoption, the rights and responsibilities of parenting are transferred entirely from the birth parent to the adoptive parent. The legal relationship between birth parent and birth child is severed; often, physical contact and communication between child and parent is lost as well.

Adoption is hardly a new phenomenon. It has been practiced in cultures across the globe for centuries. Instances of adoption can be found among some of the most famous characters in the Bible,[3] and it is noted in texts from ancient Greece, Rome, and Babylonia.[4] Historically, adoption was typically used to secure a hereditary line in order to pass property and/or wealth to a new generation. Boys were usually adopted in preference to girls, and older children[5] were the most likely candidates for adoption.[6] As the colonies formed in the United States, adoption continued to be utilized for many of the same reasons as in earlier years; however, it was also used as a strategy to secure labor in a sparsely populated country with a fledgling economy.[7] And it was used informally, of course, among different ethnic and cultural groups to ensure a degree of economic security for children.[8]

Adoption policy in the United States goes back to 1851, when the Massachusetts Adoption Act was passed, codifying legal procedures surrounding adoption. The law served to ensure the rights of birth and adoptive parents, and it also identified the needs of children as important constituents in the adoption triad (i.e., the birth parent, adoptive parent, and child).

Private adoption of infants flourished in the twentieth century,[9] particularly following the steep rise in out-of-wedlock births during and following World War II.[10] Social workers were closely involved with private adoption practice, carefully matching children to prospective adoptive parents—particularly with regard to race, ethnicity, religion, and physical features. Social workers assessed children as either "normal" or "defective,"[11] and prospective adoptive parents were closely investigated to determine the appropriateness of their home environment.

In the 1960s, as birth control methods became more widespread and social mores adjusted to accept single parenthood more readily, fewer infants became available for adoption. At the same time, foster care caseloads were rising and research studies were revealing disturbing trends about children's experiences in out-of-home care, including indeterminate stays in care and successive placements over time.[12] The large majority of the children in foster care had special needs. Many were children of color, they were older, some belonged to sibling groups, and others had physical or emotional challenges that might require more thoughtful parenting styles. Although in previous eras these children might have been considered "unadoptable," child welfare practice shifted over time, and adoptive parents were located in increasing numbers to make permanent homes for such children.[13]

Adoption from the foster care system, although underutilized as a permanency alternative for many years, was patterned on the models used in private adoption. Adoption social workers were separate from foster care social workers in the same agency, and they were usually required to submit to higher standards of training and education. Adoption files were kept separate from foster care files, and rules of confidentiality surrounding adoption files were very strict. Also following the model of private adoption, adoption files were "closed," severely limiting information about birth parents, adoptive parents, and children from other members of the adoption triad. Estimates dating back to 1982 indicate that approximately 17,000 children were in "adoptive placements," although we have no firm data on the number of finalized adoptions that may have occurred at that time.[14] By 1992, about 20,000 children were adopted from the public child welfare system.[15] That number rose markedly, to about 37,000 by 1998.[16] But even with this and subsequent increases, adoption remains the least likely permanency outcome for children.[17] In 2004–2005, about 4 years following placement in care, only about 16% of children were adopted in California— the majority were Caucasian infants placed in foster care at or near birth.[18]

The low adoption rate relative to other permanency outcomes for children suggests that there are substantial barriers limiting adoption out of foster care. First, the legal bar for involuntarily terminating parental rights is set very high. Because legal action of this nature so fundamentally interferes with the private affairs of families, judges must determine that the parent is "unfit" through "clear and convincing evidence" and demonstrate that the adoption is in the best interests of the child.[19] The finality associated with adoption also gives pause to social workers, who may hold onto the hope that birth parents will yet change if given ample time and services.[20] But the public policy messages shaping child welfare practice have varied significantly over time, with some policies favoring family preservation and extended reunification services and others promoting adoption and permanency with new families.

Why Adoption, Anyway?

In spite of the barriers, adoption has long been seen as a promising opportunity for some children. If an aggressive approach to permanency—as suggested in the previous chapter—is to be pursued, the documented benefits of adoption must outweigh indeterminate stays in foster care. In fact, evidence from a number of studies suggests that outcomes from adoption are largely very positive.[21] Adoptive parents are generally satisfied with their adoption experience and would recommend adoption to others.[22] Disruption rates following adoption are also very low. Importantly, as a comparison to the alternatives children might otherwise face, the stability and durability of adoption is notably stronger than either long-term foster care or reunification. Adoption disruption rates are markedly lower than rates of re-entry for children returned to their birth parents, rates of guardianship disruption, or rates of placement change for children remaining in long-term foster care.[23]

Outcomes for children are generally positive as well. Studies indicate that children adopted from foster care—particularly children adopted while very young—bear great similarities to those for children from the general population. Between one-third and one-half of special needs children and children adopted at older ages evidence a range of problems; however, these rates are also less than or comparable to rates of problems among children remaining in long-term foster care.[24] Adopted children are more likely to report a sense of security about their living arrangements and clarity about their position within the family compared with children living in long-term foster care.[25] And outcomes in adulthood suggest that children adopted from foster care fare very well.[26] Decidedly, although the public costs of supporting increasing numbers of public adoptions have grown markedly in recent years,[27] a cost comparison of adoption to foster care clearly favors adoption.[28]

The benefits of adoption and the harms that accrue to children remaining in long-term foster care grew increasingly evident throughout the 1990s. These trends, coupled with the spike in child welfare caseloads, brought about renewed interest in adoption. Some families lived through this subtle yet important shift in child welfare culture from one oriented principally toward family preservation to an evolving system focused more on permanency for children.

When Reunification Fails

Although she was drug-involved for most of her adult life, Janelle never had trouble with Child Protective Services (CPS) when she was raising her first two children. But her addiction worsened, and by the time she gave birth to her fifth child, CPS officials were concerned about the safety of her little ones. The new infant, Shane, 1-year-old Richard, and 3-year-old Mandel were all placed in foster care together, and Monica (age 13) and Olivia (age 16) were placed separately. Janelle was encouraged to enroll in a 12-step program and locate affordable housing. She was required to submit to random drug testing and was urged to leave her abusive boyfriend.

Janelle partially complied, although reluctantly. Hostile interactions between Janelle and her child welfare worker were frequent, and she railed at the authority and power of the state's intervention in her private family life.

When they told me to go to a 12-step program I was already angry. They wouldn't hear what I had to say so how you going to tell me to go into a program when you not even listening to what I'm dealing with? … So it made me kind of rebellious.

Janelle never enrolled in drug treatment, but she was drug-free within a year and was testing clean. She found work with a bus company and had a place to live, but she was still involved with her boyfriend. Because she had complied with most of her reunification plan, child welfare workers returned her children to her care. The lure of her boyfriend, the stress of her job, and years of addiction caught up with her: within a month she had relapsed and CPS was again knocking on her door.

The year was 1997. For Janelle, it turned out to be a turning point in her life. Only a year earlier, President Clinton had issued a memorandum urging states to increase the number of adoptions and challenging states to double the number of completed adoptions by the year 2002.[29] Presidential interest in adoption spurred congressional interest in the topic and, by the end of 1997, the Adoption and Safe Families Act (ASFA) was signed into law, pushing hard on the adoption agenda.[30]

Under ASFA, states were given financial incentives to increase the number of children adopted, with $4,000 bonuses offered for each regular adoption and $6,000 bonuses paid for special needs adoptions.[31] Children could be freed for adoption, however, only if time lines for agency decision making were tightened and birth parents were given clearer signals about the need for rapid change. Therefore the time allowed for parents to reunify with children was shortened from 18 months to 12, agencies were required to begin termination of parental rights (TPR) proceedings for children who were in care 15 of the 22 most recent months, and exceptions to the provision of reunification services were more clearly specified.[32]

The offer of reunification services had been part of child welfare policy and practice since 1980. As described in the previous chapter, under the 1980 Adoption Assistance and Child Welfare Act (AACWA, P.L. 96–272), states received some of their federal Title IV-E funding contingent on the provision of reasonable efforts toward reunification. Yet as congressional representatives debated the ASFA legislation, reservations about reasonable efforts were expressed, resulting in a clearer articulation of the circumstances in which reunification services might be denied.

ASFA identified five specific conditions that would allow states to bypass the provision of reunification services to parents. These exist when the parent has (1) murdered one of his or her children; (2) committed voluntary manslaughter of one of his or her children; (3) aided, abetted, attempted, conspired, or solicited to commit such murder or manslaughter; (4) committed felony assault resulting in serious bodily injury to any of his or her children; and (5) had parental rights to a sibling of the subject child involuntarily terminated. The law also allowed states to develop a set of "aggravated circumstances" that could be used to exempt agencies from the requirement to provide reunification services to parents. California has been particularly vigorous in establishing its list of aggravated circumstances, with a total of 15 conditions that could be applied to deny reunification services to families.[33] Parents who are denied services face a permanency planning hearing within 30 days of their child's entry to care, with TPR (termination of parental rights) proceedings occurring simultaneously or shortly thereafter.

Under ASFA and California's "aggravated circumstances" laws, the child welfare agency serving Janelle could have denied reunification services when her children re-entered care.[34] Instead, Janelle was granted a new 12-month time line and reunification services resumed. Her experience with the child welfare agency thereafter, however, speaks to the cultural shift taking place in child welfare more broadly during this time, when permanency priorities were beginning to take hold.

> So eventually I had gotten out of this abusive relationship, right? And I went back and I got clean again. So when I got clean this time I was sincerely, sincerely clean. I was driving for (the bus company). ... I had— what you call that—a reunification plan that I had to go by. Now when I was clean during that time I kept getting these abscesses in my mouth so I had to keep going to the dentist, right? Now I was on codeine. I was drug testing at this particular time. Now my worker had called me a day before—I talked to her a day before court and I asked her, I said, "What are they going to do in court?" She said, "Well, we'll see when we get there." She did not tell me on the phone I had a dirty drug test, of morphine.... That was not even a drug of choice for me! I never did morphine a day in my life, you understand? And I was clean and sober at the time and, plus, I was a driver. At the company I worked for they do random drug testing. Do you actually think I would use drugs and go to work and not knowing when they going to drug test you?

So when I went to court, you know, I'm thinking everything was okay. All of a sudden she brings up a dirty drug test. And I'm trying to explain it to the judge. And it was like every time I tried to say something the DA would shut me off. And being that I really wasn't that intelligent in my speaking or wasn't real educated on what to say or how to say it, you understand, I didn't know how to say it—how to defend myself.[35]

Janelle was given a month's reprieve, but a subsequent test again revealed morphine use.

See, at that time I didn't know the codeine shows up as morphine. But when I tried to fight (the social worker) didn't tell me to get doctor's approval. By that time they had—whatever. It was her word against my word. So they put my kids up for adoption 'cause they thought I was still using.

Some child welfare decisions are made with less than adequate information. Was Janelle taking prescribed medication for a dental problem or had she relapsed? In the murky world of he said/she said, child welfare workers make recommendations to the courts based on their professional judgment, and judges are left as ultimate arbiters, sealing the fate of children and their parents. In Janelle's case, the judge acted decisively. Mandel's status was changed to "planned, permanent living arrangement" (previously known as long-term foster care), and Janelle's young children—then 2 and 3 years old—were placed in an adoptive home together. Several months later, Richard and Shane were adopted out of foster care.[36]

The circumstances surrounding Janelle's permanency planning hearing come back vividly as she recounts her story. Her impressions of the day are detailed, and the felt injustice of the proceedings is as raw 7 years later as the day they occurred. She believes kin should have been considered more thoughtfully—a sister who was passed over because her own children had been in care previously, and Janelle's daughter, then 18, who was deemed inappropriate since she had only recently emancipated from foster care herself.[37]

When the children were adopted, Janelle slid into a deep depression.[38] She lost all contact with her children and—importantly—lost all knowledge of them: their health, their well-being, their developmental milestones, their talents.

I haven't seen them. I don't know who they with, their nationalities, I don't know anything.

Janelle tried to make contact. She composed a letter to the adoptive parents, explaining the circumstances surrounding her early parenting, assuring them of her recovery, and asking for contact.[39]

I let them know about my childhood issues back then I never had addressed up until now and I didn't know how to be a good mother and— you understand. And see, they don't understand what I went through— they don't understand what happened with me and the CPS worker in order for me to have lost my kids. I didn't just give my kids up. See, they don't under[stand]—they think—they—I don't know what impression they're under. I don't know if they're under the impression that this was a drug addict who just didn't want her kids. I fought for my kids to the best of my ability. It ain't that I just gave them up like that, you know.

The adoptive parents responded.[40] In their letter they told Janelle that they were not ready for contact; that they wanted to wait until the boys were older. Further, they provided no information, pictures, or drawings that might give her a hint of a connection to her sons.

Haunted by Memories

When I first met Janelle, it had been 7 years since her sons' adoption. Over the course of the 2 years I spent with her, the piercing ache associated with their separation never diminished. Pursued at night by dreams and haunted by day with visions of her lost children, Janelle was almost paralyzed, unable to work or go to school. Care for her older son, Mandel, was almost mechanical, as she was constantly distracted by thoughts of the past, of her lost children, and of the awesome power of the state. Sometimes she spent her days boarding one city bus after another, watching out the window in hopes of glimpsing two familiar boys, now about 9 or 10 years old, playing in the street.

According to federal law, the child welfare agency handled Janelle's case appropriately. They made "reasonable efforts" twice, and when a permanency decision was required, they made a firm and clear choice, moving expeditiously to place her young children into an adoptive home.[41] Because her children were relatively young at the time, child welfare workers seized the opportunity to secure their permanency.[42] Being separated from his siblings was undoubtedly traumatic for Mandel, and according to Janelle, it disturbs him still. But the Solomonic choice child welfare workers faced at the time was clear: improve the life chances for two out of three children or leave all three children together, buoyed by their sibling bonds but facing a highly uncertain future in foster care.[43]

Implementation of the policy may have been appropriate, but an examination of Janelle's lived experience would suggest that its effects were substantial. Could alternatives be devised that would allow children the opportunities afforded by adoption but also give birth parents and their children the advantages of a continued connection?

Open and Semiopen Adoption Alternatives

When the first U.S. adoption law was passed, provisions were made to open adoption records to the public and to the adoption triad. It was not until the twentieth century that adoption records were sealed.[44] In the broad terrain of adoption transactions, private adoptions dominated, and these usually involved infants of single mothers. Because of the public shame associated with what was then termed "illegitimacy," efforts to close adoption records were propelled by an interest in protecting women from public opprobrium and sheltering children from the knowledge of their family origins.[45]

But during the 1960s and 1970s, adult adoptees crafted a social movement that mirrored the civil rights movement of the time, claiming their right to know their birth origins, their birth history, and their birth family.[46] These nascent grassroots efforts grew rapidly, shaping public sentiments and shifting private adoption practice. At the same time, adoptive mothers initiated a call for greater openness, in part owing to the dramatic shift in the supply/demand equation. With an expanding pool of potential adoptive parents[47] and a diminishing number of birth parents willing to relinquish their infants to adoption, birth mothers grew increasingly involved in selecting adoptive parents for their children and setting the terms for future contact.[48] Adoption professionals also joined the rising chorus. Some therapists argued that closed adoptions resulted in identity confusion for children and youth and unresolved feelings of loss and pain.[49]

"Open adoption" emerged as a new practice paradigm with loose boundaries but similar features of connectedness. The model was largely embraced by private adoption agencies, many of which offered birth and adoptive parents an assortment of open arrangements that might suit their individual needs.[50] Open adoption really should be considered a "continuum of openness" that can vary by degree, by frequency and type, and may change over time.[51] At one end of the spectrum are *confidential* adoptions with little or no information shared between parties. At the midpoint are *mediated* adoptions, in which nonidentifying information is shared between parties but a third-party agency or individual is used as the pass-through. *Fully disclosed* adoptions fall at the other end of the spectrum, where birth and adoptive families have direct contact with one another and have worked out plans for visitation or other types of contact. Even among fully disclosed adoptions, some children have face-to-face contact with their birth parents, whereas others simply exchange information such as cards and letters. Open arrangements may change over time and space as parties move, marry, or make other lifestyle adjustments. Some state legislatures are even developing statutes to enforce postadoption contact.[52] These arrangements, however, are not without their critics, as complete openness among all parties may not always be in the best interests of the children.[53]

Research findings on open adoption are somewhat mixed. Almost all of the literature pertaining to openness comes from the world of private adoption and largely concerns adoption of infants at or near birth. Overall, the studies suggest that adoptive parents are generally satisfied with their arrangements. While most adoptees report few if any identity development problems,[54] some experience identity confusion; some birth parents also report protracted feelings of grief for the loss of their child.[55] Unfortunately, none of the studies utilize comparison groups, so it is unclear, for example, whether the grief that birth mothers experience is any greater in open adoption than what has been demonstrated previously in closed adoption arrangements. What is clear is that open adoption arrangements often change over time and that possibly half of the arrangements that initially include frequent contact evolve and, at the birth parents' instigation, result in less contact over time.[56] Whether these changed relationship patterns have effects on children has not been studied. Importantly, much of the open adoption research does not distinguish between *types* of contact. In one study, birth parents in closed adoptions were asked about their perspectives on open adoption. Parents overwhelmingly favored information exchange, but most were wary of direct contact, fearing its impact on the child and adoptive parents but also worrying about the effects on their own mental health.[57]

Information on public agency open adoption is relatively sparse. It appears as though open adoption may be increasingly common and is promoted as a feature of high-quality service,[58] but that the age of the child, the circumstances of the birth parent, and other factors may play a role in determining whether or not to pursue such arrangements. In one study of public adoptions, even those families who had arranged contact with birth parents had direct contact only infrequently.[59] In some cases, direct contact with birth parents may not be advisable, but some connections with other birth relatives could be appropriate. The emerging evidence on public agency adoption would suggest that mediated open arrangements or semiopen arrangements would probably be beneficial to many birth parents, as information could be exchanged that did not upset the privacy of the new family but that honored women's connection to their children.

In Janelle's case, a fully disclosed open adoption would have been problematic, but a semiopen or mediated arrangement might have worked. Janelle's unresolved anger and other mental health issues would have been highly troubling to the adoptive parents and potentially unsafe for the children. It is uncertain whether a card, a picture, or a drawing from her children might have helped her to heal. But *not* knowing—how they were, what they looked like, or what flavor ice cream they preferred—clearly contributed to her mental instability. From Janelle's perspective and that of many birth mothers, she never severed her psychological or emotional ties to her children, even though her legal relationship to them was irrevocably altered.

Using Peers to Help Start Again

The limited information available about birth parents subject to the involuntary termination of parental rights is that they feel highly isolated and deeply stigmatized.[60] Family members may not be supportive, as they too may have lost contact with the child through adoption. Friends may be critical and may ostracize the parent from her original community.[61] Isolation is unlikely to support a woman's recovery from grief and loss, but for most birth mothers, there is no natural support system to which they might otherwise turn. Birth parents involved in earlier stages of the child welfare system (i.e., prior to termination of parental rights) indicate that supportive networks might be helpful to them, whether these supportive circles include professionals[62] or peers.[63]

Increasingly, child welfare agencies are making use of peer support networks to assist in many aspects of service delivery.[64] Foster parents and kinship caregivers often derive great benefit from sharing their personal challenges in raising foster children,[65] and parents at risk of maltreating their children can experience common ground and support for positive parenting from their peers.[66] The evidence base for using peer-support models in child welfare, however, is thin. Instead, peer support has been used extensively in the field of mental health. One review of the empirical evidence in mental health interventions indicates that peer support may be an important contributor to improved mental health and quality of life.[67] And there is some support for the use of peer supports in combating alcohol addiction.[68]

While peer support models may not yet have proven their effectiveness in child welfare, they seem to make sense on theoretical grounds. That is, there may be features of mutual support that could be especially relevant for birth parents following adoption.[69] Shared experiences may promote a deeper understanding of the birth parents' circumstances and an opportunity to reduce their sense of isolation. Because of the similarities of women's backgrounds and conditions, one might expect greater honesty about events leading up to the adoption and openness in expressing emotions. Structured groups may also allow women to assume new roles, taking them out of the position as *patient* or *client* and giving them new, valued responsibilities, such as mentor or role model. Mutual support can create a context for developing new skills, strategies, and self-awareness. And cognitive changes may emerge through exposure to new world views and ideologies. Importantly, women may feel comforted by the opportunity to express intense emotions in a shared, safe environment.[70]

Janelle's case raises questions about the birth mother left behind after adoption. She received neither support nor information to help her cope with her grief. Her experience, like that of thousands of women before her, was shut away by a child welfare system that views the world in either/or terms—where children are considered family *either* to birth *or* to adoptive parents but where the blending of families is neither attempted nor acknowledged because the alternative is both messy and complicated. Janelle's experience was also dismissed in part because of who she was—a drug addict who had neglected her kids. Indeed, she behaved badly and, as a result, lost her children. But in stripping her of her legal right to her children, was it also necessary to absolutely deny her a connection to her children? And would postadoption support of some kind have made any difference at all?

A large body of literature speaks to the importance of postadoption services for adoptive families,[71] but little is written about the birth mothers touched by involuntary adoption. Although we know something about the experiences of birth mothers in the private adoption triad, birth parents in public adoption remain in the shadows, with little information available about their coping, their emotional landscape, or their needs.[72] The few studies that have explored the effects of involuntary adoption on birth parents come from England. Findings from these studies all point to significant anguish for birth parents, with feelings of grief and anger most prominent. Birth parents in these studies experienced short- and long-term effects that were both psychological and physical; many reported extended periods of "emptiness," "isolation," and "shame."[73] Some birth parents complained that they received little support during the process and that relatives and friends were often excluded from case conferences and other group meetings; many were baffled by the process and assert that they did not understand court proceedings; and still others worried that their attorneys were ill prepared for the task and did not provide adequate legal services.[74] Birth mothers describe adoption as highly traumatic, and many are desperate to have contact with their children. In one study, birth parents were particularly keen to communicate with their children, to tell them *why* the adoption had taken place and to reassure these children of their ongoing love.[75]

If the push for permanency is taken seriously by child welfare agencies, more children will likely be reunified, but more children will also be adopted. For children subjected to concurrent planning practice (described in Chapter 3), birth parents and concurrent foster parents are likely to experience almost a year of contact and visitation prior to the termination of parental rights. At the point of adoption, thoughtful planning about all members of the adoption triad should prevail. If kin, kith, and concurrent foster parents are supported in enacting *open foster care*, these arrangements should be encouraged after adoption.

Birth mothers involved in public agency adoption are disproportionately low-income women of color; most have a limited education, and many struggle with other life challenges, such as substance abuse, mental health issues, or domestic violence.[76] They are largely powerless in their dynamic exchange with child welfare workers, lawyers, and judges.[77] Termination of parental rights is surely a harsh punishment for their parenting behaviors, but a life sentence of silence may be too extreme.[78] In spite of their history of parenting, studies conducted with birth mothers indicate that they love their children and view them as central to their identity.[79] When the state strips women of their rights to their children and their role as parents, care should be taken to recognize the women left behind. At the very least, facilitated support groups may allow women to come to terms with their separation from children, and open, semiopen, and mediated adoption hold the promise of helping birth mothers heal from the trauma and maintain a human connection to their children.

A Chance to Move On

One spring day, I paid a visit to Janelle. I found her waiting for me with a bright, broad smile. She had received a letter and felt a glimmer of hope. Months earlier she decided to take action, to try to correct the injustice she perceived, and to regain custody of her children.[80] She had composed a letter approximately three pages in length, detailing her interactions with the child welfare agency, her powerlessness in the face of a dominating bureaucracy, and the pain resulting from her children's departure. In part the letter reads:

> Part of my life has been destroyed. I have to take psychiatric medication to help me cope with the part of my life that was taken away from me and the heartless way CPS went by doing it. When they took my babies they also took a part of my soul from me.

She mailed her letter to President Bush, her state senator, her congressional representative, and a host of others. Months later, the responses began to arrive. In each letter, Janelle was informed that her concern was "out of [their] jurisdiction," but each individual had done something to try to help.[81] Janelle was thrilled. President Bush's letter stated that he had sent her inquiry "to the Department of Health and Human Services." Senator Feinstein had encouraged her to contact Governor Schwarznegger, and the governor had recommended she address her concerns to the Office of the Attorney General. In each response, Janelle felt as though she had been heard. Most of the letters she received were sympathetic in tone and sincere in regret for her circumstances. The experience was cathartic. Janelle's outreach to various political actors resulted in neither a return of her children nor hope of future contact. But the connection to figures of authority made human the face of bureaucracy and in one case resulted in a sincere apology for the pain that was caused—an apology that Janelle had been waiting for for years. Today, Janelle's pain has not healed, but she is ready to engage in the world, if modestly. She is clean and sober, she has reenrolled in her community college, and she has begun to look for work. Most days she just tries to stay focused on Mandel—her last remaining child at home.

5
Kinship Guardianship:
Finding a Home Between the Family
and the State

"I wanted to keep it in the family."

The steep rise in the foster care caseload from the mid-1980s through the end of the century was accompanied by child welfare administrators' worst fear: the number of foster parents available to serve children during this time declined precipitously. Some estimates suggest that nearly one-third of foster parents left the field in the decade from 1980–1990.[1] The imbalance in supply and demand and the pressing need for care providers left state officials with few choices: to expand care provided in institutional settings (an alternative that would raise costs considerably and clash with philosophical sentiments about the best interests of children) or to develop alternative placement settings. As relatives had long provided care to children outside of the auspices of the child welfare system,[2] they were turned to as a potential placement resource.

By the mid-1990s, kinship foster care had become the fastest-growing service funded by the child welfare system.[3] In some states, the rapid expansion of kinship foster care continued thereafter. In California, for example, the utilization of kin peaked in 1998, with 45% of all children placed in kinship foster care[4]; Illinois showed similar trends, with approximately half of their child welfare population placed with kin.[5] In recent years, utilization of kin has declined somewhat and stabilized. Today, kinship foster care accounts for roughly one-quarter of all placements nationwide, although it still predominates in many large states.[6]

Kinship caregivers are those related to children by blood, law, or marriage. In some contexts "kin care" also includes care provided by "members of [a] tribe or clan, godparents, stepparents, or other adults who have a kinship bond with a child," although these caregivers are more widely referred to as "kith."[7] The large majority of children's kinship caregivers are maternal grandmothers.[8] They differ from nonrelative foster parents in several respects. First, they are older, on average, than the typical foster parent; they have less education, they are more likely to be single parents, and they are more likely to come from an ethnic minority group.[9] Importantly, they are much poorer than the average foster parent. In a study conducted by Ehrle and Geen, almost two-fifths of children in kinship foster care were living below the federal poverty level, compared with about one-fifth of children in nonrelative care.[10] Of course kin caregivers' approach to the child welfare system differs from that of nonrelative foster parents in that they often have not anticipated becoming caregivers, nor have they made personal, familial, or financial arrangements to accommodate their new role.[11]

With the advent of kinship foster care, child welfare agencies across the country have struggled to develop new practice strategies to respond to the unique circumstances and needs of relative caregivers. Unlike traditional foster parents, kin do not participate in preservice training; therefore many are unaware of agency rules and regulations and court-mandated responsibilities. Child welfare workers are thus left with the task of explaining this complicated system to kin, and a good deal of evidence suggests that this information loop is inadequate. Rather than providing kin with more services to support their significant needs or more contact with child welfare workers to help them understand their role vis-à-vis the child welfare agency, much of the research on kinship care indicates that child welfare workers offer *less* contact and *fewer* services to kin than to non-kin.[12]

Kinship care developed amid a sea of controversy. Were these caregivers truly capable of providing quality care to children? Had not social workers been taught that there were intergenerational patterns associated with maltreatment, drug addiction, and other socially marginal behaviors?[13] Did not these grandparents raise parents who ultimately maltreated their children, and did this not speak to their own limitations as parents? Or were these just vulnerable older adults who had raised other children, many of whom were now fine citizens? And although socially disadvantaged, did not their love and concern for children override other considerations?

The evidence on these questions is equivocal. One study suggests that maltreatment with kin may be more likely than with foster parents[14]; another indicates that maltreatment with kin is less likely[15];

and still another shows that the quality of care is roughly equivalent.[16] Beyond the attributes of the caregiving relationship, most studies indicate that children placed in kin care largely experience more socially disadvantaged environments.[17] Outcomes associated with kin care are also mixed. Some studies show few if any differences between children placed in kin and non-kin care in behavioral, educational, health, or social domains.[18] Others show benefits to children from placement with kin[19]; still others suggest negative effects, including higher rates of delinquent behaviors[20] and lower cognitive scores.[21] One study indicates that the longer children reside with kin, the more detrimental the effects, including a greater likelihood of delinquent behavior, sexual activity, substance use, arrests, and lower grades.[22] Studies examining adults who spent time in kin and non-kin care as children generally show mixed or no differences.[23]

While child welfare practice with kin evolved throughout the 1990s, kinship policy was slower to change and mirrored the uncertainties associated with this newer placement option. By the end of the decade, variations in state approaches to kinship policy were numerous[24]; in some states, kin were excluded from the foster care system unless they were fully licensed as foster parents; in others, kin were considered equivalent to foster parents whether or not they met the same licensing standards. In some states, kin were paid a foster care subsidy similar to that paid to a regular foster care provider; in other states, kin were paid a lower rate—usually equivalent to a Temporary Assistance for Needy Families (TANF, or welfare) grant. In many states, standards for care were relaxed, resulting in environments of highly uneven quality.

Federal guidance in the area of kinship care was lacking until 1996, when policymakers showed their support for kinship care placements. The Personal Responsibility and Work Opportunity Reconciliation Act (P.L. 104–193) largely focused on reforms to the welfare program,[25] but Congress also addressed child welfare by requiring states to "consider giving preference to an adult relative over a non-related caregiver when determining a placement for a child, provided that the relative caregiver meets all relevant State child protection standards." Guidelines regarding placement preferences were a helpful starting point; however, the federal government remained silent on the issues of foster care subsidies and licensing standards. With the Adoption and Safe Families Act of 1997 (P.L. 105–89—ASFA), policies pertaining to both these issues were clarified.[26] The resulting regulations made it clear that kinship caregivers would be eligible for federal IV-E foster care payments only if they met the same licensing standards as nonrelatives in each state.[27] Perspectives on kinship care had shifted somewhat. Extended family were to be included as caregivers whenever possible, and the system's previous ignorance of their needs and limitations was recognized as unhelpful to children. Kinship caregivers required services and supports in order to provide care, children had rights relating to the parameters of that care, and kin had to abide by their responsibilities to children and to the state.

Blending Bureaucratic Systems and Family Dynamics

Taken together, these policies showed lawmakers' support for kinship foster care, tempered by an interest in ensuring some measure of safety and quality for children. But the tangled issues of kinship care have not been settled entirely. The introduction of kin into the child welfare system has ushered in a wholesale shift in philosophy, where the stark lines between *family* and *stranger* have blurred. Kinship care does not fit the traditional paradigm of foster care; in many cases children know their relative caregivers and in some cases they have lived with them previously.[28] Sharp dividing lines between out-of-home and in-home care are more murky. Indeed, some have questioned whether kinship care should even be categorized as foster care or as family preservation.[29]

In part because of the differences in the nature of kinship care, the experiences of children in care and their pathways through care are quite different from those of children in non-kin care. A good deal of evidence suggests that children in kinship care visit with their birth parents more often than do children in non-kin foster care[30]; they also have more frequent contact with siblings, either because they are placed together in the same household or because visitation is facilitated by the caregiver.[31] Children's placement experience while in care is more stable—they are less likely to move, and when they require replacement, they frequently move from the home of one relative to that of another.[32] Once children are placed in kinship care, their stay is likely to be much longer than the average stay of children with non-kin. Research indicates that for some groups—particularly African-American children—placement duration may be more than two times greater than that for children placed with nonrelatives.[33] Although kinship care is more stable than regular foster care,[34] long-term care with kin is still no guarantee of security.[35] Some research shows that the longer the duration in care, the greater the likelihood that children placed with kin will also experience changes in placement.[36]

Responding to Children's Permanency Needs With Relatives

Although rates of reunification are relatively similar between children placed with kin and non-kin, it takes children in kin care longer to reunify with their parents than it does for children placed in foster care.[37] Children's lengthy duration in kinship care is explained in part by the lack of available permanency alternatives for these children. Some evidence suggests that adoption, for example, is frequently rejected by relatives—usually maternal grandmothers—who are reluctant to terminate their daughters' parental rights and may be hopeful that their daughters will one day change their behavior enough to reunify with their children.[38] Growing evidence from one study in Illinois, however, indicates that relatives will indeed adopt if they are adequately informed about the option and told of the potential benefits[39]; in some states, relatives represent the fastest-growing segment of the adoptive parent population.[40] But for those children whose caregivers are unable or unwilling to adopt, long-term foster care is often the answer.

Current policy shuns long-term foster care for children placed with nonrelatives, but federal lawmakers continue to show their ambivalence about the unique circumstances of kin, determining that long-term care with kin may be appropriate. Under ASFA, states are required to initiate termination of parental rights (TPR) proceedings when a child has been in a non-kin care for 15 of 22 consecutive months. If, however, a child is being cared for by a kinship caregiver, states are allowed to extend this time frame and can consider relatives as part of a "planned, permanent living arrangement."

The combination of presumed adoption obstacles and the tacit promotion of long-term care result in lengthy stays in out-of-home care for children placed with kin. But permanency alternatives are emerging in several states that may offer new options for some families. Subsidized kinship guardianship programs allow the custodial rights of the child to be transferred from the state to an adult caregiver. Rather than terminate parental rights altogether—as in adoption—and rather than grant all rights back to the parent—as in reunification—legal guardianship represents a midpoint wherein parents retain limited rights (e.g., visitation[41]) but guardians are extended a wide range of rights in order to care for the child free from state intrusion.[42] Under legal guardianship, for example, caregivers are vested with the authority to make everyday health, educational, and disciplinary decisions on behalf of the child. They can also represent the child in court, consent to marriage and enlistment in the military, and make determinations about major medical treatments.[43] Unlike the situation in the adoption process, child welfare workers conduct minimal screening to determine the appropriateness of the adult guardian and her caregiving capacity.

Legal guardianship is not a new phenomenon. Evidence dates back to the Roman era for its use in offering care and protection to children whose parents had died or deserted them.[44] In the context of child welfare in the United States., Hazeltine Taylor promoted subsidized private guardianship in the mid 1960s[45]; as of the early 1990s, the idea had taken hold in several states. Until recently, legal guardianship was used relatively infrequently as a permanency planning option, but in those states that allowed legal guardianship, most included kin and non-kin as prospective guardians.[46] Some states pay guardians a foster care rate after the assumption of guardianship; others restrict these payments only to non-kin, while still others offer payments based upon a means test. Importantly, a few states provide payments to guardians only if the state retains joint custody of the child with the guardian.[47] In these cases, the child welfare case remains "open," child welfare services are sustained, and social workers continue to supervise and support caregivers and children.[48]

Kin seeking legal guardianship for their relative children *outside* of the child welfare system have always been free to petition the courts when parents were unable or unwilling to care for their child. Custody was a private, family matter and probate courts were involved to the extent that the legal change in relationship needed state sanction. Following the change in custody, however, the role of the state faded. Legal custodians were not compensated for the care of the child; however, they were allowed to apply for welfare[49] in the form of a child-only grant to help offset the costs of care.

A new alternative, the subsidized guardianship program, has grown substantially in the past decade. Today, almost two dozen states have developed such programs as a means of encouraging relatives to assume a legal custodial relationship with the child, thus terminating child welfare involvement. The programs vary by state in design, and they are financed through different channels. Some of the programs are financed with federal IV-E funds through state waiver requests. Others are funded through TANF, and still others use state funding mechanisms.[50] Some states limit guardianship based upon the age of the child (e.g., age 10 or older),[51] while others restrict the program to those caregivers who have provided foster care to their relative child for some period of time (e.g., 12+ months). Depending on the state, payments are made at or near the basic foster care rate and Medicaid services are continued. Other services, including case management, are terminated and court oversight of the case is withdrawn.

A number of benefits of subsidized guardianship are widely reported. First, states stand to accrue significant financial gain, with some estimating that each guardianship may represent up to a 50% cost savings.[52] Subsidized guardianship also allows children to experience the security of a legal relationship with their kin caregiver in addition to the affective relationship they likely enjoy. It gives children living in kinship foster care a way out of the child welfare system and allows relatives to continue caring for children into adulthood with no intrusions from social workers or others monitoring their parenting and their children's well-being.

In spite of the purported benefits, subsidized guardianship with relatives is complicated, as it carries with it some of the same challenges associated with kinship foster care. Kinship guardianship does not fit the traditional paradigm of stranger-based guardianship; thus certain assumptions about the degree of distance between and protection from the birth parent and child may not necessarily fit. The boundaries between parent and child may be more porous, and the relationship between guardians, parents, and the state may be more difficult to define.

Grace and LaDonna—A Family Affair

Grace, age 44, has a full household. At 16 she had her first child and 20 years later had her last. All of her children were born into her addiction and all experienced a troubled childhood. It was not until her youngest was in preschool that she sought help and became clean and sober. Since that time, she has altered her life unimaginably, attending church and school and conscientiously working to improve her parenting skills. But her children are challenging. All of them were raised with drugs, inconsistency, maternal absence, and unpredictability. Grace recounts stories of her early parenting:

> There is still pain that hovers over me and it's painful when I think about how the two oldest boys was probably 3 or 4 years old and
> I think about how they was so hungry one time and they wanted to—me to feed them, but I was so doped up and loaded I couldn't get up to feed them. And what woke me up was a fire and they was actually trying to cook theirself and the whole house was almost catching fire. And when I think about the little ages of those kids, when I think about that, that is painful for me.
>
> Then when I think about my daughter that's 18 and one that's 15 now, how I had moved into an apartment one time and I left them, just babies, inside the house. And I remember there wasn't much in that house because I just moved in there. And I had left to go get a hit of dope and I never came back for three or four days and what happened? How did they fend for theirself in there? When I think of those times it's painful for me because I'm still being healed from that, you know, and because I'm human now, you know, and I have a conscience now and I love children. I always did love them.

If they weren't raised by her, they were raised by Grace's family members in the initial days of kinship foster care. In California, during the 1990s, foster care caseloads were so high and the pressing need for caregivers so great that little was done to assess kinship caregivers' capacity or quality of care. When her children were removed to foster care, Grace told workers from Child Protective Services (CPS) that she wanted her children placed with her sister Tabitha; social workers did a background check and found that her sister had no criminal record and therefore placed all but the two youngest children with her.[53] But it is not clear that social workers ever visited Tabitha's home or inquired about others who might live there. Six months after placement, Grace's second-oldest daughter, Lacy, was molested by Tabitha's boyfriend.

Grace was so upset by her daughter's treatment that she brought all her children home, told social workers that she had decided to reunify then and there, and that her recovery was sufficiently stable. As a consequence, CPS closed the case. A year later, she relapsed and a new placement was made—this time with her sister Vicky. Again, social workers did nothing to assess Vicky's home. She too was abusing drugs, and a year later Lacy ran away. Eventually Lacy returned to Grace's home and Lacy and her mother lived together for some months until Grace's child welfare worker made a home visit and discovered Lacy's living arrangement. Once again, Grace asserts that she refused to return her daughter to placement. Instead, all four of her children under the age of 18 were returned to her while she received several months of court supervised in-home services and continued in her drug treatment program.

After the second reunification, Grace experienced a religious awakening and her drug treatment began to take hold. She changed everything—the town she lived in, her children's schools, her daily routines, her circle of friends. Four years later, she remains clean and sober and works hard to parent her children thoughtfully.

Grace's eldest, LaDonna, never lived in foster care, but because of her tumultuous childhood in Grace's care, her young adulthood was also troubled. She gave birth to her first child at the age of 17; by the time she was 25, all three of her children—Elaine, Tara, and Lenore—had been placed under the custody of the child welfare agency. Child welfare workers asked LaDonna about her preference for placement and she named her mother, Grace.

Although Grace's recovery was still fresh and her own case was terminated just months earlier, her household grew from four children to seven, including the infant Lenore. Recently a client of the child welfare system, Grace had now become a paid kinship foster parent. After 3 years of caring for LaDonna's children, Grace was told by her social worker about California's KinGAP program. The Kinship Guardianship Assistance Payment program (KinGAP) was designed for relatives caring for their kin children in a safe and stable placement.[54] Under guardianship, custody of the child is transferred from the state to the caregiver and the case is closed. Caregivers also receive a regular monthly payment at a rate similar to their foster care payment for each child in their custody. Grace describes it this way:

My oldest daughter, she won't move, she won't budge. She will follow me. She ended up in prison and she followed in my footsteps, everything I did she did. I got hooked, she got hooked, everything, you know. She went to prison a couple of times and she was on her way back this time and I really believe the reason why she was trying to—why she went back [to prison])—is because she was trying to take the baby. See, I've been having that baby since she [Lenore] came out of the hospital. She was in jail when she had the baby so I had to get the baby. And I took care of the baby while

I was getting my education and everything and she wanted to take the baby and God didn't want her to take the baby, so she ended up going to jail the next day when CPS was getting ready to give her the baby back. And I say okay. The next day she went to jail. And that's how come I still have the baby.

Grace now sees the efforts of child welfare workers as helpful, but during her addiction she was reluctant to accept their help. Now, LaDonna is reliving her mother's prior experience. She resents child welfare's involvement in her family and resists their requirements.

See, with CPS with LaDonna it's a little different than when it was with me. Like when they tried to help me all the time, she got something in her heart like they ain't trying to help me do nothing, they ain't trying to do this or—she just hate them, you know. And so with that she's not going to get anything out of them. She don't do nothing they tell her to do. She don't do nothing they tell her to do.

When the social worker talked with Grace about guardianship, she was eager to press forward. She did not really mind the monthly visits or the help she received with the children's clothing allowance, but she felt that guardianship would allow her children and grandchildren to slip into the private sphere of family life, giving Grace the authority to manage family decisions that were now publicly controlled. Simply put:

With legal guardianship it'll be easier for my family. It'll be my decision when it's time for LaDonna to get her kids and not theirs. I know if I can keep her close to me, then I'll know when and if she's ready to have her children.

Grace also felt the push for permanency from her child welfare worker. Knowing that there was an implicit possibility of adoption, that her social worker could recommend a placement change for her grandchildren, and recognizing that child welfare agencies try to keep to a time line for reunification, Grace wanted to slow down the process and allow LaDonna's recovery to unfold more naturally.

I'm still working with her. And then I'm not in a hurry, you know, because I found out that you can't be in a hurry with this thing because everybody is different and if you rush a person they ain't going to do nothing but miss something. Then they got to fall all the way back down to get what they missed to get up again, to start over again. It's just like classes. You know, you can't go to the first grade if you don't complete the kindygarten, you know, so you really have to take your time with people. You can't rush them. You know, you have to have patience. Patience is a virtue and that's something, CPS, they have a lot of patience with people but they give them 'til like six months to get theirself together, to get their kids back.

Grace's interest in a more fluid arrangement for her grandchildren stemmed in part from her own experience with the child welfare system. Her children had shuttled back and forth between her sister's kinship foster home and her home, usually outside the gaze of the child welfare system.[55] It also reflected the natural flow of living arrangements in her extended family. She often had nieces and nephews "staying" in her home for a month or more, and her own children moved easily from her household to that of one of her sisters. When children are under the jurisdiction of the child welfare agency, social workers and the courts determine when and if parents can visit, whether these visits are supervised or unsupervised, when children can remain overnight in their parents' home, and when their stay can be extended over several days or even weeks. Although guardianship arrangements assume that parents can not and should not care for their children, the actual circumstances of these provisions are more porous as children move among family members outside of the gaze of public officials. As for little Lenore,

[LaDonna] keep Lenore, I keep Lenore, [my sister] keep Lenore. Lenore's a little rolling stone, you know. But I have not, you know, released her from KinGap. I still get her income and she still be here and I still take her over to the nursery [school]. But, you know, her mother wanted to spend a couple of days with her, so [my sister] took her over there yesterday, you know.

As for Lenore's sisters, Grace returned them to LaDonna several months after the guardianship was established.

I didn't go back to court. I just made the decision to give LaDonna her kids and let her get the money for her kids. I didn't have to go back to court. You know, they gave me the power to make the choices because I'm the legal guardian and today I'm still the legal guardian.[56]

These private arrangements make sense for individual families, but they raise questions of equity, and legitimacy when considered within the context of the state. Grace, for example, receives approximately $1,500 per month to care for her three grandchildren under KinGAP.

She keeps $500 for Lenore's care but gives $1,000 to LaDonna for the other girls' care. Grace receives an annual letter from the social services agency asking about the status and well-being of the children and asking her to verify that they continue to live with her. She routinely checks the boxes and returns the form, knowing that no more oversight or investigation will be forthcoming.

But Grace's guardianship agreement stipulates that she will not return the girls to their mother barring a change in legal custody by the courts. Further, the financial arrangement they have devised may fit their family's needs, but it subverts the intention of the law. If the girls were in LaDonna's legal custody, she would receive TANF payments for their care.[57] TANF is means tested, her own income would be considered in the calculation, and assuming that she had no income of her own, LaDonna's monthly income would total about $550—far below the KinGAP rate.[58] Further, TANF is time-limited (5 years total), whereas KinGAP payments remain in place until the child turns 18. The private arrangement between Grace and her daughter undercuts notions of equity for other parents and kin, and—ultimately—also makes illegitimate the entire notion of kinship guardianship if increasing numbers of families use this innovation in child welfare as a mechanism to increase their family's economic well-being outside of the structure of the state.

Uptake and Outcomes of Kinship Guardianship

Subsidized guardianship for kin was established because of a long-standing concern about rates of permanency for children in kinship foster care. Assuming that reunification rates were similar and that adoption would be shunned by blood relatives, children in kinship foster care were much more likely to remain in long-term foster care under the continued supervision of the state. Proponents of subsidized guardianship for kin estimated that legal guardianship could result in cost savings, and some purported that a legally binding relationship would offer children a greater degree of emotional security and lead to a stronger attachment between child and caregiver than could be provided by long-term foster care.[59] Guardianship was not without its detractors, however. Some expressed concerns that it was not necessarily a permanent setting for children, since the guardianship could be easily overturned by disillusioned or disgruntled caregivers. In short, guardianship was considered less *binding* and therefore less *secure* than adoption.[60]

What does the research tell us about guardianship to date? Ten states now have waivers from the federal government to implement subsidized guardianship programs for kin, utilizing funding from Title IV-E.[61] The largest and most comprehensive study of subsidized guardianship comes from the state of Illinois. In that state, research involving experimental and control groups randomly assigned to groups allowed for subsidized guardianship to be tested against the availability of unsubsidized guardianship. Children in the experimental condition, where subsidized guardianship was available, had a greater likelihood of achieving permanency (either through reunification, adoption, or guardianship) than the children in the control condition, and the availability of subsidized guardianship did not significantly reduce children's opportunities for other permanency options (i.e., reunification or adoption).[62]

Maryland's study of subsidized guardianship pointed to the importance of adequate funding in order to attract kin caregivers. That is, in that state, some kin providing foster care services receive a regular foster care payment averaging about $600 per month; other kinship caregivers who are not licensed foster parents receive a TANF child-only grant close to $200 per month. Under the subsidized guardianship program, relatives were offered about $300 per month. Not surprisingly, relatives previously receiving TANF child-only grants as foster parents were enthusiastic about electing kinship guardianship, whereas kinship foster parents receiving the higher payment rate under foster care were disinclined to change their status to guardianship.[63]

These studies suggest that if a subsidized guardianship program is offered and is adequately funded, long-term kinship caregivers will select this permanency option, offering children an exit from foster care. Although the studies tell us that the children have left foster care, they do not necessarily tell us where the children are now living, nor do they speak to children's well-being.

Once children are in guardianship, some research suggests that they are relatively safe. Shlonsky's study of over 8,000 cases in California's KinGAP program examined whether or not these children were reported for child maltreatment or returned to foster care up to 2 years after the guardianship placement.[64] About 2% of children were subsequently reported to child welfare authorities for maltreatment following guardianship, and about 1% were once again placed into foster care. These rates of re-entry are especially low and compare favorably against re-entry rates from reunification with birth parents, but this study still tells us remarkably little about children's day-to-day living arrangements.

Only one study has included the perspectives of children in kinship guardianship. That study included children in kin guardianship compared with those adopted by relatives; it assessed their sense of safety, attachment, and well-being with their adoptive parents or guardians. Findings from the study suggest that the two caregiving arrangements were roughly similar from the children's vantage point.[65]

Lifting the Veil of Uncertainty in Kinship Guardianship

Outcomes from kinship guardianship studies are promising. They indicate a strong sense of safety and attachment for children, protection from maltreatment, and very low rates of re-entry to foster care. Subsidized kinship guardianship can result in cost savings as compared with long-term foster care, and it allows increasing proportions of children—particularly children of color—to exit the child welfare system. Programs such as these—now well under way in almost two dozen states—should be expanded to all states and given the documented cost savings, should be federally funded and supported.[66] But promotion of subsidized guardianship with relatives should not be considered in a *no-strings-attached* policy environment. Efforts should be made to formulate a monitoring mechanism that ensures the safety of children's custody arrangements and that these arrangements remain intact following case closure.

Children's experience of living with relatives is different from the experience of living with non-kin, whether that care is provided through foster care, adoption, or legal guardianship. But care by kin that is publicly funded highlights the inevitable conflict between the private sphere of the family and the public domain of the state. Legal guardianship policy can therefore be developed further by focusing principally on the *family* aspects of care, or it can evolve from a purely *bureaucratic* perspective.[67] Each viewpoint suggests a different path for policy formation.

Concentrating entirely on the family aspects of kinship care means ignoring the likelihood that boundaries between family members may be elastic; it assumes that the constellation of family members' strengths, problems, and needs remains static until the child reaches adulthood; and it considers the financial subsidy as a means of supporting the child, regardless of his or her living arrangements. Such a perspective is adopted when we promote unsupervised subsidized guardianship for the duration of childhood. This is the stance most states have accepted thus far; the perspective honors family, but it does so with a blind eye to the intricate family dynamics that play out in many kinship arrangements.[68]

Legal guardianship can just as easily evolve by focusing more clearly on the role of the state in protecting children. Using this paradigm, one assumes that children have been removed from their parents' care to protect their safety and well-being and that continued separation from parents is warranted unless circumstances change. Under this model, boundaries between parents and children are more firm, the state plays a modest role in monitoring the custodial arrangements for the child, and payments are designed to compensate caregivers for extending themselves to the child.[69] The exact monitoring arrangement that might occur in kinship guardianship could take many shapes, including social worker visits, phone calls, or references from third parties. The point is not to determine the nature of continued state contact but to contend that some ongoing state contact might be prudent over time.

Testa has argued most eloquently in favor of legal guardianship for kin, forwarding the *interactionist* perspective, based on the notion that kin have natural inclinations to behave altruistically toward their relative children but that these social attachments need reinforcements from the state in order to be sufficiently stable and secure.[70] Testa claims that the monthly subsidy plays an important role in activating relatives' altruistic motivations toward their kin children and, absent the subsidy, kin may not be sufficiently motivated to provide care or may lose their sense of obligation over time. But the interactionist theory misses an important component suggested by other family theorists. According to the work of Giddens,[71] altruism will diminish if it is not sufficiently rewarded or if the altruistic relationship is not amply reenforced by moral and/or legal standards. In the case of subsidized guardianship with kin, the rewards are apparent and ongoing via the monthly subsidy, but there is no enforcement of either moral or legal standards—by way of continuing social worker contact or other means of meaningful monitoring—once the legal relationship has been established.

Subsidized guardianship is an important component in the array of permanency options available to children placed with kin. But because care provided by relatives has features that distinguish it considerably from care provided by strangers, ongoing connections to the state are important. The contemporary family is adaptable, fluid, and diverse.[72] Patterns of living arrangements among low-income families are also permeable and, understandably, patterns of economic cost and resource pooling are prevalent.[73] Therefore kinship care that is publicly subsidized should be structured in such a way as to support caregivers' natural obligations toward family members but also monitored so that it is made more transparent to the state than is private care.

Children placed in kinship foster care need reasonable options to live in safe, stable, permanent homes. When reunification is not possible and adoption is not preferred, legal guardianship—with mechanisms that assure safety and well-being before placement and systems that ensure children's long-term stability—affords children a special opportunity for permanency—a place to call home.

6

Quality Foster Care:
My Home for Now

*"Why would you put them someplace where it is not
okay to be?"*

On any given day, there are over half a million children in out-of-home
care in the United States. Surely some of those children could be
prevented from coming into care, and some of them could probably go
home more quickly, but the essential fact remains that many children
live in out-of-home care each year; some of them throughout childhood.
According to the U.S. Department of Health and Human Services, the
average length of stay for children in foster care is 31 months; almost
one third of children stay for 3 years or more. Nationwide, almost half of
children in out-of-home care live with nonrelatives (46%), another quarter live in kinship foster care (24%), and another fifth live in group homes
or institutions (18%).[1]

Although kinship care has grown in prominence in recent decades,
nonrelative foster care dominates as the central type of caregiving
environment for children removed from their homes. In spite of its
prevalence, family foster care is plagued by significant problems. There
are too few foster parents available to care for the thousands of children
needing care, support for caregivers is woefully inadequate, subsidies to
caregivers are insufficient, and monitoring of caregivers' quality of care
is minimal.

The shortage of foster homes is so severe that the U.S. Department
of Health and Human Services has indicated that demand exceeds
supply by over 30%.[2] Foster parent recruitment is only part of the
problem; some estimates indicate that almost 40% of foster parents quit
during the first year of service,[3] and an additional 20% report plans to
discontinue care in the foreseeable future.[4] The shortage may be due to

any number of problems, including low reimbursement rates, an increase in the number of women working outside of the home, perceptions that children in care are increasingly challenging to care for, changes in demographic patterns, and concerns that agencies are not sufficiently supportive of caregivers.[5] This scarcity can be resolved by a number of different methods. First, kinship care could continue its expansion across the nation. But with preferential policies already in place and licensing standards imposed since the Adoption and Safe Families Act (ASFA), kinship care may have reached its saturation point. That is, each year since 1998, the proportion of all children residing with kin in out-of-home care has declined slightly and stabilized around 24% nationwide.[6] This may suggest that most states are already utilizing kin to the greatest extent possible.

Other options might include the expansion of group or residential care. The use of group care has hovered between 16% and 19% over the past several years.[7] Cost certainly keeps in check the utilization of group care, however. Depending on the state and the circumstances of the child, group care placement can run from approximately $4,000 to $5,000 per month.[8] Some critics of child welfare have called for the expansion of group care and orphanages,[9] but on cost considerations alone, group care is an unlikely candidate for large-scale development. Group care is limited by cost and by federal law and philosophical considerations that point toward home-based family-like settings.[10]

Serving as the backbone of the child welfare system, then, traditional foster care is nonetheless given scant attention by public policymakers, administrators, and child welfare reformers. The clamor for prevention may be loud, and adoption may also receive occasional public attention, but calls to bolster or improve the core intervention of the child welfare system – foster care – are heard less frequently. The neglect of foster care has resulted in a remarkably uneven quality of care for our nation's most vulnerable children.

Research on children's experiences of out-of-home care paints a mixed portrait. On the one hand, a number of studies suggest that children's opinion is largely positive. In a nationally representative sample of children having contact with the child welfare system, about 90% indicated that they "liked" the people they were living with and felt as though they were part of their families.[11] Other large-scale studies of children from Illinois suggest a high degree of satisfaction with their placement experience.[12] Many of the other studies attempting to elicit children's perspectives on care are small in scale; most show that children have more favorable views of foster care and kinship care than they do of group care.[13] The study findings largely converge in suggesting children's generally positive views of care, although all of the studies suffer from sample biases, as children's social workers, their caregivers, or the children themselves often opt out of participation in the studies.[14] And in spite of children's regard for their caregivers and their caregiving experience, most studies also point to general inadequacies in accessing appropriate educational,[15] health,[16] or mental health services[17] for many children in care.

The rather spotty yet generally positive evidence on the quality of children's care experience is encouraging; however, these data are coupled with increasing information on children's poor-quality experiences as well. Maltreatment in foster care represents the far end of the spectrum in considering quality care. There is no doubt that children who are abused by their foster caregivers are receiving care of very low quality. So what do we know about maltreatment in care? Official reports of maltreatment in foster care suggest that this is a relatively rare phenomenon. The federal government sets an upper threshold of tolerance for maltreatment in out-of-home care of less than 1%.[18] In the most recent government reviews, about half of the states were in "substantial conformity" with this goal.[19] We know from rather dated studies, however, that maltreatment used to be relatively common. In a follow-up study involving interviews with 61 adults who entered care between the years 1951 and 1969, some 40% reported experiencing severe physical punishment but not necessarily confirmed cases of abuse, in at least one foster home during their tenure in the system.[20] In another follow-up study involving interviews with 106 young adults who were Casey Family Program foster youth between the years of 1966 and 1984, 25% reported that they experienced severe physical punishment in their Casey home of longest stay.[21] More recently, large-scale studies have suggested that poor-quality care may still be a serious problem. In one retrospective study of young adults' perceptions of their caregiving experience, almost 40% had run away from their placement setting during their stay in care; of these, about 60% had run away more than once. About one third indicated that they had been "mistreated" while living in foster care.[22]

The disjunction between official reports and client surveys is troubling. Further, whether the data show a marginal problem or a system riddled with abuse, these statistics mask the profound injustice done to some children residing in care and to the powerlessness parents feel when they can not respond to their children's needs.

A Mother's Perspective on Poor-Quality Foster Care

Rachel knows that feeling of helplessness first hand. She knows she was not there for her children. She is well aware of her mistakes and is penitent daily. Regardless, she still can not forgive the state for taking her children only to have them suffer at the hands of another. She tells her story like this:

It was a hot summer night and Rachel wanted to get high. She knew she was struggling with addiction, but she had no idea how to escape. Her boyfriend was using, most of her family members were using, she was surrounded by drugs everywhere in her neighborhood. But it was discomforting to be around her kids when she was in her addiction; she hated it when the kids saw her. If only she could get some time away from her children, she could get loaded and she could hide from them … for just a while. She boarded the city bus with her 9-year-old, Steven, and her 4-year-old, Michael, in tow. They reached the bus stop across town late in the evening …

> And the bus is a block—you can see my sister's house from the bus stop, okay. And I told my son, I say, "You sure y'all can make it from here to the corner? And he was like "yeah." And then I had to go—I was all caught up.

The boys made their way, alone, to their aunt's house. The aunt was in no position to care for the boys, and she was angry that they had been left without supervision in her dangerous neighborhood. Unable to contact Rachel, she phoned the child abuse hotline and the police, and reported the boys for maltreatment. Court reports from that period indicate "child neglect" as the primary reason for foster care.

> It's weird, though, because they, the reports, when they first start them out the first thing they say is the kids were not properly housed, clothed, or fed. But my kids had all that. You know what I mean? The only thing was I was on drugs and I wasn't here for them, you know what I'm saying? I wasn't being a mommy, okay.

This was not the first time she had had contact with the child welfare agency. Rachel had struggled with addiction for over 10 years. She was first reported to Child Protective Services (CPS) in 1996. Reports from that time show that the children were living in badly deteriorated conditions with their grandmother, little food was available, and the oldest son, Daniel, was not attending school. Child abuse investigators examined the situation and closed the case. A year later, a new child abuse report was filed. Conditions were similar, and this time the children were taken into care.

Daniel and Steven lived in foster care for 3 years. Michael—just an infant at the time—lived with his mother in her residential drug treatment program. Then, after the conditions of her case plan were met, all three children were returned to Rachel's care.

> *But I relapsed. I ended up thinking, "Okay, I could just take one, I'll be okay." And it didn't turn out that way. This time, I guess I could say I know what they mean when they say one is too many and a thousand is never enough. And so I went—after that I was gone. I was back out on the street.*

A new child abuse report was filed shortly thereafter, but the children were living with their father at the time, so child welfare authorities thought they had sufficient care; the case was closed. Another month passed and one more report was filed, this time by schoolteachers. The family was homeless and Daniel had run away. Because Rachel promised that their housing would soon stabilize, social workers again closed the case. Three months later, in late 2002, Daniel called the child abuse hotline himself; but nothing was done. By mid-2003, Rachel was often gone for days at a time. Her sister frequently took care of the children when Rachel was off on a binge. This time, though, Rachel's sister had had enough. When the children again showed up unaccompanied by their mother one evening, Rachel's sister called the police and the children were taken into custody.

Steven and Michael re-entered foster care. Rachel anticipated that her children would receive good care in a foster home, and her early impressions were confirmed. Although Daniel was on the run, moving from one relative's home to the next, the younger boys were placed together in Lynette and Ray Dunn's foster home, where they were enrolled in school and taken to therapy. The Dunns brought the boys to the social service agency each week for visitation sessions with their mother, and each week the boys looked well fed and appropriately clothed. Rachel does not know what happened next, but after a couple of months in care, strange problems began to emerge.

> *I had a visit and my son came and he had a black eye. So he has all these scratches and stuff on his face and then he got this black eye and I'm just looking, you know. And I was at a supervised visit and I didn't say*

anything but my boyfriend seen it and then I say, "Yeah, you saw it
too?" So I told Lynette, I said, "What happened to my baby?" And then
their excuse is when he's at school he jumps off stuff and he hurts hisself,
right? So then—so my kids are coming to me on the visits, right, and
they're telling me the stuff that's going on in the foster home. The lady's
grabbing them by they collar and hitting on them and throwing—just
torturing them.

At first, Rachel held back. Fearing retribution from the foster parent and inattention from the social worker, Steven insisted that his mother remain quiet. *"Mama, she ain't going to move us and we have to go back,"* he would say. She honored her son's request at first but finally called her social worker to report the problem. Ms. Williams, Rachel's social worker at the time, said she would investigate, but the boys claimed they never saw their social worker and the situation worsened. Each time Rachel visited with her sons they would tell her about the escalating maltreatment. Alarmed, Rachel called Ms. Williams again, insisting that she do something.

So I called Ms. Williams and I'm saying, "You need to move my kids!
You need to do something 'cause there's something going on." And
every time I told her something she said, "Well, I'm going to investigate
it," right?

Rachel called the hotline to report the maltreatment, but the call was simply referred to Ms. Williams, who did not respond. Weeks went by and Rachel called Ms. Williams' supervisor. She, too, claimed that an investigation would be done, but nothing seemed to change. Rachel's despair was beyond compare when her son called during an altercation at the foster home:

My son call me on the phone one day and he said, "Mama, please
come get me 'cause I'm scared." I say, "Steven, what's wrong?"
He say, "Lynette just threw a vase." He says, "Glass everywhere.
Mama, please come get me." And I'm like "Man ..." I'm sitting up
here and I start crying and everything. I'm like, "Steven, I can't."

After 8 months, the boys were finally moved to another foster home, not because of the quality of care they were receiving in the Dunn's home but because Lynette accused Michael of harming another foster child in her care. When the boys moved, the new foster parents discovered that Michael had not been attending school, as Lynette had indicated, and the court reports reflected, that the boys had only attended one therapy session, and that all of their clothes but for a few were tattered or too small. Nothing in the court reports suggests that an investigation for maltreatment took place, and social workers later assigned to the case were unaware that there had ever been a problem in care.

A year later, well after Steven and Michael were reunited with their mother, Rachel was watching the evening news when she learned that Lynette and Ray killed a foster child in their care. In spite of her efforts to save her own sons, someone else's child was not as lucky.

Foster Parenting and Good Parenting: What Is the Connection?

The Dunn's lack of proper care for Rachel's children was extreme, but what do we expect of typical foster parents? How should they treat children, what skills should they possess, and how can we account for their behavior? High-quality foster parenting should mirror strong parenting. One might argue, however, that good foster parents may need even better parenting skills than the average parent, given that they care for exceptional children with challenging emotional and behavioral problems.[23] Among average families, parenting skills associated with children's social and emotional development include warmth and acceptance of the child's natural skills and abilities,[24] minimal parent–child conflict,[25] disciplinary practices that are not harsh,[26] and a high degree of monitoring and supervision.[27] In addition to parenting skills, other factors appear to play a role in children's healthy development. These include the general quality of the home environment, family functioning, marital functioning,[28] the parents' positive mental health, social support, some demographic characteristics,[29] and the interaction between the children's and parents' temperament. Unfortunately, the evidence base to suggest that social service personnel consider these characteristics when reviewing foster parent applicants is sparse. Some assessments of these caregiving qualities may indeed go on, but systematic data to describe how they are applied or the extent to which the average foster parent possesses these qualities is missing.

Researchers John Orme and Cheryl Beuhler conducted a review of almost three dozen studies to better understand how foster parents and foster homes reflect the characteristics of homes in the general population – homes that are commonly associated with positive family life and favorable outcomes for children.[30] Based on their review, they estimate that approximately 15% to 20% of foster parents "have problems in their home environment, family functioning, and parenting."[31] Further, they indicate that data which might speak to foster parents' mental health, marital conflict, social support, and temperament are almost entirely absent. In their own study of foster parent applicants, following those who were ultimately approved and not approved to foster, they determined that about 15% of approved families had four or more psychosocial problems and a full one quarter of approved foster parents had problems in showing empathy for children.[32] Researchers at the Urban Institute have also examined characteristics of nonrelative foster parents. In their study, about 10% of children were living with caregivers who showed symptoms of poor mental health, and about one quarter of the children surveyed were living with caregivers who were "highly aggravated."[33] In the National Survey of Child and Adolescent Well-Being (NSCAW), the home environments of foster parents were identified as "much less stimulating" than the home environments of children in the general population, and caregivers were described as "on the whole, providing marginally adequate environments" for children.[34] Combined, these studies point in a similar direction: a significant minority—probably somewhere around one fifth of foster homes—are not appropriate settings for seriously vulnerable children. Startling perhaps, but not surprising, given the degree to which foster care is prioritized in the child welfare system.

Foster caregiving has long been a relatively low-status activity,[35] with low pay, long hours, and little public recognition. Standards for acceptance into the community of caregivers are minimal. According to Richard Barth, standards of care may have fallen so low that social service agencies have allowed a new standard to predominate: a "minimum sufficient level of care plus a smoke detector."[36]

In 1997 the federal government set baseline standards for foster parent licensing, requiring, at least criminal background checks for prospective caregivers. Additional standards, however, are set at the state level, resulting in some variability nationally. Foster parents usually must participate in preservice training prior to accepting children into their homes, although the amount and type of training varies. Following an in-home inspection and one or more interviews with a licensing staff member from the social service agency, foster homes may be licensed if they meet the following general requirements:

• Adequate space in the home to accommodate a child[37]
• Basic health and safety standards of the home[38]

- Adult caregivers (one or more) age 21 or older[39]
- Caregivers with sufficient income to meet family needs[40]
- Caregivers who have cleared the state's criminal registry and central registry for child abuse[41]
- Caregivers in good physical and mental health[42]
- Caregivers who adhere to disciplinary practices that do not include corporal punishment of foster children

The licensing process may take from a few to several months,[43] depending upon the ability of foster parents to gather all relevant materials and the ability of social service staff to assess the home and the caregivers.

The basic standards are fairly straightforward—assessing caregivers' age and physical health and the square footage of a home are routine tasks. But more is at stake when care is offered to vulnerable children. Part of the assessment process for caregivers is clinical in nature and therefore subject to error, bias, and variable application by social workers.

Until recently, very little research was available to help social service agency personnel assess or select appropriate foster parents. In the 1960s and 1970s, research conducted by David Fanshel and by Patricia Cautley suggested that higher-quality care could be distinguished from lower-quality care by foster mothers who were considerate of children's behavioral issues and their emotional needs.[44] In the 1980s, a small-scale study conducted in England examined how foster parents' motivations to foster affected the quality of their caregiving.[45] In that study, foster parents who were childless and unable to conceive and those who had experienced difficulties in their own childhoods were rated higher by social workers than foster parents with other motivations. Similarly, foster parents who were driven by a spirit of altruism were also more likely to be considered stronger caregivers than others.[46]

More recently, John Orme and his colleagues developed the Foster Parent Potential Scale to help licensing workers make decisions about foster parent applicants.[47] The scale measures the major domains of parenting generally considered relevant for promoting children's well-being. Further efforts to determine the measure's success in predicting quality care is necessary.

Quality Care From a Mother's Perspective

Rachel's experience with foster care for her children was harrowing. But today her children are home. Today Rachel is clean and sober. She goes to community college, her children attend school, and they live in a clean, simple apartment in a quiet part of town. As I approached their home on more than one occasion, I heard Rachel laughing and the boys giggling. Now that they are safe, Rachel can talk freely about the good and the bad. The differences between high and low quality care are stark. Once the children were moved from the Dunn's home, their care improved measurably while they lived with the Lowe family:

> *Those foster parents are very good, okay. They [the children] stayed at the same school. The people drove them out there. Oh, girl, they are so cool.*

The children's placement change both reassured and slightly threatened Rachel. Although the quality of care was high, Mr. and Mrs. Lowe did not have children of their own, and they were looking to adopt. But Rachel knew that Michael's challenging behavior would make them think twice about adopting her son, and she felt confident in the strength of her recovery. She was especially reassured one day when Mrs. Lowe stated emphatically:

> *We know how it is. We want families to reunite, okay. That's what we got into this for.*

The foster parents did everything they could to maintain Steven and Michael's connections to school and family, driving Steven over 20 miles each day back and forth to school as well as taking both children to weekly therapy sessions and weekly visits at home. And the children had easy access to a telephone, so that they could call Rachel several times a day. Mr. and Mrs. Lowe were kind and loving to the boys, but they were always focused on the family's eventual reunion.

> *You don't find foster parents now that really go all the way to the limit for nobody's kids that's not their own. And they just—[my kids] were happy. I mean they was doing so good and at first I was like "Well, they taking them here and they doing this and they doing that, and I can't do that and I don't want them to get used to it." But they [my kids] still wanted to come home. They'd come for the visit and then Steven's like "Mom, why can't we stay?" He was like "I like being where I'm at because they're good people, they take care of us— but I want to come home." And then he came in and he sat in that chair and then he leaned back and then he looked around. He says, "Mom, I miss being at home. Why we can't stay?"*

*And I'm sitting up here, I'm like "Okay, well, just give me a minute.
You'll be able to come." I got to come up with something really quick
'cause I swear—I was sitting here and started bawling big time and
I didn't want to do that to them.*

Explaining Variability in Foster Care Quality

Clearly some foster parents provide exceptional care for children. They
are the unsung heroes of our community. They are the ones who open
their homes to children who often have serious health or behavioral
problems. They facilitate frequent visits with parents and siblings. They
welcome birth parents into their homes to model strong parenting and
to provide emotional support. They drive children to numerous medical
appointments, attend meetings with teachers and school administrators,
and arrange recreational activities to develop children's natural talents.
Moreover, they act as emotional buffers between children and chaotic
court and social service systems and the parents who are unable to care
for them.[48]

But support for foster parents is woefully inadequate. In study
after study, caregivers point to their real frustration: payment rates that
are unfathomably low, there is not enough or no respite from the relent-
less nature of the work, social workers are unresponsive and unsupport-
ive during times of crisis, and caregivers get little assistance in finding
appropriate services to meet children's needs.[49] In one study of foster
parents, caregivers were asked about the principal rewards of fostering
and its most significant challenges.[50] Although foster parents were quick
to describe a number of benefits associated with their work, such as
making a difference in a child's life and watching a child grow and
develop, the list of problems they faced was lengthy. Chief among these
was a concern about the social service agency's inadequacy or workers'
incompetence vis-à-vis the child and family. Some foster parents raise
concerns about the serious behavioral problems of some of these children, difficult interactions with birth parents, or problems between
foster and birth children in the home.[51] But the large majority of studies
examining issues associated with foster parent satisfaction and retention
suggest that foster parents' source of discontent largely lies with the
child welfare system itself; it's bureaucracy, its workers, its reimbursement rates, and the supports it provides.[52]

A Look at Foster Parents in the United States

National studies of the foster parent population have not been conducted for many years; some of our understanding about foster parents comes from the National Survey of Current and Former Foster Parents carried out in 1993.[53] In that study, the majority of foster parents were married, Caucasian, Protestant high school graduates with some college education; the majority were working outside of the home. In the more recently commissioned National Survey of America's Families (a study not specifically focused on foster care but including a foster care sample), the majority of children living in nonrelative foster care were residing in families whose finances were less than optimal. Almost one fifth of children in nonrelative foster care were living in homes with incomes below 100% of the poverty level, and an additional two fifths of children were living in homes with incomes below 200% of the poverty level.[54] About one quarter of children were living in homes where their caregivers were unable to pay their rent or mortgage, and one quarter had experienced food insecurity in the previous year.[55] Data from the National Survey of Child and Adolescent Well-Being indicate that foster parents are older, less educated, and with fewer financial resources than U.S. families in the general population. The majority of caregivers are married (73%), almost two thirds have a high school diploma or less (58%), about two fifths work full time, another two fifths do not work at all (39% and 41% respectively), and about two thirds have provided foster care for less than 6 years.[56] Although the average family size in non-kin foster homes is 5.6, one-fifth of families have annual incomes below $25,000, and 15% have annual incomes between $25,000 and $35,000.[57]

Considerable research indicates that family income has a strong impact on children's home environment and their well-being.[58] When upwards of one-quarter of foster parents are struggling financially such that they can not even offer food or housing security, foster children's well-being is far from protected. Further, foster care board rates do almost nothing to raise family income and in many cases reinforce standards of living at or near the poverty line.

A Look at Foster Parent Subsidies

How much do we pay foster parents? The U.S. Department of Agriculture (USDA) sets benchmarks based on the cost of rearing a child in low-, moderate-, and high-income families. Although this branch of the federal government sets standards for the cost of rearing children, another branch (the Administration for Children and Families) does not use these standards to help states set their foster care payment rates. In fact, there are no minimum standards for payment rates, and an examination of foster care payments across the states suggests that on the average, such payments are 37% *below* the minimum the USDA deems necessary for raising a child in a *low-income* family. [59] In many states, these financial conditions deteriorate annually. California foster parents, for example, have not had a cost-of-living adjustment to their base rate since 2001.[60] According to the federal government, the average monthly foster care payment for a young child across states is $387; but these payment rates vary dramatically by state and sometimes within states.[61] In Omaha, Nebraska, for example, where subsidies fall at the lower end of the spectrum, foster parents receive $226 per month to care for a baby under the age of 2; in Washington, D.C., that same foster parent would receive $869 per month. One national study examining foster care payment rates concluded that average payments across the states would have to be increased substantially in order to pay for children's basic needs. The study's authors recommended average payment increases from 29% to 41%, depending on the age of the child. In five states, payment rates are so low that the authors recommended over a 100% increase in order to meet children's basic needs.[62] Although we have few empirical data linking foster care payments to the supply of foster parents,[63] one could imagine that recruitment is especially difficult in states such as Alabama, Idaho, and Missouri, where reimbursements fall well below $250 per month.[64]

Some would argue that foster parents should not be richly remunerated – that their work should not be motivated by self-interest.[65] Based upon the work of Richard Titmuss,[66] some suggest that foster care is an act of altruism and that it should remain in the realm of volunteerism, reflecting its essential quality as a community service to others.[67] Current payment rates, therefore, are designed to reimburse caregivers for basic expenses but are not intended to cover additional services or needs.[68] If payments were to rise, foster parents' motivations might become suspect, and community members who would otherwise shun this work could be drawn into caregiving for less than charitable reasons.[69] Reimbursement rates for foster parents also reflect beliefs about the nature of the care provided. If one assumes that care of foster children requires no special talents or skills, only an outlay of "emotional labor,"[70] then payments associated with that unskilled labor should be quite low—certainly lower than payments made to skilled professionals.

The distinction between professional wage and volunteer subsidy is important. The foster care payment is not a *wage* and is guarded against such by social service bureaucracies. Efforts to unionize foster parents have met with stiff opposition in some states.[71] And if the typical California foster parent were to calculate her average $500 monthly payment as a wage, she would quickly learn that she was earning about $0.73 per hour.[72] Theorists connecting the decline in the foster parent census with the growth of the female labor market need few data to support their claims[73]; even employment in day care, one of the lowest-paying sectors in the service economy,[74] offers considerably higher wages than a foster care subsidy. Women who work in child-care centers at least get some respite at the end of the day, and their weekends may be free.

Foster parents are not only unrewarded in the market over the short term but also significantly disadvantaged in the long run, as their labor does not qualify them for social security benefits. Caregivers who make a commitment to raise others' children through their working years are financially penalized when they withdraw from the labor market at retirement. Certainly social service agencies do not offer pensions to offset these substantial financial losses.[75]

If there are financial gains for caregivers, they are minimal, as monthly payments are not taxed. But the advantages end there. Payments include neither work-related benefits nor insurance. Foster children automatically qualify for Medicaid, yet foster parents have no access to health insurance for themselves or other family members.[76] And in most jurisdictions, caregivers do not receive assistance with liability insurance—an issue of some importance if foster parents are caring for children with significant behavioral challenges. In short, foster parents are underresourced for the care they offer. In at least one state, monthly payments for dog shelters exceed what is paid to foster parents.[77]

With exceptionally low reimbursement rates and long-term financial hazards for families, it is a wonder that anyone is willing to care for foster children. Caregivers are not recognized publicly for their honored social status or their influential effects on children's lives. Those who take up the challenge are offered modest training and little support in their day-to-day work.

A Look at Training and Support

Training has grown more lengthy and comprehensive in recent years, covering topics such as children's development, the effects of maltreatment, how to manage children's disruptive behavior, and child welfare and court requirements. Although training is widely considered important in ensuring quality care and improving foster parent retention rates,[78] evidence on the effectiveness of traditional training has been disappointing. A few studies have examined the effects of foster parent training programs and have shown only modest gains in positive parenting techniques.[79] In one study examining foster parents exposed to standard training versus those without such training, the trained foster parents improved in only 2 of 12 parenting domains.[80] Only one study has shown significant effects. In this study, the *Incredible Years* intensive parent training program was used with foster parent/birth parent dyads, improving parenting and relationship-building between caregivers.[81] Given the significant psychological and behavioral challenges posed by the majority of foster children,[82] intensive clinical training to prepare caregivers to respond appropriately to these children's needs is likely warranted.[83]

But foster parents need more than training. Much is written about including foster parents as team members in decision making vis-à-vis foster children, but several studies indicate that worker shortages, turnover, and agency red tape conspire to minimize foster parents' meaningful participation.[84] Efforts to engage foster parents into the organizational framework and decision making processes affecting foster children are infrequent, but efforts to engage social workers into the daily lives of foster parents are less common still. When something goes wrong in foster care— emergencies relating to children's behavior, birth parent difficulties, or other matters— foster parents routinely complain that they simply cannot get phone calls returned from overburdened child welfare workers.[85]

A Look at the Monitoring of Quality Caregiving

If foster parents receive little support for the care they offer children, even less is done to monitor the quality of care provided.[86] The federal Child and Family Service Reviews require states to report on the maltreatment rate in foster care, but otherwise little is done to systematically examine the quality of caregiving. In California, for example, foster parents used to receive annual visits by licensing workers to monitor basic quality standards. In recent years, however, these rules were relaxed and foster parents see a licensing worker only twice a decade.[87] Focus groups with foster youth consistently indicate that they would like more frequent licensing visits and that these be made unannounced, so that workers can see honest representations of children's homes and the conditions of their care. But even if the care provided is inadequate, protocols for removing foster parent licenses are administratively burdensome. Once social workers identify poor-quality foster homes, they have few alternatives but to move children and then hope that their peers will avoid that home for future placements.[88]

Caring for Children: The Centerpiece of a Reformed Child Welfare System

The picture that emerges suggests that the screening and selection of foster parent applicants is variable, training is often inadequate, payments are minimal, supports from service agencies are lacking, and the resulting quality of care tends to be highly uneven. That is, many caregivers are providing high-quality services *in spite of the system*, and a significant number of caregivers are providing low-quality services *because of the system*.

When the deficiencies of foster care are revealed, it is remarkable that abuse and neglect are not more frequent. With inadequate financial compensation, monitoring, and support, quality foster care relies on the private decisions of individual caregivers to do the "right thing" for the children in their care each and every day. Such a system, built upon the goodwill of private individuals, may have been sufficient in earlier days, but today, with over half a million children living in out-of-home care, these quaint service systems are inadequate. Indeed, mandated public service systems such as foster care should not have to depend on the goodwill of saints.

Some reforms are under way. The Annie E. Casey foundation, for example, has launched a new initiative to improve the services provided to foster parents.[89] Through the Family-to-Family program, foster parents are invited to participate as team members in decision making for children in their care. The approach responds to many foster parents' previous concerns that they were not taken seriously as informants vis-à-vis children, and it honors their knowledge of and perspective on a child's individual needs. The initiative also attempts to prepare foster parents for their work with birth families, helping to build bridges between children and their families and to maintain a focus on children's eventual reunification with their parents.

Initiatives such as these move in the right direction; they elevate the role of foster parents from simple caretakers to contributing team members, and they raise expectations of foster parents to expand their role beyond caring for children alone to caring for and about birth parents and the children's other family members. But increased responsibilities should be accompanied by improved recognition and support. The quality of foster care is not likely to advance appreciably until a more comprehensive approach is taken toward large-scale reform.

Foster Parent Recruitment

Some foster parents are identified by birth parents at the point of entry to care. That is, team decision making and other types of family conferences are used increasingly to help identify kith who might be available to care for children when kin are otherwise unavailable. But neither kin nor kith care will be sufficient to handle all of the children who need foster care services. In California alone, where outreach to kith care has been fairly aggressive in recent years, only about 4,000 children (out of a total of about 74,000 children in out-of-home care) reside in kith care.[90] Recruitment to the larger community will probably always be required to locate a sufficient pool of foster caregivers.

Foster parent recruitment efforts typically target the faith-based community and friends and acquaintances of current caregivers. Outreach to the wider community is usually accomplished through billboards, fliers, bus stop advertisements, and public service announcements.[91] In recent years, foster parent recruitment efforts have also targeted adults living in the neighborhoods from which children are removed. While these communities should not be excluded from foster parent recruitment activities, it is questionable whether they should be targeted as the central focus for recruiting children's caregivers.

The large majority of children are removed from challenging, distressed neighborhoods. A number of researchers have shown significant correlations between high child maltreatment rates and neighborhoods with low social and economic resources,[92] high poverty rates, and significant neighborhood mobility.[93] Geographic mapping technology now confirms that entries to foster care are most prevalent from the neighborhoods that pose the greatest risks to children's safety and well-being. And evidence from a number of community-oriented studies shows that some neighborhoods pose corrosive risks to children's well-being. That is, parents exert substantial influence on children's development, and parents' income, education, and employment play out powerfully in shaping the course of that development.[94] But neighborhoods have both direct and indirect effects on children's well-being. High poverty rates, unemployment rates, rates of welfare receipt, large numbers of single-parent families, elevated crime rates, low community cohesion, and poor schools affect children's outcomes.[95] These characteristics also affect adults living in these communities; they affect parenting practices (and therefore substitute parenting practices), they affect maternal depression, and they affect overall family functioning.[96]

Although the benefits of maintaining children's ties to their community may be significant for some, these advantages must be balanced against the hazards that can result from living in a distressed community. Caregivers living in vulnerable neighborhoods are likely to have demographic characteristics that provide less social capital than adults living in possibly adjacent, more affluent neighborhoods.[97] Given the odds that potential caregivers will reflect the characteristics of the neighborhoods where they live, screening for caregivers who *can* differentiate themselves from their neighbors, who can moderate the effects of the surrounding community, and who have the capacity to provide exceptional care for exceptional children is essential. The evidence showing how to promote children's well-being indicates that the odds for improving outcomes are increased when children are exposed to positive parenting practices, particularly with caregivers who use their social capital to children's advantage.[98] Therefore foster parent recruitment efforts that target children's neighborhoods of origin run the significant risk of enlisting caregivers who may not be capable of providing the rehabilitative care that children in foster care often require.

Using an aggressive concurrent planning approach for those children unlikely to return home (described in Chapter 3), recruitment efforts should focus on the hundreds of thousands of parents in the United States who might become adoptive families. According to recent estimates, one third of American families have seriously considered adoption. Over a million women have taken steps to look into adopting a child, and child welfare agencies across the nation log almost a quarter of a million phone calls a year from adults considering adopting a child from foster care.[99] If qualified adoptive parents were welcomed into the child welfare agency, given clear and honest information about the children available for adoption, and supported during the time-limited period of concurrent planning, many adults with a vague interest in adoption might step forward to parent a child. Further, finalized adoptions would not necessarily result in a withdrawal from the concurrent foster parent pool. One study suggests that many foster parents in the United States play both roles simultaneously, adopting some children while still fostering others.[100]

With a large pool of concurrent parent applicants, child welfare agencies could implement assessment strategies that screened in only the most qualified individuals likely to offer strong parenting skills, a stimulating home environment, and committed, unconditional care. Abundant concurrent foster parent resources would allow social workers to make thoughtful placement decisions, appropriately matching children's characteristics and needs with caregivers' strengths and abilities.[101]

Foster Care Subsidies

And what about foster care payments? Research on foster care pay has been limited to studies of caregivers with relatively low reimbursement rates, some of whom have received supplements of marginal value. These studies have shown that somewhat higher payment rates may do little to attract additional caregivers to the field, although they may help to retain existing caregivers over time.[102]

Only one study has examined the use of "professional" foster care. In that study, professional foster parents were paid an annual salary of $16,000 per year plus a monthly subsidy of $600 per child. Outcomes in that study included measures of the distance between the child's birth home and foster home, number of siblings cared for, placement stability, restrictiveness of care, and permanency. Overall, professional foster care outperformed traditional foster care.[103] The study provides a very useful starting point but falls short of fully informing the field about the potential of professional care.[104] The study was limited to children in large sibling groups and does not speak to care for children in smaller families. Further, only partial evidence exists to describe the characteristics of the caregivers; we do not know whether the professional foster parents possessed greater social capital than traditional foster parents or whether they were similar in characteristics but simply paid more. Relatedly, we still do not know whether child well-being was enhanced by a professional foster care placement or whether the quality of their care was improved.

The evidence base for treatment foster care is substantially greater. In this model, foster parents are specially trained to care for emotionally or behaviorally challenged children, no more than two children are placed in the treatment foster home, caregivers are closely supervised and supported, and they are paid at a higher rate (usually substantially higher) than traditional foster parents. Programs such as these show improvements in children's behavior and well-being—particularly as compared with children who might otherwise be served in more restrictive settings.[105] The principal element limiting its widespread utilization is its cost. As an alternative to group or residential care, treatment foster care has proven its effectiveness; but as an alternative to traditional foster care, it is more expensive. This limitation, however, is shortsighted and speaks to the value we place on foster children, our commitment to their care, and the short horizons we use as our metric. That is, if treatment foster care results in fewer placement changes in the short run and better child well-being outcomes in the long run, its benefits may actually outweigh its costs.

Both the professional foster care study and research on treatment foster care suggest that a hazard of care is the dampening effect on alternative permanency for children. That is, when children cannot reunify with birth parents, it is more difficult to achieve adoption or guardianship, presumably because the higher rate of pay is forfeited and caregivers have to rely on traditional adoption subsidies[106] for children's long-term support. Using an aggressive concurrent planning approach in a reformed child welfare system, this shortcoming is substantial. But rather than shun treatment foster care, we could experiment with alternatives that might lead to equivalent permanency outcomes. For example, treatment foster parents might be willing to forgo higher monthly adoption subsidies if they were assured of a lump sum payment upon the child's emancipation that could be used for college or vocational education; similarly, experiments that reduced adoption subsidies, but maintained social and mental health services might be sufficiently attractive to engage treatment foster parents in alternative permanency decisions. Or adoption payment rates that exceeded typical foster care rates by some margin might also be sufficiently attractive to promote adoption decisions among caregivers.[107] Much is still unknown about the potential of using treatment foster care, and the research agenda is therefore substantial. What we do know about the effects of treatment foster care and about its potential to serve children better than traditional care, is very promising for children.

The evolution of foster care has shifted the nature of the work considerably. The "natural systems" approach from earlier years—wherein foster parents were simply asked to provide love and support to children in need—has evolved into a "rational system" of care,[108] where foster parents are expected to go well beyond love and support, creating a rehabilitative environment for children, offering modeling for birth parents, serving as an active link between children and multiple service systems, advocating for children's special needs, and serving as a bridge between children, birth parents, social service agencies, and the courts. The "emotional labor"[109] involved in these intensely intimate relationships is significant.

More research is needed to determine the right combination of pay, support, availability of outside services, and training. Pay is probably only one component of our search for high-quality care, but it is no doubt important.[110] Whether significant increases in payment levels might attract a larger pool of foster and concurrent foster parent applicants and whether these applicants might be drawn from a wider range of individuals than the group typically attracted to foster care is unknown.[111] That is, were payment levels to rise sufficiently that adults would forgo outside employment in nursing, social work, or education, for example, individuals from a wider variety of backgrounds might consider leaving the labor market in order to pursue care for children. Elevating services and supports while increasing foster parents' rights and responsibilities might increase caregiver quality and commitment. Children likely to go home to birth parents within a limited period of time would receive the rehabilitative care they needed. And children for whom reunification was not possible would receive unconditional love and permanent care with new parents who were prepared to raise them through their childhoods.

Foster Parent Support

Some evidence suggests that when foster parents are specially trained and well supported, they can improve child welfare outcomes and children's developmental well-being. For example, the Early Intervention Foster Care program[112] has shown substantial effects on placement stability and permanency. The program has also improved young children's attachment behaviors[113] and symptoms associated with stress.[114] Foster parents in this program are provided intensive preplacement training; moreover, once children are placed in their homes, they work closely with a foster parent "consultant," have daily phone contact for supervision and support, participate in weekly support groups, and receive 24-hour on-call assistance when needed.[115] Other programs based upon a similar model have shown promising results.[116]

The key to these programs' success and that of treatment foster care more generally may be the limited placement of two children per home; it may be the intensive preservice training; or the higher payment rates to caregivers. But the role of the caregiving "coach" also may be essential. A look at typical parents in the United States hints at the need for some type of close consultation.

In early 2005, a television show called *Super Nanny* first aired in the United States. It featured Jo Frost, a nanny with 15 years of experience, who could arrive on the doorstep of an otherwise tumultuous home and bring about peace. Frost serves as a parenting coach to adults who are at their wits' end. *Super Nanny* was an instant success and won national praise from a number of media outlets. Shortly thereafter, the book *Supernanny: How to Get the Best From Your Children*, spent 4 months on the *New York Times* bestseller list.[117] The show has been wildly popular and has even received support in the academic literature.[118] Its producers may have known that the show would hit a nerve; parents have been seeking advice from Dr. Spock and other parenting consultants for decades. Today, many parents who can not get what they need from television and books are turning to in-home consultants for advice on matters such as potty-training, infant sleep patterns, and behavior management.[119] This is the state of American parenting for average parents raising average children, some of whom kick up a tantrum, others who are jealous of siblings, and a number who have trouble sharing. But children in foster care are not necessarily typical; in many cases they are exceptional. The parenting they need ranges from the average to the extraordinary. In short, foster parents need a Super Nanny to help them get through the bumps along the road in caring for very special children.

Overstretched social workers who cannot respond to foster parents' calls for help are the antithesis of the Super Nanny that foster parents need. Foster parents are hungry for adult human contact, and substantial help – including coaching to manage children's emotions and behaviors, services for children's special needs, occasional respite from the demanding nature of the work, and aid during times of crisis.[120]

The beneficial results of treatment foster care may be attributed as much to the ongoing and sometimes intensive consultative services made available to caregivers as it is to the higher subsidies foster parents receive. Regular, knowledgeable, responsive assistance in times of need can help foster and concurrent foster parents weather the difficult times so that they can more regularly experience the joys that accompany parenting.

Increased Accountability

The effect of a Super Nanny would ensure greater support and assistance for children's daily care, but it would also serve a substantial monitoring function. Foster care is an intensely private activity. Foster parents are not subject to video surveillance in their homes; their younger charges are limited in their capacity to call attention to poor-quality care. Therefore frequent, close supervision to monitor the care children receive must be developed to assure ongoing quality; pairing the monitoring function with the coaching function meets two objectives simultaneously. Regular, unannounced visits that include private interviews with children must be part of a strategy to supervise children's placement settings.[121] A single incident of maltreatment in foster care not only harms the child and family but also tarnishes the important work of high-quality caregivers and disables community trust in the child welfare system at large. Building in more intensive quality controls for foster care will improve the experiences and outcomes for children, and will renew public faith in a badly eroded public service system.

Creating Quality Foster Care

When Rachel recalls her children's experience of foster care, her indignation flares. Try as she might, she still can not make sense of her children's experience in care, the social worker's apparent indifference, or the system's passivity. Although speaking to me, she directs her anger squarely at the social worker and at the system that worker represents:

> You sent them through eight months of hell because of your laziness. Why would you take my kids from me and put them someplace where it is not okay to be?... It's not fair and it's not okay. Something needs to be done, you know what I mean? It just has to. Because if not, the same thing is probably happening right now with somebody, another family, you know? There's probably another child being beaten in foster care right now, probably hungry, you know, because the workers want to sit

on their ass and eat donuts and not go look at—It ain't going to kill you to get in your car. It's not going to kill you to get up, take a ride, just knock on the door, and say well I'm just, you know, just was in the neighborhood. I just stopped in, you know. But they don't want to do that. That's too much like work. It's bad because these people are in charge of protecting these kids and that's not what they doing.

Children in out-of-home care must be protected from harm. Focused attention to improve the quality of foster care not only raises awareness about the role of quality caregiving as the centerpiece of the child welfare system but also improves the likelihood of long-term beneficial outcomes for children and minimizes the need for ancillary services. A glance at the legislative roster of any state signifies the current approach to child welfare reform. New programs to assist transition-age youth prepare for independence after foster care, programs to support children moving from one school to another, or initiatives designed to prevent placement "breakdown" all add layers of service providers and new bureaucracies that may be helpful but that avoid the real issue: good parents provide unconditional love and support, they are their children's most fierce advocates, and they take pains to prepare their children for adolescence and adulthood. Parents do not begin to groom youth for independence at age 16. Starting in early childhood, these tasks preoccupy good parents as they build children's competencies, which will later be called upon during emerging adulthood. Similarly, when parents move and change their children's schools, they serve as their children's champions, making enrollment decisions, ensuring appropriate placements, and – for those children with learning challenges – pushing school and service systems to meet their children's needs appropriately.[122] When parents fall in love with their children they make unconditional, lifetime commitments; they don't give up, and they fight to see their children succeed. Foster parents, if properly trained, adequately compensated, and sufficiently supported, also can be foster children's greatest allies—in the home, at their school, and in their community.

Child welfare reform that squarely tackles the issue of quality foster care can make irrelevant many of the smaller reforms underway. But foster care has few advocates. The federal policy framework itself shifts our focus to the front and back-ends of the child welfare system, but is largely silent on children's placement experiences in out-of-home care. With the implementation of ASFA, child welfare agencies are pushed to reunify children expeditiously or to adopt them into new families. Termination of parental rights must occur within 15 out of 22 months in care, and "long-term foster care" has been abolished from child welfare nomenclature altogether.[123] The emphasis on keeping kids out of care or pushing them out quickly has relegated interest in foster care to all but a footnote in child welfare practice.[124] For child welfare workers, foster care provides neither the sigh of relief offered by successful prevention services nor the happy ending of adoption. But quality foster care can present both of these to children otherwise suffering under the care of their birth parents. Foster care can be more than a bed to sleep in at night. It can offer children a therapeutic environment in which to recover from trauma and a richly stimulating setting in which to catch up on previously lost opportunities. Changing foster care will make legitimate the protective function of the child welfare system and will have a transformative impact on children's lives. Importantly, it has the potential to provide desperately needed love and security for the nation's most vulnerable children.

7

Take Me Home

Today's child welfare system could be different. It could be reformulated, redesigned, and reconstructed. It could be entirely abolished. Importantly, we can choose. We can organize government services in ways that reflect our values and our priorities. And in so choosing, we can decide to do away with child welfare as a state-sponsored protective system.

Perhaps that is the direction in which we are moving, today. As our disillusionment with foster care grows, there are signs suggesting that we may follow such a path. The U.S. Supreme Court has time and again supported the view that the family is the fundamental building block of our society,[1] and the concept is not disputed. Therefore we just could do nothing. We could decide that family is best regardless; that the protective child welfare system is so badly flawed that it must be dismantled and children must remain with their birth or extended families in order to avoid being touched by child welfare. If we were faced with such a decision, we would proceed based upon our values—not on solid evidence. Federal law is no different. It has been constructed upon principle more than data. Our values guide the determination that children should receive services to prevent placement. Our values also guide our beliefs about reunification.[2] Unfortunately, the research evidence is not sufficiently sophisticated to answer the question at the heart of the child welfare system: Are children better off remaining with their families or placed in foster care?

Although the practice of foster care is hundreds of years old and the resources dedicated to the current foster care system are substantial, the number of well-designed studies that might hint at the outcomes and effectiveness of foster care is small. Further, findings from these studies are contradictory and somewhat perplexing. Some of the early research examining the effects of foster care on children's well-being indicated that outcomes for children reunified with their parents or for children who were never removed to care were worse than outcomes for children who were placed or remained in foster care. None of these studies, however, were able to control for children's behavioral problems or other characteristics at entry to care, they included small samples, and they are dated.[3] Among the more recent studies, only a few are sufficiently rigorous to allow a detailed examination. Because proponents of foster care are quick to suggest the benefits of care and critics charge that foster care damages children, a close examination of each of these studies may shed a brighter light on the state of our developing knowledge in this critical area.

At the turn of this century, an important new contribution included a paper published in the influential *Pediatrics* by authors Heather Taussig, Robert Clyman, and John Landsverk.[4] These investigators examined a cohort of approximately 150 children who entered foster care in San Diego, California, in the early 1990s and who remained in care for at least 5 months. The children were interviewed shortly after their entry to care and again about 6 years later. At 6 years, about 40% of the children had returned to their birth parents and the other 60% remained in out-of-home care.[5] The outcomes of the children who returned home were considerably worse than those of children who remained in foster care. Reunified children showed more self-destructive behaviors and more substance abuse. Overall, they had higher "risk behavior" scores than did the children remaining in care. Children who were reunified were more likely to have been arrested, to have received a traffic ticket, to have dropped out of school, and—if still enrolled in school—to have lower grades; these children were also more likely to report greater internalized problems, such as feeling anxious or depressed, withdrawn, or having somatic complaints. Controlling for children's behavioral problems at entry to care, their age, and their gender, the children who were reunified had more negative outcomes in multiple domains than did their peers who remained in care. The foster care experience of the children remaining in care was considered average—these were not children participating in a specialized or enriched foster care program.

Similar to the findings of Taussig et al., a study of almost 300 young children from the Southwest region of the United States examined children's exposure to violence following a stay in foster care.[6] At age 6, 37% of the children had reunified, 31% had been adopted, 16% were living in kinship foster care, and 17% remained in non-relative foster care. Drawing upon interviews with children and their caregivers, Litrownik and associates determined that reunified children experienced significantly higher rates of family violence and higher rates of witnessing family violence compared to children living in kinship, foster, or adoptive homes.

A later study, conducted in Israel with a rather smaller sample size, is provocative because it assessed a group of children who were placed in foster care compared to another group who were maltreated but were not placed in care. Findings from that study—while more limited—indicate that children placed in care had a higher "quality of life" than children remaining with their families of origin.[7] Other measures of well-being were not included in this study, however.

To add complexity to our understanding of the matter, Catherine Lawrence, Elizabeth Carlson, and Byron Egeland examined almost 200 children in the state of Minnesota, approximately a quarter of whom experienced a stay in foster care during childhood (an average of 13 months' duration), another quarter experienced maltreatment but did not experience a foster care placement, and half were considered "at high-risk" but experienced neither maltreatment nor foster care placement.[8] Controlling for developmental well-being and family poverty at the beginning of the study, these authors found that children experiencing foster care had more behavioral problems than children in either comparison group. The nature or severity of the maltreatment children sustained, however, was not captured in their study—presumably, children placed in foster care had experienced greater trauma at the hands of their parents, which might account for poorer outcomes overall.

Research conducted by Michelle Jonson-Reid and Richard Barth included a very large sample of children and youth (over 150,000), all of whom were reported for maltreatment, some of whom were placed in foster care, some who received in-home services, and others who remained at home with no services. On average, children who received services from the child welfare agency—including foster care placement—were less likely to experience subsequent juvenile incarceration.[9]

Most recently, Joseph Doyle examined outcomes for children placed in the Illinois foster care system compared with children who were reported for maltreatment but were not placed in care.[10] The study included only those children who were considered "marginal" cases. Among these "marginal" cases, some children were placed in care and others remained at home (using a unique statistical strategy, these children were, in essence, almost randomly assigned to home versus foster care). Importantly, children for whom protective care was clearly warranted were excluded from the study. Following children into adolescence and examining administrative data from several sources, the author concluded that outcomes for some children experiencing foster care were worse than outcomes for children who remained with their birth parent(s). On measures of delinquency, earnings, and—to a limited extent—teen pregnancy, children "at the margin of placement" yet placed in care had more negative outcomes.[11]

Taken together, the findings from these studies paint a murky picture. For cases considered "marginal," children may do better at home, without the disruption and uncertainty that follow a foster care placement. For children who require protective care away from their parents, however, outcomes may be better in foster care than remaining at home. Studies inviting foster youth to share their perspective surely suggest a wide range of program changes that could improve their experience, but they also indicate that protective care away from parents is often essential to children's safety and well-being.[12]

If research has not yet answered the most critical question facing child welfare, why not design a study that could quiet the debate? The definitive study would involve random assignment to condition. That is, a large sample of children, all needing protective care, would be served at random either at home with their parents, or away from their parents in foster care. Researchers would follow both samples of children over some period of time and examine their physical and emotional well-being. At the end of the study, we would have greater certainty about the protective or damaging effects of foster care and the benefits and hazards of remaining at home. For ethical reasons, however, such a study has never been launched. When pressed, most people agree that some children must be protected. We have indeed decided. A child welfare system that sometimes separates children from their parents simply must exist.[13]

Although a controlled research study has not been initiated, large-scale experimentation nevertheless is currently underway. Few data are being collected and we have not solicited informed consent, but in fact new models of child welfare services are emerging that fuse traditional child welfare practices with freedom from government intervention.

These new models increasingly rely on kin caregiving, but they depart from historic models of formalized kin care and instead draw on help from relatives outside of the auspices of government oversight and support.

When kinship care first emerged in child welfare, it reflected an *institutional* approach, in that kin were identified as potential caregivers and then were drawn in to the formal child welfare system. This bureaucratization of kinship care was most pronounced in Illinois, where, in the late 1980s and early 1990s, vast numbers of kin previously caring for their relative children under private family arrangements were deemed foster parents under the public child welfare system.[14] Federal legislation clarified the institutional perspective, making clear through the Adoption and Safe Families Act (ASFA) that kin could receive federal foster care subsidies if they were made formal members of the child welfare system as foster parents. This fully bureaucratic model shifted with time, and subsidized guardianship programs (described in Chapter 5) emerged as a hybrid model where kin entered into their relationship with the child welfare agency through the bureaucratic front door (as foster parents) but exited through a public/private back door, taking with them the monthly subsidy (public) but leaving behind the support, services, and supervision of the state-sponsored system (private).

Newly emerging initiatives designed to fully embrace the values of family-centered practice increasingly appeal to kin as a natural support upon which birth parents and the state can rely. For example, child welfare reforms going on in many jurisdictions are especially aggressive in their efforts to locate relatives who might care for children in need of protection.[15] In some cases, relatives are assessed and approved as formal foster parents, are offered minimal training and support, and they are given a modest degree of oversight. In many jurisdictions, however, kin are used as a diversion from the child welfare system altogether. These kin, given the term "voluntary kin" by Rob Geen and Karin Malm,[16] are neither foster parents nor private caregivers making their own family living arrangements. Voluntary kin represent those caregivers identified and solicited by the state as potential caregivers for children needing protective care away from their parents. Once identified, however, they serve as children's caregivers outside of the auspices of the state.

Some states use voluntary kin in subsidized kinship guardianship arrangements early on in the case,[17] moving children expeditiously into the arms of grandma and out of the reach of government. And still other states have a long history of voluntary kinship care,[18] where social workers redirect children entirely out of public child welfare's authority and into the hands of private family members, thus absolving themselves of responsibility for children's ultimate fate.

One of the benefits of this new nonsystem of private protective care is that it has the potential to dramatically shrink the foster care caseload in the United States and to reduce public expenditures substantially. If relatives can be identified from the start and they can take responsibility for children's care and protection, then the only children remaining in a fully public system would be those without any viable family support.

The hazard is that such a private arrangement relieves public agencies of their responsibility for children's protection, alleviates them of an obligation to support parents in their efforts to reunify, and absolves them of any accountability for child and family outcomes. Moreover, evidence from the National Survey of America's Families indicates that children residing in voluntary kinship care are living in significantly disadvantaged circumstances. These kin are more economically and socially disadvantaged than kin providing formal foster care and are even more disadvantaged than kin who have made private arrangements with family members (fully outside of the child welfare system) to care for children.[19] Intentionally diverting vulnerable children to these especially challenged caregivers at the same time that we turn a blind eye to children's outcomes and well-being may not necessarily serve to protect their needs. More importantly, the children most likely diverted into voluntary care are disproportionately African American and Native American, as historical trends suggest that these communities are far more reliant on kin care than are other ethnic groups.[20] The resulting two-tiered system—one that is formalized, funded, supervised, and supported will largely serve Caucasian children and one that is informal, poorly funded, loosely supported, and unsupervised—will largely serve African-American and Native American children.[21] Efforts to devolve authority for child welfare out of the hands of government and into the hands of family reflect deep sentiments regarding one view of culturally sensitive child welfare practice. But these culturally sensitive practices could be viewed with a different lens—one oriented toward children's developmental needs, particularly with the knowledge that maltreated children may need more recuperative care than they are likely to receive in unsupervised voluntary kinship settings. In short, a two-tiered system such as the one we may be constructing, may further disadvantage African-American and Native

American children who already suffer disproportionately along a number of social indicators.

Ironically, the new approach to voluntary kinship practice pits child welfare advocates' interests against one another as each claims an abiding interest in serving children. Bruce Fuller has characterized this tug of war between competing visions of progressive political thought as a debate between *institutional liberals* and *decentralized progressives*.[22] While both political orientations fall to the left of center, institutional liberals see the benefits of government-supported protective care for children. Decentralized progressives, claiming a position further to the left than the institutional liberals, advocate the devolution of responsibility away from government to the community, and ultimately to the family. In fact, a close examination of decentralized progressives' ideology in the field of child welfare suggests an orientation that aligns closely with the conservative right as they renounce the benefits of government, advocate less government in the lives of families, and define "family" narrowly by blood.

The two perspectives both share a passionate desire to shelter children from harm and to support children's well-being. Using a developmental framework, one could argue that children thrive when they live with a caregiver who is loving and stable, and when the caregiver has sufficient social capital that the child can be buffered from community extremes including poverty and violence.[23] Using a cultural continuity perspective, one might suggest that children's development is best supported within the context of the family and the community to which they were born.

The differences are probably not so great when the generalities are removed and the needs of an individual child are presented. Indeed, any child will do best living in a healthy, loving family where the child experiences a caring, stable, life-time relationship. Even in a "marginal" situation, where the parent's care may not be ideal, that child should not be separated from his parent. When protective care is required – the pivot point on which all protective child welfare decisions should be made – family continuity should certainly be pursued, if family members can provide love, support, stability, and shelter from the extremes of poverty and violence.

When kin are available, however, caution is probably warranted when we rely on their services entirely outside of the public child welfare system. Extended family members should be solicited as part of a network of support for children in marginal cases[24] and thoughtfully screened kin should be enlisted as kin foster parents whenever available. Yet it is less clear, when protection is clearly warranted, whether family members should necessarily serve as children's caregivers outside the child welfare system. As suggested in Chapter 5, family dynamics are complex, and children who need protective care are vulnerable. Relegating these children to a nonsystem that accepts no accountability for their protection may be an injustice to their obvious need.

For some children, then, publicly supported foster care is a necessity, and that state-sponsored care should be provided by licensed relatives or close friends when safe and appropriate[25] or by nonrelative foster parents who offer quality caregiving when relative placements are inappropriate.[26] But some system of state-supported foster care must exist. Some children live in family situations that are so gravely dangerous or unhealthy that they must live apart from their parents either temporarily or permanently.

If we can agree that a foster care system should exist for children who must be protected, then it should be used only when protection is clearly warranted. But how many children need protective care, and what are our standards for determining children's safety? Clearly, much greater efforts are required to make more rational—and therefore more equitable and just—placement decisions in foster care. Decision making about when to remove children from their parents' care varies considerably by child welfare worker.[27] Worker discretion about child removal allows for differences of philosophical framework (family preservation versus child protection, for example) to override more objective conditions about child safety. Worker bias—particularly with regard to the child's race and ethnicity—can also play a significant role in decision making about child removal when these factors should not be relevant to the case. Much attention has been paid to the disproportionate representation of African-American and Native American children in foster care.[28] To the extent that this representation is a reflection of racial bias in child removal decisions, it simply must be stopped; using evidence-based tools that standardize decision making about foster care entries will make significant inroads in this important area. Extensive, ongoing training is also essential to ensure that common perspectives regarding children's protection needs are uniformly understood. And decision making regarding child removal should be a team endeavor. These decisions are possibly the most significant in all of child welfare; they should be recognized as such, institutionally supported with time for thoughtful information-gathering, and closely supported in a team context so that the "marginal" cases about which Doyle writes[29] are kept out of foster care. Once the child welfare system can claim that the protective needs of its children are equivalent, we will then better understand the nature of racial and ethnic disproportionality, if it still exists.

But concern about racial and ethnic overrepresentation—in and of itself—again distracts us from the central issues in child welfare. That is, if African-American children are overrepresented in foster care because of racial bias, then developing standardized processes for objectively measuring safety, removal, and readiness for reunification will appropriately adjust the proportion of African-American children in care.[30] Simply reducing the number of African-American children for the sake of addressing disproportionality—either by narrowing opportunities to enter care or prematurely exiting children—is foolhardy if those children require protective care.[31]

Significant progress has been made in the past decade to develop and use research-based instruments that gauge safety and risk.[32] Much more research and more practice improvements are still needed, however, to ensure that only those children who require protective care are removed from their parents' homes.

Assuming that some children need protective care to assure their safety and that decision making is standardized about who qualifies for protective care, then the children who receive foster care should be enrolled in a system with clear parameters guiding reunification decisions, with safe, stable, and reasonable opportunities for alternative living arrangements if reunification fails, and with restorative care that allows children to heal and thrive during their separation. Neglecting the protective arm of the child welfare system does as much damage to children as the maltreatment children sustain at the hands of their parents— sometimes more. If we choose to intervene authoritatively in families' lives yet do so with an instrument that is careless with regard to parents' opportunities for reunification, that is thoughtless about the parents left behind after adoption, that is cavalier about children's care once they are living with kin, and that ignores the dimension of quality in foster care, we do no more than perpetuate the maltreatment children received at the hands of their parents.

We do not live in an either/or world. We do not have to choose between prevention and intervention in our armory of child and family services. In fact, federal and state lawmakers already provide funds to support a variety of child maltreatment prevention and family preservation activities, and funding is also available to support the infrastructure for out-of-home care. The point is not to divest from prevention services or minimize children's connections to family. But we cannot call for the reallocation of protection dollars to serve prevention interests, if we do not know how to prevent maltreatment, and when the protective arm of the child welfare system is already massively under-funded and woefully inadequate. Further, the scarce resources that are currently available for child maltreatment prevention and family preservation services should be invested in a rigorous research enterprise to help determine how those dollars can be used effectively. Once an effective prevention approach can be articulated, the clamor for additional support will be deafening and well justified. Finally, other agencies that are responsible for health, education, criminal justice, and public assistance outcomes must be enrolled as leaders in a renewed family support agenda, capitalizing on the known benefits that accrue to children and families who receive high quality family support services.

What we need is a corrective—a reprioritizing of our mission and purpose. Child welfare services in the areas of reunification, permanency, and foster care are not prochild and antifamily. Far from it. Time-limited, concentrated reunification services put children and their birth parents at the center of good child welfare practice. Maintenance of family ties after adoption recognizes and honors children's lifetime connections to birth parents. Kinship guardianship with a modicum of state oversight bridges the important elements of family and protection. And quality foster care respects *family* as the central building block of child development—whether children live with birth parents or alternative caregivers.

Children should live in their parents' homes whenever that is safe and appropriate, and child welfare services should be at the forefront of developing evidence-based practices that can keep children safely at home with their birth parents. But in the event that children are removed to out-of-home care to support their safety, we should honestly engage with parents to help bring their children home. If they can not, we must find new homes that offer unconditional love and support for a lifetime. In the end, children need to be home. Children need safe homes where they can grow and thrive; vulnerable children in out-of-home care are desperate to live in such homes today.

APPENDIX

Talking to Parents Involved in the Child Welfare System

Six case studies are included in this book. Their inclusion was deliberate for a number of reasons. Consumer voices are faintly heard in the field of child welfare research. Aggregate data on child welfare pathways and placements, particularly those emanating from administrative data, have grown in prominence in child welfare research in recent years. This development is entirely positive. Large-scale administrative data now tell us so much more than we ever knew previously about patterns of services across and between states and localities. Research that is reliant on case file information can also provide in-depth information about a range of child, family, case, and court variables, and a body of literature supports this methodological practice. The recent emphasis on strengths-based, family-focused services might suggest that new research enterprises eliciting the subjective realities of child welfare's clients would be emerging. But inclusion of client voices into the child welfare literature is still the exception more than the rule.[1]

Diorio suggests that the absence of parents' voices from the child welfare literature may reflect the "child saving" focus of traditional child welfare services or the inherent power imbalance between professional "expert" (i.e., the child welfare worker) and lay individual (i.e., the parent).[2] Regardless of its origins or meanings, greater attention to child welfare consumers' experiences of the services they receive is warranted.

The case study approach not only features parents' voices but also allows for the complexity of child welfare cases and child welfare–involved families to be revealed. The typical child welfare family is not likely to include an intact two-parent family and their two children; instead, child welfare–involved families are more likely to include several children, multiple fathers, and multigenerational relations that may be sources of strength or struggle. Capturing the dimensionality, heterogeneity, and complexity of family life is an important aspect of understanding child welfare practice and ultimately potential changes to child welfare policy.

The case study approach allows for an in-depth, detailed examination of a single person, family, or community.[3] It provides for a closeup view of the human experience in a naturalistic setting[4] and—importantly—reveals the subjective experience, and meaning of that experience from an emic perspective for each individual studied.[5]

The stories told through this book were derived using qualitative methods to collect data on the lived experiences of families exposed to the child welfare system. Birth parents were invited to share their personal stories and were followed over the course of approximately 2 years. Data collection for this longitudinal, qualitative study was conducted between 2004 and 2006.[6]

Families were selected from a single county in the San Francisco Bay Area. Reasons for selecting a single county were many: first, the ethnographic approach is designed to illustrate typologies of family experiences and families are purposively selected as illustrative examples of particular experiences. The approach in ethnography is not to select a sample that will be generalizable to the larger public but rather to examine certain experiences in depth. Given these criteria, it was not necessary to include a variety of counties, particularly since county practices may differ. Second, given the population under study, it was expected that gaining a sample and retaining it would be very challenging. The author's previous work with families aided by welfare[7] had shown that attrition can be especially problematic, and simply locating families in their homes or other agreed upon settings might be challenging. Maintaining a sample that is geographically near the researcher offers the benefit of maximizing time and funding when study participants are not available or are not home for scheduled interview appointments.

Social service agencies often have an inclination to be protective of their clients. Researchers asking for direct contact with clients can face a number of bureaucratic obstacles; as a result, the ideal research design can be compromised.[8] I therefore worked in collaboration with the public child welfare agency to determine an approach for contacting families that would be amenable to administrators and staff. Once a common approach was devised, the study methodology was approved by the university's committee for the protection of human subjects.

In 2004, I attended a number of staff meetings in the public child welfare agency, focusing specifically on those units providing "back end" services to families, including reunification services, long-term-care services, postreunification services, and concurrent planning. At these meetings, I described the study to child welfare staff and distributed several copies of a brochure that explained the nature and purpose of the project. Staff were asked to identify birth parents on their caseload who "typified" their average client. Staff were then asked to distribute the brochure to these birth parents. Staff were also given a common script to use as a guide in their interactions with clients, so that clients would not feel coerced into participating; that they would know that their participation would not affect their case or be known to their current social worker. The brochure included an 800 number for phone contact in addition to a stamped, preaddressed envelope. Birth parents contacted me directly and I then explained the nature of the project in more detail. Those agreeing to participate were scheduled for an interview where they received detailed consent materials.

Twelve families agreed to participate. Each family participated in at least two interviews. Six families were then selected from the twelve to be followed over time. Each interview lasted approximately 2 hours, and participants were paid for each interview. Interviews occurred quarterly.

Interview sessions were designed to be inclusive and flexible. Using semistructured interview questions and observer–participant methods, each session was guided by a predefined set of themes focused on respondents' experiences as parents, and their experience with the child welfare system. Themes included the following: (1) a general introduction to the family, family members, characteristics, personality, strengths, and challenges; (2) genograms and life histories; (3) precipitating events leading to child welfare involvement; (4) recollections of initial child welfare contact; (5) chronological description of child welfare involvement thereafter for each child; (6) experiences with the child welfare worker including respect, cultural competence, knowledge, assistance; (7) experiences with foster and/or kin provider(s), including contact, quality, relationship, access; (8) experiences with the court system including judge(s), parent's attorney(s), and child's attorney(s); (9) case plan goals, initially and over time; (10) child welfare services pre-, post-, and during child placement; (11) child(ren)'s current well-being, needs, hopes, and expectations for the future; (12) parent's current well-being and needs, including current parenting strategies; and (13) suggested changes to child welfare systems and/or processes.

Interviews were informal, and although each had a theme, they were wide-ranging, since parents took our conversations into those directions that mattered most to them. As Burgess notes, the interviews took on the characteristics of "conversations with a purpose,"[9] flexibly allowing for data collection on the questions of import to me while allowing for the inclusion of information of importance to parents.

All interviews occurred in birth parents' homes. Most interviews occurred in private, although some interviews were interrupted by children coming in and out of the home or the room. All interviews were audiotaped and transcribed by a professional transcription company. Following each interview, extensive field notes were taken, capturing events, emotions, or other contextual factors that might not otherwise be revealed in transcription.

In addition to parents' perspectives on their child welfare case and their families' circumstances, 2 out of 6 birth parents provided copies of many—if not all—of their court reports. The court reports offer insight into the child welfare workers' perceptions of the family and their circumstances at that time. Although efforts were made to triangulate the data for the other families in the study, some parents could not locate court reports and/or were reluctant or fearful about giving consent to contact child welfare workers associated with their case.

Throughout the period of data collection, I developed field notes and descriptive memos. Early on, I developed a genogram for each family to help organize and plan for future interviews. I also developed timelines showing the major events in each mother's life and then confirmed these events with mothers during subsequent interviews. Information obtained from mothers that was unclear or confusing was reviewed in subsequent interviews. An abbreviated timeline for each family portrayed in this book is included below.

At the beginning of the study, all of the mothers had at least one child in out-of-home care. Most mothers saw at least one child or all children return to their care during the course of the study, allowing continued observation of the family postreunification. Most mothers were in recovery from addiction, and most had spent some time in jail or prison. Names, some dates, and some selected characteristics of parents or children have been changed in order to protect confidentiality.

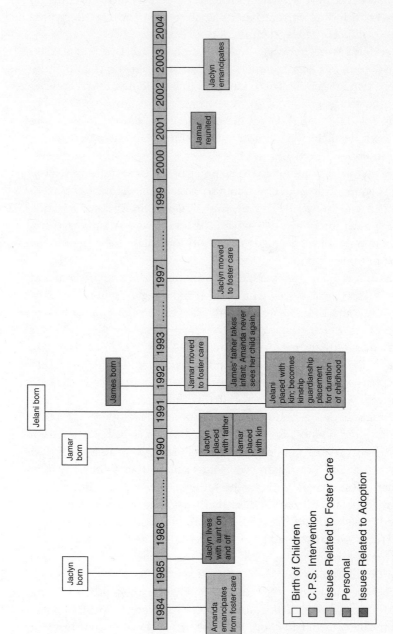

FIGURE A.1 Case Study of Amanda.

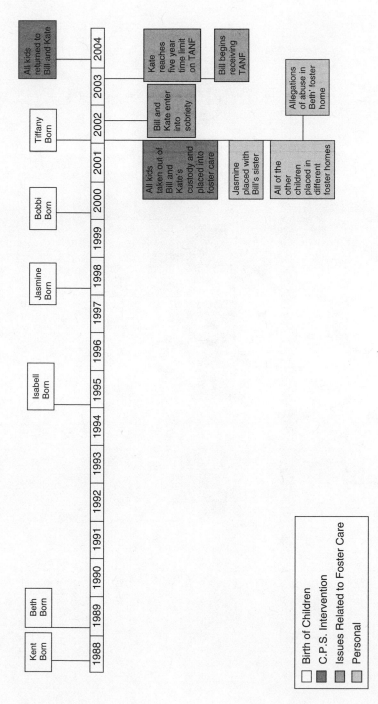

FIGURE A.2 Case Study of Bill and Kate.

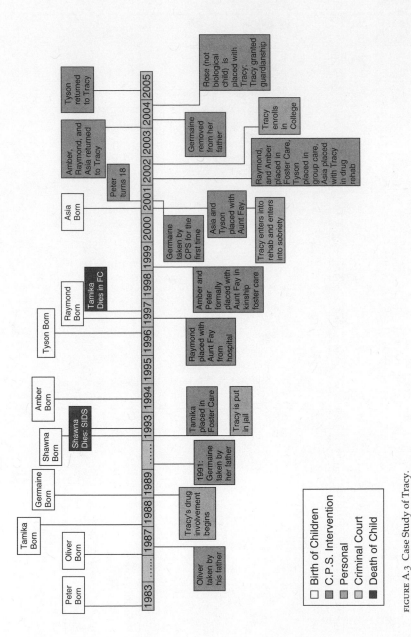

FIGURE A.3 Case Study of Tracy.

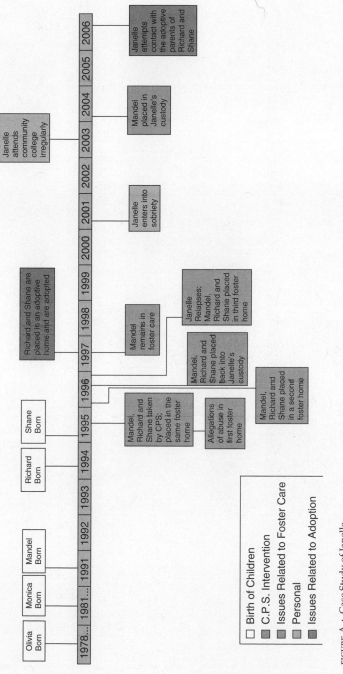

FIGURE A.4 Case Study of Janelle.

The timeline shows the following events:

Legend:
- Birth of Children
- C.P.S. Intervention
- Issues Related to Foster Care
- Personal
- Issues Related to Adoption

Timeline (years): 1978... 1981... 1991 1992 1993 1994 1995 1996 1997 1998 1999 2000 2001 2002 2003 2004 2005 2006

- Olivia Born (1978)
- Monica Born (1981)
- Mandel Born (1991)
- Richard Born (1994)
- Shane Born (1995)
- Mandel, Richard and Shane taken by CPS; placed in the same foster home (1995)
- Allegations of abuse in first foster home
- Mandel, Richard and Shane placed in a second foster home (1996)
- Mandel, Richard and Shane placed back into Janelle's custody (1996)
- Mandel remains in foster care (1997)
- Richard and Shane are placed in an adoptive home and are adopted (1997)
- Janelle Relapses; Mandel, Richard and Shane placed in third foster home (1998)
- Janelle enters into sobriety (2001)
- Janelle attends community college irregularly (2003)
- Mandel placed in Janelle's custody (2004)
- Janelle attempts contact with the adoptive parents of Richard and Shane (2006)

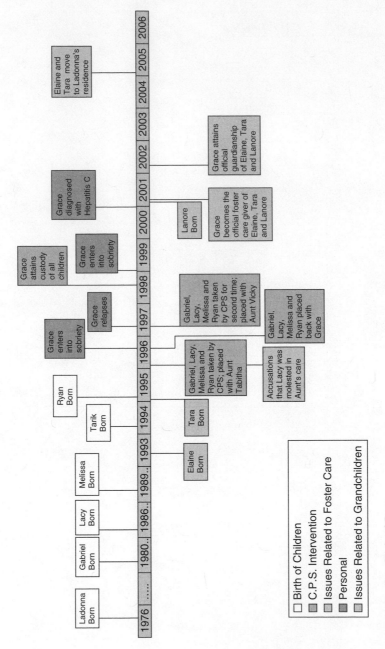

FIGURE A.5 Case Study of Grace.

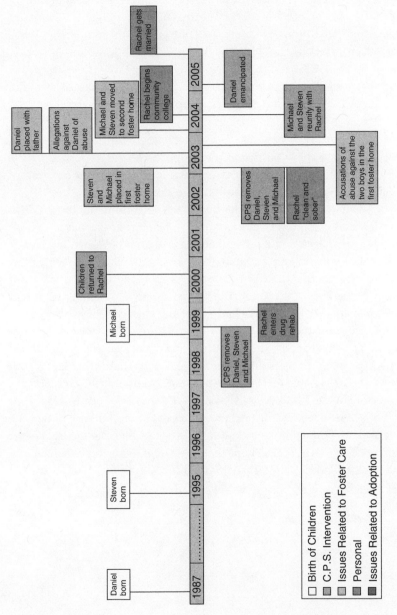

FIGURE A.6 Case Study of Rachel.

Birth of Children
C.P.S. Intervention
Issues Related to Foster Care
Personal
Issues Related to Adoption

1987 1995 1996 1997 1998 1999 2000 2001 2002 2003 2004 2005

Daniel born

Steven born

Michael born

CPS removes Daniel, Steven and Michael

Rachel enters drug rehab

Children returned to Rachel

Steven and Michael placed in first foster home

CPS removes Daniel, Steven and Michael

Rachel "clean and sober"

Accusations of abuse against the two boys in the first foster home

Daniel placed with father

Allegations against Daniel of abuse

Michael and Steven moved to second foster home

Rachel begins community college

Michael and Steven reunify with Rachel

Daniel emancipated

Rachel gets married

Some critics of qualitative studies point to their limitations with regard to reliability and validity.[10] Interviews with individuals about their lived experience indeed describe their subjective understanding of experience but may be less accurate in relating the objective circumstances and conditions of family life. Subjects in this study may have suffered from recollection bias in recreating their child welfare histories, they may have idealized their role or their actions over time, they may have forgotten or intentionally ignored or skipped important pieces of information, or they may have reinterpreted events, experiences, or emotions over time.[11]

Efforts to review case file documents allowed for triangulation of data and a data check on parents' accounts. Where these court reports were obtained, there was remarkable consistency in parents' accounts of events and social workers' accounts as described to judges.

It is somewhat difficult to determine the nature and degree to which selection bias was present in the sample of families agreeing to participate in this project. Some researchers have warned against the overinclusion of respondents in qualitative research who are "articulate, insightful, attractive, and intellectually responsive informants."[12] But surely the families that volunteered to participate in this study represent a select group. They may have had especially strong feelings about their experience with the child welfare system (good or bad), motivating them to participate in the study. Or they may have been especially proud of their recovery process and therefore eager to share their story with others. It is impossible to determine how these parents differ from others connected to the child welfare system. Because the study was used largely as a device to bring a richer and more textured description of the child welfare population to the reader and not to generate theory, policy, or practice on a large scale, I hope that these limitations can be considered in context and viewed as largely inevitable.

Notes

CHAPTER 1

1. According to the U.S. Department of Health and Human Services, there were approximately 513,000 children in out-of-home care on September 30, 2005. See: http://www.acf.hhs.gov/programs/cb/stats_research/afcars/tar/report13.htm. That number has declined considerably from a high of approximately 550,000 in 2000.

2. According to the U.S. Department of Health and Human Services, approximately 1,400 children die annually as a result of child maltreatment. For additional information relating to child maltreatment–related deaths, see Lindsey, D. (2003). *The welfare of children* (2nd ed.). New York: Oxford University Press; Sabotta, E. E. & Davis, R. L. (1992). Fatality after report to a child abuse registry in Washington State, 1973–1986. *Child Abuse and Neglect, 16*(5), 627–635; U.S. Department of Health and Human Services, Administration on Children, Youth and Families. (2007). *Child maltreatment 2005.* Washington, DC: U.S. Government Printing Office.

3. For information on national trends see: U.S. Department of Health and Human Services, Administration on Children, Youth and Families. (2007). *Child maltreatment 2005.* Washington, DC: U.S. Government Printing Office. For information on California, see: Child Welfare Services Stakeholders Group (2003). *CWS Redesign: The future of California's child welfare services.* Sacramento, CA: California Department of Social Services.

4. Testa and associates indicate that in 2002, over 185,000 children were in care for 17 out of 22 months nationwide. These children were living in a state of impermanency. Although some number of these children will eventually reunify with their parents or achieve another permanency goal such as adoption or legal guardianship, some will remain in foster care for many years. Data from California suggest that between 10% and 15% of children who enter out-of-home care are still in care 4 years later. Needell, B., Webster, D., Armijo, M., Lee, M., Cuccaro-Alamin, S., Shaw, T., et al. (2006). *Child welfare services reports*

for California. Retrieved May 16, 2006, from University of California at Berkeley Center for Social Services Research website. URL: http://cssr.berkeley.edu/cwscmsreports/cohorts/exits/exitsFrameset.asp?data=data&year=2000&crit= G&co Phelan unty=0. According to the U.S. Department of Health and Human Services, over 300,000 children enter foster care in any given year. See: http://www.acf.hhs.gov/programs/cb/stats_research/afcars/trends.htm. If national data mirror statistics in California, approximately 28% of children return home within the first 5 days in care, but the remainder stay for more extended periods.

5. Child and Family Service Reviews were mandated as part of the Adoption and Safe Families Act of 1997 as a mechanism to make states more accountable for child welfare outcomes. For more information relating to the CFSR's see: http://www.acf.hhs.gov/programs/cb/cwmonitoring/index.htm

6. Kosanovich, A., & Joseph, R.M. (October 2005). *Child welfare consent decrees: Analysis of 35 court actions from 1995–2005*. Washington, D.C.: Child Welfare League of America.

7. States that do not meet the standards set by the Child and Family Service Reviews must develop Program Improvement Plans (PIPs) that identify how they will improve outcomes in the following 2 years. States that do not come into substantial conformity with the standards when reassessed may face significant federal financial penalties. For more information see: http://www. acf.hhs.gov/programs/cb/cwmonitoring/general_info/pipstatus.htm

8. The National Survey of Child and Adolescent Well-Being provides information on a national sample of children coming to the attention of the child welfare services system, including those closed to services, those served in-home, and those served out-of-home. The study suggests that families coming to the attention of the child welfare system have a wide range of problems and challenges. See: NSCAW (2005). *CPS sample component wave 1 data analysis report*. Washington, D.C.: Department of Health and Human Services, Children's Bureau. For other information pertaining to the characteristics of parents whose children are involved with the child welfare system, see: Needell, B., & Barth, R.P. (1998). Infants entering foster care compared to other infants using birth status indicators. *Child Abuse and Neglect, 22*(12), 1179–1187.

9. In California, the prevalence of children living in out-of-home care (for 5 days or longer) has varied from a high of 11.6 per 1,000 in 1999 to 7.7 per 1,000 in 2006. See: http://cssr.berkeley.edu/CWSCMSreports/Pointintime/fostercare/childwel/prevsFrameset.asp?whichForm=&data=data&pyear=ju12006.

Wulczyn and Hislop point out that there is considerable variation in foster care utilization and placement patterns by state, however, and even in regions within states. See: Wulczyn, F., & Hislop, K. (2003). *Foster care dynamics in urban and non-urban counties*. Chicago: Chapin Hall Center for Children.

Although the proportion of children living in out-of-home care is very small relative to the total child population, increasing policy interest has been focused on foster care due to the mounting costs of care, and – until recently – rising caseload size. In 1990, there were about 400,000 children in out-of-home care in the United States, increasing to over 550,000 by the end of the decade.

As Wulczyn and Hislop point out, these significant increases occurred despite the fact that child poverty rates across the country were relatively stable, federal lawmakers had devoted significantly more resources to preventive services, and the crack cocaine epidemic had subsided considerably by middecade. See: Wulczyn, F., & Hislop, K. (2003). *Foster care dynamics in urban and non-urban counties*. Chicago: Chapin Hall Center for Children.

10. The appendix offers more information about the families portrayed in each chapter of the book. As described in the appendix, names of all of the individuals described in this book and some other identifying features have been changed to protect confidentiality.

11. In this excerpt, Amanda is talking about "home," but "home" at that time meant any place where she could find a bed or couch. Sometimes it was with family, sometimes with friends, sometimes in abandoned buildings, and sometimes in a car. For the first year of Jamal's life, Amanda and her children roamed from place to place. She also refers to "positive tox for cocaine," meaning that hospital officials tested the baby at birth and learned that Jamal had traces of cocaine in his system, because of Amanda's drug use.

12. Amanda is referring to exchanging drugs for sex.

13. SRO—single-room-occupancy hotel.

14. Although Jaclyn had never before lived with her father, when she was moved into his home, she was "reunified" according to court documents and her case was closed. When Jaclyn moved in with Amanda's friend, the arrangement was made privately, outside of the auspices of the child welfare system.

15. Amanda had a fourth child thereafter, who was also removed from her care and given to his birth father. The father disappeared with the baby and Amanda never saw either of them again.

16. There is substantial evidence that with each move, children's behavior problems increase. See, for example: Newton, R. R., Litrownik, A. J., & Landsverk, J. A. (2000). Children and youth in foster care: Disentangling the relationship between problem behaviors and number of placements. *Child Abuse and Neglect, 24,* 1363–1374; Rubin, D. M., O'Reilly, A.L. R., Luan, X., & Localio, A. R. (2007). The impact of placement stability on behavioral well-being for children in foster care. *Pediatrics, 199,* 336–344;

17. This statement was made by a child welfare professional during discussions among various "stakeholders" involved in California's Child Welfare Redesign initiative. This 3-year planning process included individuals from across the state (myself among them) working together to improve the service design in child welfare. Because I did not ask for permission from the speaker to attribute the quote, I offer it as an anonymous statement. My personal experience on the redesign committee was not terribly dissimilar to my experience a decade earlier, when California conducted a strategic plan to reform child welfare, and then my subsequent and most recent experience on the Blue Ribbon Commission for Foster Care Reform.

18. This statement is taken from the document California used to "redesign" its child welfare system. I have no intention of singling out California from the rest of the nation, as all states share this enthusiasm for prevention. The California

statement simply serves as an example in this instance. See: Child
Welfare Services Stakeholders Group (2003). *CWS Redesign: The future of
California's child welfare services*. Sacramento, CA: California Department of
Social Services.

19. Adoption and Safe Families Act of 1997, Pub.Law No. 105–89, 111 Stat.
2115. (1997).

20. The term is taken from Fein and Staff's 1993 article on reunification
services: Fein, E., & Staff, I. (1993). Last best chance: Findings from a
reunification services program. *Child Welfare, 72*(1), 5–40.

21. According to federal data, over 300,000 children entered foster care in 2005.
This includes children whose stay was very short (less than 5 days in care), and
children whose stay was especially lengthy. The California data archive held at
U.C. Berkeley indicates that in recent years about 30,000 children entered or
reentered care. These numbers, however, include only children whose stay in
care lasted 5 days or longer. Since California represents about 16% to 17% of
the U.S. caseload, I estimate that the corresponding national figures for entries
to out-of-home care (for 5 days or longer) are probably closer to 150,000, than
to 300,000. For federal data see:
  http://www.acf.dhhs.gov/programs/cb/stats_research/afcars/tar/report13.htm
  For California data see: http://cssr.berkeley.edu/cwscmsreports/cohorts/
firstentries/

CHAPTER 2

1. Smothers, R. (November 7, 2003). Manslaughter charge in Newark neglect
case. *New York Times*.

2. Richmond mother arrested in murder, torture of son (October 31, 2006). CBS-
5. Retrieved June 19, 2007. http://cbs5.com/local/local_story_303165544.html.

3. Burt, C. (May 25, 2006). Mom who drowned kids takes stand. *Oakland
Tribune*.

4. Child welfare services stakeholder group. (2003). CWS Redesign: The
future of California's child welfare services. Sacramento, CA: State of
California, Department of Social Services, p. 7

5. A new beginning: The future of child welfare in New Jersey. (June, 2004).
Retrieved June 25, 2007. http://www.state.nj.us/humanservices/cwrp/index.htm

6. Maltreatment is defined differently in each of the 50 states, and each state
also defines the categories of citizens and/or professionals who must report
maltreatment. At a minimum, the federal government defines maltreatment
as "Any recent act or failure to act on the part of a parent or caretaker which
results in death, serious physical or emotional harm, sexual abuse or
exploitation; or an act or failure to act which presents an imminent risk of
serious harm." U.S. Department of Health and Human Services, Administration
for Children, Youth, and Families. (2007). *Child maltreatment: 2005*. Washington,
D.C.: U.S. Government Printing Office.

7. Although David Finkelhor and associates claim that maltreatment may
be on the decline, their evidence rests upon various data sources using
mixed methods and disparate samples. See: Finkelhor, D., & Jones, L. (2006).

Why have child maltreatment and child victimization declined? *Journal of Social Issues, 62*(4), 685–716.

8. For information on the National Incidence Studies (there have been three to date, and the fourth – NIS4 – is currently under way), see:

http://www.childwelfare.gov/systemwide/statistics/nis.cfm.

The NIS-3 identified very large numbers of children who were never reported to child welfare agencies for maltreatment. Whereas recent estimates from official child abuse reporting indicate that about 900,000 children are victims of maltreatment, the NIS-3 uncovered closer to 3 million children.

9. Cicchetti, D., & Toth, S. (1996). A developmental psychopathology perspective on child abuse and neglect. *Journal of the American Academy of Child and Adolescent Psychiatry, 34*, 541–565; Crouch, J. L., & Milner. J. S. (1993). Effects of child neglect on children. *Criminal Justice and Behavior, 20*(1), 49–65; Egeland, B. (1991). A longitudinal study of high risk families: Issues and findings. In R. Starr & D. A. Wolfe (Eds.), *The effects of child abuse and neglect* (pp. 33–56). New York: Guilford; Gaudin, J. M. (1999). Child neglect: Short-term and long-term outcomes. In H. Dubowitz (Ed.), *Neglected children: Research, practice and policy*. Thousand Oaks, CA: Sage.

10. U.S. Department of Health and Human Services, Administration for Children and Families. (2007). *Child maltreatment: 2005*. Washington, D.C.: U.S. Government Printing Office.

11. In each of the NIS studies, findings related to the race/ethnicity of the child were repeated. These findings are perplexing, as African-American children are markedly overrepresented in the child welfare system, from child abuse report investigation to substantiation to out-of-home care. The findings are especially curious in light of the fact that African-American children are more likely to hail from low-income, single parent families, with larger sibling groups, where mothers are less likely to be engaged in the labor market. Each of these factors also contributes to the likelihood of maltreatment, so one might think that the risk of maltreatment for African-American children would be especially high. In recent analyses of the NIS-3 data, Sedlak and Schultz account for these characteristics and point out that the risk of maltreatment for African-American children in the United States is actually considerably *lower* than the risk for maltreatment among Caucasian children. The additional factors listed above increase African-American children's risk, but only such that it reaches a level on par with the risk of maltreatment among Caucasian children who are not typically as socially disadvantaged. See: Sedlak, A., & Schultz, D. (2005). Race differences in risk of maltreatment in the general child population. In D. M. Derezotes, J. Poertner, & M. F. Testa (Eds.), *Race matters in child welfare*. Washington, D.C.: Child Welfare League of America.

Regarding subsequent child welfare involvement, findings from a variety of studies suggest that African-American children are significantly overrepresented, particularly the deeper one is drawn into the child welfare system. African-American children are much more likely to have their child maltreatment report investigated by child welfare personnel and to be placed in foster care. Once placed in foster care, they are less likely to return home, less likely to be adopted, and more likely to remain in out-of-home care for the long term. Placement into care can be explained in part by their greater utilization of kinship care. One study found that the availability of kin may play a role in child welfare workers' greater willingness to use foster care as a placement resource for African-American children [see: Goerge, R. M., & Lee, B. J. (2006). The entry of children from the welfare system into foster care: Differences by race. In D. M. Derezotes, J. Poertner, & M. F. Testa (Eds.), *Race matters in child welfare*. Washington, D.C.: Child Welfare League of America]. Their long stays in care are also partly explained by the greater use of kinship care, where kin are less likely to adopt (discussed in more detail in Chapter 5). While there are ongoing and important debates about the role of racial bias among child welfare workers in decision making about foster care placement, the evidence is mixed [see: Derezotes, D.M., Poertner, J., & Testa, M.F. (2006). *Race matters in child welfare*. Washington, D.C.: Child Welfare League of America]. In short, the disproportionate representation of African-American children in the child welfare system is a sobering and complicated topic but one with no clear culprit. Greater efforts to understand the phenomenon will go a long way toward developing strategies that appropriately respond to this pressing issue.

12. Stein, T. J. (1998). *Child welfare and the law*. Washington, D.C.: Child Welfare League of America.

13. For a review of these issues see: Duncan, G.J., & Brooks-Gunn, J. (Eds.). (1997). *Consequences of growing up poor*. New York: Russell Sage Foundation. See also: Berrick, J.D. (2006). Neighborhood-based foster care: A critical examination of location-based placement criteria. *Social Service Review. 80*(4), 569–583.

14. The other four children were living with Kate's parents during most of this 2-year period, but her oldest child, Kent, from about 9 to 11 years of age, stayed with her throughout this turbulent time.

15. Bill remained in prison on drug-related charges.

16. Programs to assist Bill and Kate before they had become a family might have been of some assistance. For example, the work of David Wolfe indicates that programs targeted to adolescents to help them make healthier partner choices may be effective. In Wolfe's study, 158 adolescents who had experienced maltreatment in childhood were assigned to treatment and control conditions. Adolescents in the treatment condition were exposed to a 18-session intervention for the prevention of dating violence. At the 2-year follow-up, students in the treatment condition were less likely to have experienced a violent incident or emotional abuse than were youth in the control group. See: Wolfe, D. A., Wekerle, C., Scott, K., Straatman, A., Grasley, C., & Reitzel-Jaffe, D. (2003). Dating violence prevention with at-risk youth: A controlled outcome evaluation. *Journal of Consulting and Clinical Psychology, 71*(2), 279–291.

17. Kent also had significant health and developmental problems. Bobbi and Jasmine had vision and hearing problems. Tiffany was born completely deaf.

18. Some of the problems associated with drug treatment engagement include child-care problems and transportation difficulties. See: Friedmann, P. D., D'Aunno, T. A., Jin, L., & Alexander, J. (2000). Medical and psychosocial services in drug abuse treatment: Do stronger linkages promote client utilization? *Health Services Research, 35*, 443–465; Marsh, J. C., D'Aunno, T. A., & Smith, B. (2000). Increasing access and providing social services in drug abuse

treatment for women with children. *Addictions, 20*(95), 1247–1287; Marsh, J. C., & Miller, N. (1985). Female clients in substance abuse treatment. *International Journal of the Addictions, 20*(6–7), 995–1019.

19. Gregoire, K.A., Schultz, D.I. (2001). Substance-abusing child welfare parents: Treatment and child placement outcomes. *Child Welfare, 80,* 433–452. The state of Illinois has experimented with "recovery coaches" – women who are individually assigned to help support child welfare–involved clients in engagement, compliance, and treatment. These coaches appear to be effective in increasing the likelihood that parents will engage in substance abuse treatment. The effects of recovery coaches on reunification rates are statistically significant (families with recovery coaches are 1.28 times more likely to reunify than families accessing typical services), although reunification rates in both groups of drug-involved women are exceedingly low (7% vs. 12%). See: Ryan, J. P., Marsh, J. C., Testa, M. F., & Louderman, R. (2006). Integrating substance abuse treatment and child welfare services: Findings from the Illinois Alcohol and other drug abuse waiver demonstration. *Social Work Research, 30*(2), 95–107.

20. The large majority of studies that have been conducted examining women, substance abuse, and treatment outcomes are quasi-experimental and most include small sample sizes. See: Porowski, A., Burgdorf, K., & Herrell, J. (2004). Effectiveness and sustainability of residential substance abuse treatment programs for pregnant and parenting women. *Evaluation and Program Planning, 27*(2), 191–198. New funding for research on substance abuse treatment must insist upon more rigorous designs that can inform the field about the most effective treatment methods.

21. Lindsey, D. (2003). *The welfare of children* (2nd ed.). New York: Oxford University Press; Pelton, L. H. (1989). *For reasons of poverty: A critical analysis of the public child welfare system in the U.S.* New York: Praeger.

22. Barth, R. P., Wildfire, J., & Green, R. (2006). Placement into foster care and the interplay of urbanicity, child behavior problems, and poverty. *American Journal of Orthopsychiatry, (76)*3, 358–366

23. Mead, L. (1992). *The new politics of poverty: The non-working poor in America.* New York: Basic Books.

24. Loprest, P. J., Zedlewski, S. R. (2006). *The changing role of welfare in the lives of low-income families with children.* Washington, D.C.: Urban Institute.

25. During California's 3-year redesign process, the river analogy was frequently used to describe the proposed approach to developing prevention services. Although the final report does not refer to the river analogy, the logo describing the process to redesign services includes a picture of a river ambling through a grassy pasture. See: Child Welfare Services Stakeholder Group. (2003). CWS Redesign: The future of California's child welfare services. Sacramento, CA: State of California, Department of Social Services.

26. Cohn-Donnelly, A. H. (1997). An overview of prevention of physical abuse and neglect. In M. E. Helfer, R. S. Kempe, & R. D. Krugman (Eds.), *The battered child* (5th ed.). Chicago: University of Chicago Press; Newman, M. R., & Lutzker, J. R. (1990). Prevention programs. In R. T. Ammerman & M. Hersen (Eds.).

Children at risk: An evaluation of factors contributing to child abuse and neglect.
New York: Plenum.

27. Guterman, N. B. (2001). *Stopping child maltreatment before it starts: Emerging horizons in early home visitation services.* Thousand Oaks, CA: Sage; MacLeod, J., & Nelson, G. (2000). Programs for the promotion of family wellness and the prevention of child maltreatment: A meta-analytic review. *Child Abuse & Neglect, 24*(9), 1127–1149.

28. Adams, P. (1994). Marketing social change: The case of family preservation. *Children and Youth Services Review, 16*(5/6), 417–431.

29. Some of the early studies, lacking a control or comparison group, found that upwards of 90% of children participating in Intensive Family Preservation Services were not placed in foster care. Lacking a comparison group, however, one could not be assured that placement rates would be any different if families had not participated in services. See, for example: Behavioral Science Institute. (1990). *Homebuilders evaluation summary.* Federal Way, WA: Author.

30. In fact, children in the intensive family preservation group were statistically *more likely* to have an "indicated" report of maltreatment 3 years following services than children in the typical program group. For detail on this study see: Schuerman, J. R., Rzipnicki, T. L., & Littell, J. H. (1994). *Putting families first: An experiment in family preservation.* New York: Aldine de Gruyter. Subsequent analyses of the data determined that the program was not effective for any of the subgroups within the child welfare population, including substance-abusing clients, clients with housing issues, clients with mental health problems, or clients with parenting challenges. Further, findings were no different regardless of the duration of services, the intensity of services, or the number of concrete services provided. See: Littell, J. H., & Schuerman, J. R. (2002). What works best for whom? A closer look at intensive family preservation services. *Children and Youth Services Review, 24*(9/10), 673–699. For a review of other family preservation studies see: Blythe, B. J., Salley, M. P., & Jayaratne, S. (1994). A review of intensive family preservation research. *Social Work Research, 18*(4), 213–224; Fraser, M. W., Nelson, K. E., & & Rivard, J. C. (1997). Effectiveness of family preservation services. *Social Service Review, 21*(3), 138–153. Littell, J. H., & Schuerman, J. R. (1995). A synthesis of research on family preservation and family reunification programs. Washington D.C.: Office of the Assistant Secretary for Planning and Evaluation, Department of Health and Human Services.

31. William Meezan and Jacklyn McCrosky have argued that close attention to placement prevention has been too limited and that other important outcomes can and have been effected by family preservation services. These include improvements in parent–child interactions, family support, and family stress. For a discussion, see: McCroskey J., & Meezan, W. (1998). Family-centered services: Approaches and effectiveness. *The Future of Children, 8*(1), 54–71.

32. Efforts continue, however, to study the potential effects of family preservation and other services designed to serve families as a diversion from foster care. Illinois has just launched a new statewide program to use thorough

family assessments coupled with clinical services to reduce foster care entries. The program will be tested using random assignment to condition.

Other efforts – variously called Differential Response, Multiple Response, or Alternative Response – are taking hold in jurisdictions across the country. These programs are designed for those families who are *not* at imminent risk of foster care placement but who might benefit from services to reduce the likelihood of a future maltreatment report. Studies have been conducted in five states and the findings have been contradictory. In Minnesota and Missouri, families receiving Differential Response were less likely to be rereported for maltreatment, while in Washington and North Carolina there were no differences in rereport rates for families receiving Differential Response compared with families receiving traditional services. Findings were also mixed with regard to future placement in out-of-home care. See: Center for Child and Family Policy (2004). *Multiple Response System (MRS) evaluation report to the North Carolina Division of Social Services (NCDSS)*. Retrieved online March 15, 2005 from the Center for Child and Family Policy Web site: http://www.pubpol.duke.edu/centers/child; English, D. J., Wingard, T., Marshall, D., Orme, M., & Orme, A. (2000). Alternative responses to child protective services: emerging issues and concerns. *Child Abuse and Neglect*, 24(3), 375–388; Loman, L. A. & Siegel, G. L. (2004a). *Differential response in Missouri after five years*. Retrieved online April 5, 2005 from the Institute of Applied Research Web site: http://iarstl.org/papers/MODiffResp2004a.pdf; Loman, L. A. & Siegel, G. L. (2004b). *Minnesota alternative response evaluation final report*. Retrieved online March 20, 2005 from the Institute of Applied Research Web site: http://iarstl.org/papers/ARFinalEvaluationReport.pdf; Virginia Department of Social Services (2004). *Evaluation of the differential response system*. Retrieved online April 20, 2005 from the Virginia Department of Social Services Web site: http://www.dss.virginia.gov/files/division/dfs/cps/reports/eval_drs_2004.pdf

33. Geeraert et al.'s original study included 40 studies; however, the majority of these relied upon very weak research designs. In a critique of their study methods, Miller suggested a more rigorous approach, only including studies with stronger research designs. In the subsequent analysis, Geeraert and associates included only the 19 studies with a control group selected either at random or by means of matching. Their review examines 11 indicators of risk reduction or abuse reduction. The overall effect size across all indicators was 0.21. The effect size for reductions in maltreatment reports was 0.16. They include a category of "indirect indication" of abuse reduction. The effect size for this measure is 0.20. When the effect size for "reports" and "indirect indication" are combined, they arrive at the effect size of 0.19. The original study can be found at: Geeraert, L., Van den Noortgate, W., Grietens, H., & Onghena, P. (2004). The effects of early prevention programs for families with young children at risk for physical child abuse and neglect: A meta-analysis. *Child Maltreatment*, 9(3), 277–291. For the revised analysis see: Van den Noortgate, W., Geeraert, L., Grietens, H., Onghena, P. (2006). The effects of early prevention programs for families with young children at risk for physical child abuse and neglect: A reply on the comments of Miller. *Child Maltreatment*,

11(1), 98–101. The critique is: Miller, M. G. (2006). Letter to the editor. *Child Maltreatment, 11*(10, 95–97.

MacLeod and Nelson included over 50 studies in their review, including family support programs, child maltreatment prevention programs, and placement prevention programs. They also combined studies that used relatively weak designs, and others that relied on strong designs. See: MacLeod, J., & Nelson, G. (2000). Programs for the promotion of family wellness and the prevention of child maltreatment: A meta-analytic review. *Child Abuse and Neglect, 24*(9), 1127–1149

According to Cohen, effect sizes of 0.2 or below should be considered small, medium effect sizes are about 0.5, and 0.8 or above can be considered a large effect size. See: Cohen, J. (1977). *Statistical power analysis for the behavioral sciences* (2nd ed.). New York: Academic Press.

34. See MacLeod, J., & Nelson, G. (2000). Programs for the promotion of family wellness and the prevention of child maltreatment: A meta-analytic review. *Child Abuse and Neglect, 24*(9), 1127–1149; Schoff, L. B. (2007). *Pathway to the prevention of child abuse and neglect*. Washington, D.C.: Pathways Mapping Initiative; Wulczyn, F., Barth, R. P., Yuan, Y-Y. T., Harden, B. J., & Landsverk, J. (2006). *Beyond common sense: Child welfare, child well-being, and the evidence for policy reform*. New York: Aldine de Gruyter.

35. See also Daro, D., & McCurdy, K. (1994). Preventing child abuse and neglect: Programmatic interventions. *Child Welfare, 73*, 405–430.

36. Dagenais, C., & Bouchard, C. (1996). As cited in: MacLeod, J., & Nelson, G. (2000). Programs for the promotion of family wellness and the prevention of child maltreatment: A meta-analytic review. *Child Abuse and Neglect, 24*(9), 1127–1149.

37. Karoly, L. A., Greenwood, P. W., Everingham, S. S. Hoube, J., Kilburn, M. R., Rydell, C.P., Sanders, M., & Chiesa, J. (1998). *Investing in our children: What we know and don't know about the costs and benefits of early childhood intervention*. Santa Monica, CA: Rand; MacLeod, J., & Nelson, G. (2000). Programs for the promotion of family wellness and the prevention of child maltreatment: A meta-analytic review. *Child Abuse and Neglect, 24*(9), 1127–1149;

38. For a review of the costs and benefits associated with many family support programs (not necessarily targeting parenting practices but more generally targeting a wide range of potential child and family problems) see: Aos, S., Lieb, R., Mayfield, J., Miller, M., & Pennucci, A. (2004). *Benefits and costs of prevention and early intervention programs for youth*. Olympia, WA: Washington State Institute for Public Policy. Retrieved November 20, 2007 from: http://www.wsipp.wa.gov/rptfiles/04-07-3901.pdf

39. All of the studies described here are experimental or (in only a few cases) quasi-experimental, they include good sample sizes, follow families over extended periods of time, suffer from limited attrition, and usually include standardized measures.

40. For the immediate and near-term findings and information on various program outcomes see: Olds, D. L., & Kitzman, H. (1993). Review of research on home visiting for pregnant women and parents of young children. *Future of Children, 3*(4), 53–92.

41. Olds has written extensively about the short- and long-term effects of his work. See: Olds, D. L., Henderson, C. R., Chamberlin, R., & Tatelbaum, R. (1986). Preventing child abuse and neglect: A randomized trial of nurse visitation. *Pediatrics, 78*, 65–78; Olds, D. L., Robinson, J, O'Brien, R., Luckey, D. W., Pettitt, L. M., Henderson, C. R., et al. (2002). Home visiting by paraprofessionals and by nurses: A randomized, controlled trial. *Pediatrics, 110*(3), 486–495.

42. Duggan, A., McFarlane, E., Widham, A., Rohde, C., Salkever, D., Fuddy, L., et al. (1999) Evaluation of Hawaii's Healthy Start program. *The Future of Children, 9*(1); Gomby, D. S., Culross, P. L., & Behrman, R. E. (1999). Home visiting: Recent program evaluations, analysis, and recommendations. *The Future of Children, 9*(1), 4–26; Kitzman, H., Olds, D. L., Henderson, C. R., Hanks, C., Cole, R., Tatelbaum, R., et al. (1997). Effect of prenatal and infancy home visitation by nurses on pregnancy outcomes, childhood injuries, and repeated childbearing: A randomized controlled trial. *Journal of the American Medical Association, 278*, 644–654; Olds, D., Eckenrode, J., Henderson, C., Kitzman, H., Powers, J., Cole, R., et al., (1997). Long-term effects of home visitation on maternal life course and child abuse and neglect. *Journal of the American Medical Association, 278*, 637–643.

43. Gomby, D. S., Culross, P. L., & Behrman, R. E. (1999). Home visiting: Recent program evaluations: Analysis and recommendations. *Future of Children, 9*(1), 4–2; MacMillan, H. L., MacMillan, J. H., Offord, D. R., Griffith, L., & MacMillan, A. (1994). Primary prevention of child physical abuse and neglect: A critical review, Part I. *Journal of Child Psychology and Psychiatry, 35*(5), 835–856. See also: Barth, R. (1991). An experimental evaluation of in-home child abuse prevention services. *Child Abuse and Neglect, 15*(4), 363–375; Duggan, A., Caldera, D. Rodriguez, K., Burrell, L., Rohde, C., & Crowne, S. S. (2007). Impact of a statewide home visiting program to prevent child abuse. *Child Abuse and Neglect, 31*(8), 801–827; Duggan, A., McFarlane, E., Fuddy, L., Burrell, L., Higman, S. M., Windham, A., et al. (2004). Randomized trial of a statewide home visiting program: Impact on preventing child abuse and neglect. *Child Abuse and Neglect, 28*, 597–622; Fraser, J., Armstrong, K., Morris, J., & Dadds, M. (2000). Home visiting intervention for vulnerable families with newborns: Follow-up results of a randomized controlled trial. *Child Abuse and Neglect, 24*(11), 1399–1429; Landsverk, J., Carillio, T, Connelly, C. D., Ganger, W. C., Symen, D. J., Newton, R. R., et al. (2002). Healthy Families San Diego clinical trial: Technical report. San Diego, CA: San Diego Children's Hospital and Health Center, Child and Adolescent Services Research center.

44. For information pertaining to the 15-year follow-up, see: Olds, D., Eckenrode, J., Henderson, C., Kitzman, H., Powers, J., Cole, R., Sidors, K., et al., (1997). Long-term effects of home visitation on maternal life course and child abuse and neglect. *Journal of the American Medical Association, 278*, 637–643. Where maltreatment prevention effects were seen, these were delayed effects, and effects appeared to be weakest when mothers were substance involved or troubled by intimate partner violence.

45. Chaffin, M. (2004). Is it time to rethink Healthy Start/Healthy Families? *Child Abuse and Neglect, 28*, 589–595.

46. Brooks-Gunn, J., & Markman, L. B. (2005). The contribution of parenting to ethnic and racial gaps in school readiness. *Future of Children, 15*(1), 139–168.

47. For a review, see: Caughy, M., DiPietro, J., & Strobino, D. (1994). Day care participation as a protective factor in the development of low-income children. *Child Development, 65*, 457–471; Hungerford, A., & Cox, M. (2006). Family factors in child care research. *Evaluation Review, 30*(5), 631–655.

48. Reynolds, A. J., Chang, H., & Temple, J. A. (1998). Early childhood intervention and juvenile delinquency: An exploratory analysis of the Chicago Child-Parent Centers. *Evaluation Review, 22*(3), 341–372; Reynolds, A. J., & Temple, J. A. (1998). Extended early childhood intervention and school achievement: Age thirteen findings from the Chicago Longitudinal study. *Child Development, 69*(1), 231–246; Reynolds, A. J., Temple J. A., Robertson, D. L., & Mann, E. A. (2001). Long-term effects of an early childhood intervention on educational achievement and juvenile arrest: A 15-year follow up of low income children in public schools. *Journal of the American Medical Association, 285*(18), 2339–2346.

49. National Research Council and Institute of Medicine. (2000). *From neurons to neighborhoods: The science of early childhood development.* Committee on Integrating the Science of Early Childhood Development. J. P. Shonkoff & D. A. Phillips (Eds.) Washington, D.C.: National Academy Press.

50. Reynolds, A. J., Chang, H., & Temple, J. A. (1998). Early childhood intervention and juvenile delinquency: An exploratory analysis of the Chicago Child-Parent Centers. *Evaluation Review, 22*(3), 341–372; Reynolds, A. J., & Temple, J. A. (1998). Extended early childhood intervention and school achievement: Age thirteen findings from the Chicago Longitudinal study. *Child Development, 69*(1), 231–246; Reynolds, A. J., Temple J. A., Robertson, D. L., & Mann, E. A. (2001). Long-term effects of an early childhood intervention on educational achievement and juvenile arrest: A 15-year follow up of low income children in public schools. *Journal of the American Medical Association, 285*(18), 2339–2346.

51. U.S. Department of Health and Human Services, Administration for Children and Families (2005). *Head Start impact study: First year findings.* Washington, D.C.: Author. For a detailed review of several Head Start studies, see: Gormley, W. T. Jr. (2007). Early childhood care and education: Lessons and puzzles. *Journal of Policy Analysis and Management, 26*(3), 633–671.

52. Karoly, L. A., Greenwood, P. W., Everingham, S. S., Hoube, J., Kilburn, M. R., Rydell, C. P., et al. (1998). *Investing in our children: What we know and don't know about the costs and benefits of early childhood interventions.* Santa Monica, CA: Rand.

53. U.S. Department of Health and Human Services, Administration for Children and Families (2005). *Head Start impact study: First year findings.* Washington, D.C.: Author.

54. Reynolds, A., & Robertson, D. (2003). School-based early intervention and later child maltreatment in the Chicago Longitudinal Study. *Child Development, 74*(1), 3–26.

55. If there are other studies showing the effects of child care services on maltreatment prevention, I am unaware of them, having conducted an extensive literature review. The Reynolds study, although impressive, is also

not without flaws. The study did not include random assignment and thus the comparison group may be subject to selection bias. In particular, the comparison group used in this study was less likely to suffer from severe poverty, possibly biasing the findings.

56. Mathematica Policy Research, Inc. (2002). *Making a difference in the lives of infants and toddlers and their families: The impacts of early head start*. Contract DHHS #105–95–1936. Princeton, NJ: Mathematica. Differences in children's cognitive and language development at 3 years of age were statistically significant between treatment and comparison groups, although the size of the differences were modest (e.g., a score of 91.4 vs. 89.9 on the Bayley Mental Development Index, and a score of 83.3 vs. 81.1 on the Peabody Picture Vocabulary test.) Parents who did not appear to benefit and who actually experienced unfavorable outcomes from program services were those described as having "extremely high numbers of demographic risk factors" (i.e., with four or more risk factors such as lacking a high school education, being single parents, teen parents, public assistance recipients, and not employed or in school) – factors frequently associated with families in the child welfare population.

Other studies examining the effects of high-quality infant care may suggest improved mother–infant interactions, including the nature and degree of mothers' responsiveness to her infant. See: NICHD Early Child Care Research (1997). The effects of infant child care on infant-mother attachment security. *Child Development, 68,* 860–879.

57. Some studies have targeted low-income urban preschoolers at risk for conduct problems [Brotman, L. M., Klein, R. G., Kamboukos, D., Brown, E. J., Coard, S. I., & Sosinsky, L. S. (2003). Preventive intervention for urban, low-income preschoolers at familial risk for conduct problems: A randomized pilot study. *Journal of Clinical Child and Adolescent Psychology, 32*(2), 246–257]. Other have targeted toddlers with behavior problems [Gross, D., Fogg, L., & Tucker, S. (1995). The efficacy of parent training for promoting positive parent–toddler relationships. *Research in Nursing and Health, 18,* 489–499].

58. Webster-Stratton, C., Reid, J., & Hammond, M. (2001). Preventing conduct problems, promoting social competence: A parent and child training partnership in Head Start. *Journal of Child Clinical Psychology, 30*(3), 283–302; Webster-Stratton, C. (1998). Preventing conduct problems in Head Start children: Strengthening parenting competences. *Journal of Consulting and Clinical Psychology 66*(5), 715–730.

59. The program has been adapted and implemented with foster parent–birth parent dyads and has shown effects on improved parenting. See: Linares, L. O., Montalto, D., Li, M. M., & Oza,V. S. (2006). A promising parenting intervention for foster care. *Journal of Consulting and Clinical Psychology, 74*(1), 32–41.

60. Barth, R. P., Landsverk, J., Chamberlain, P., Reid, J., Rolls, J., Hurlburt, M., et al., (2005). Parent training in child welfare services: Planning for a more evidence-based approach to serving biological parents. *Research on Social Work Practice, 15,* 353–371.

61. Although the literature reviewed here is targeted to specific families who present particular risks, using relatively tightly controlled interventions to

support targeted changes, many other family support initiatives – when placed in a community context – are highly diffuse, showing negligible or no impacts. See, for example: Center for the Study of Social Policy. (n.d.) *Community partnerships for protecting children.* Washington, D.C.: Author.

62. Brayden, R., Altemeier, W., Dietrich, M., Tucker, D., Christensen, M., McLaughlin, F., et al. (1993). A prospective study of secondary prevention of child maltreatment. *Pediatrics, 122*(4), 511–516; Fraser, J., Armstrong, K., Morris, J., & Dadds, M. (2000). Home visiting intervention for vulnerable families with newborns: Follow-up results of a randomized controlled trial. *Child Abuse and Neglect, 24*(11), 1399–1429.

63. Gormley, W. T. Jr. (2007). Early childhood care and education: Lessons and puzzles. *Journal of Policy Analysis and Management, 26*(3), 633–671.

64. MacMillan, H. L., Thomas, B. H., Jamieson,E., Walsh, C. A., Boyle, M. H., Shannon, H. S., et al. (2005). Effectiveness of home visitation by public health nurses in prevention of the recurrence of child physical abuse and neglect: A randomized controlled trial. *Lancet, 365,* 1786–1793.

65. Duggan, A., Fuddy, L., Burrell, L., Higman, S. M., McFarlane, E., Windham, A., et al. (2004). Randomized trial of a statewide home visiting program to prevent child abuse: Impact in reducing parental risk factors. *Child Abuse and Neglect, 28,* 623–643; MacLeod, J., & Nelson, G. (2000). Programs for the promotion of family wellness and the prevention of child maltreatment: A meta-analytic review. *Child Abuse and Neglect, 24*(9), 1127–1149. Effect sizes from various programs ranged from 0.17 to 0.56, with higher effects noted for family wellness outcomes and lower effects noted for child maltreatment outcomes.

66. See: Bugental, D., Ellerson, P., Lin, E., Rainey, B., Kokotovic, A., & O'Hara, N. (2002). A cognitive approach to child abuse prevention. *Journal of Family Psychology, 16*(3), 243–258; Chaffin, M., Silovsky, J. F., Funderburk, B., Valle, L. A., Brestan, E. V., Balachoa, T., et al. (2004). Parent-Child Interaction Therapy with physically abusive parents: Efficacy for reducing future abuse reports. *Journal of Consulting and Clinical Psychology, 72*(3), 500–510; Chambless, D. L., & Ollendick, T. H. (2001). Empirically supported psychological interventions: Controversies and practices. *Annual Review of Psychology, 52,* 685–716; Heinicke, C., Fineman N., Ruty, G., Recchia, S., Guthrie, D., & Rodning, C. (1999). Relationship-based intervention with at-risk mothers: Outcomes in the first year of life. *Infant Mental Health Journal, 20,* 349–374; Reid, M. J., & Webster-Stratton, C. (2001). The Incredible Years parent, teacher and child intervention: Targeting multiple areas of risk for young children with pervasive conduct problems using a flexible, manualized treatment program. *Cognitive and Behavior Practice, 8,* 377–386.

67. For a review of the evidence base for sexual abuse prevention programs and other maltreatment prevention approaches, see: Chaffin, M., & Friedrich, B. (2004). Evidence-based treatments in child abuse and neglect. *Children and Youth Services Review, 26,* 1097–1113.

68. See, for example, DePanfilis, D., & Dubowitz, H. (2005). Family connections: A program for preventing child neglect. *Child Maltreatment, 10*(2), 108–123. Project 12-Ways/SafeCare is also gaining popularity, but rigorous

studies have not yet been undertaken to show its effectiveness. Gershater-Molko, R. M., Lutzker, J. R., & Wesch, D. (2002). Using recidivism data to evaluate project SafeCare: An ecobehavioral approach to teach "bonding," safety, and health care skills. *Child Maltreatment, 7,* 277–285.

69. Substance abuse programs might also be included in the list.

70. Promoting Safe and Stable Families Amendments of 2001 (P.L. 107–281) http://thomas.loc.gov/cgi-bin/cpquery/!&db_id=cp107&r_n=hr281

71. Families could be identified as needing services either by volunteering, by referral from community professionals, or from maltreatment reports that were determined insufficiently severe that they needed protective child welfare intervention. The model bears similarities to Differential Response programs now taking shape in jurisdictions across the country, but the goal of newly developed family support efforts – in contrast to Differential Response – would not be child maltreatment and foster care placement prevention. Family support would instead target those domains of family functioning that have shown effectiveness in previous research.

72. Kate no longer receives TANF as she reached her 5-year time limit.

73. Although the specifics of their foster care experience are not detailed here, their experience was very difficult. Bill and Kate (and their children) are Native American and should have been given special consideration under the Indian Child Welfare Act (ICWA). When they asked for tribal contact and representation, the social worker did not understand their request and was completely ignorant of ICWA. Her only knowledge of issues pertaining to native tribes related to Indian gaming. Bill and Kate's efforts to assure their social worker that federal law offered them special provisions in child welfare were fruitless. After some time, Bill and Kate contacted the tribe on their own and tried to establish closer collaboration. The tribe was nominally involved in the case, as attempts to have tribal representation involved in court proceedings (via satellite) never materialized.

CHAPTER 3

1. Gendell, S. J. (2001). In search of permanency: A reflection on the first three years of the Adoption and Safe Families Act implementation. *Family and Conciliation Courts Review, 39;* Stein, T. J. (2000). The Adoption and Safe Families Act: Creating a false dichotomy between parents' and children's rights. *Families in Society: the Journal of Contemporary Human Services, 81*(6), 586–592.

2. *Reasonable Efforts.* 105th Cong. S3947 (1997). Statement of Senator DeWine. From the Congressional Record Online via GPO Access [wais.access.gpo.gov].

3. Exceptions to the reasonable efforts provisions are discussed in greater detail in Chapter 4. For additional information, see: D'Andrade, A., & Berrick, J. D. (2006). When policy meets practice: The untested effects of permanency reforms in child welfare. *Journal of Sociology and Social Work. 33*(1), 31–52.

4. These data are derived from cross-sectional analyses of federal AFCARS reports. U.S. Department of Health and Human Services, Administration for Children and Families, Administration of Children, Youth and Families,

Children's Services Bureau (2005, June.). AFCARS Report #13. Retrieved August 2, 2007, from http://www.acf.dhhs.gov/programs/cb/stats_research/afcars/tar/report13.htm. More accurate understandings of child welfare caseload dynamics may be obtained from conducting entry cohort analyses. See: Courtney, M., Needell, B., & Wulczyn, F. (2004). Unintended consequences of the push for accountability: The case of national child welfare performance standards. *Children and Youth Services Review, 26*(12), 1141–1154.

5. See: Frame, L., Berrick, J. D., & Brodowski, M. L. (2000). Understanding re-entry to care for reunified infants. *Child Welfare, 74*(4), 339–369; Reich, J. A. (2005). *Fixing families: Parents, power, and the child welfare system.* New York: Routledge; Smith, B. (2003). How parental drug use and drug treatment compliance relate to family reunification. *Child Welfare, 82*(3), 335–366.

6. Littell, J., & Girvin, H. (2004). Ready or not: Uses of the Stages of Change Model in child welfare. *Child Welfare, 83,* 341–366.

7. Given Tracy's history, it is possible that her child's SIDS death could have resulted from neglect or other causes.

8. It is remarkable that CPS made a kinship foster care placement with Tracy's sister, even though a few years earlier there was significant question as to whether Fay had been involved in Tamika's drug incident.

9. Kinship care is described in greater detail in Chapter 5. Relatives can care for children outside of the child welfare system and, in doing so, can collect Temporary Assistance for Needy Families (TANF - welfare) payments. If the children are formally placed in foster care with the relative, the relative can receive substantially higher monthly payments. Before the Adoption and Safe Families Act (ASFA) was passed, few requirements were made of kinship foster parents; standards for care were negligible in the state of California.

10. Prior to 1997, when the Adoption and Safe Families Act was passed into federal law, families were given access to 18 months of reunification services. With the new law, the time frame was shortened to 12 months.

11. Tracy's case takes an interesting turn at this point: The notion that a woman could have four children living in out-of-home care – all because of drug exposure and drug use – that the mother was still actively using, but that a 1-year-old infant would be allowed to remain in her care is curious and nonsensical. Court reports from that period indicate that Tracy's care of Tyson was "adequate." If indeed it *was* adequate (which of course it was not), what justified the state's intervention on behalf of her other four children? And if Tracy's care of her children was inadequate, what made social workers think that her sister Fay's care for the children was superior? For the state to hold different standards of care not only between families but within families calls into question the basis of the legitimacy of the child welfare system. Not only was Tyson left unprotected in Tracy's care but three of her other children were also unprotected by their placement in an unsafe kinship setting.

12. Bess, R., & Scarcella, C. A. (2004). *Child welfare spending during a time of fiscal stress.* Washington, D.C.: Urban Institute. The authors indicate that approximately $11 billion comes from federal sources, $8 billion from state resources, and $2.6 billion from local resources. Local spending increased from 2000 to 2002 at a rate double that of the federal or state governments.

According to Swann and Sylvester, comparative figures for federal spending on the Food Stamps program, WIC, and TANF were $17.1 billion, $4.0 billion, and $11.5 billion, respectively. See: Swann, C. A., & Sylvester, M. S. (2006). The foster care crisis: What caused caseloads to grow? *Demography*, 43(2), 309–335.

13. Besinger, B. A., Garland, A. F., Litrownik, J., & Landsverk, J. (1999). Caregiver substance abuse among maltreated children placed in out-of-home care. *Child Welfare*, 78(2), 221–239; Child Welfare League of America. (1998). *Alcohol and other drugs: Survey of state child welfare agencies*. Washington, D.C.: Author. According to Swann and Sylvester, a large proportion of the caseload growth in foster care in the late 1980s and 1990s can be attributed to the increased proportion of women imprisoned on drug charges and the substantially longer lengths of their prison terms. See: Swann, C. A., & Sylvester, M. S. (2006). The foster care crisis: What caused caseloads to grow? *Demography*, 43(2), 309–335.

14. Hohman, M. M., & Butt, R. L. (2001). How soon is too soon? Addiction recovery and family reunification. *Child Welfare*, 81(1), 53–67; Semidei, J., Radel, L. F., & Nolan, C. (2001). Substance abuse and child welfare: Clear linkages and promising responses. *Child Welfare*, 80(2), 109–127.

15. Berrick, J. D., Needell, B., Barth, R. P., & Jonson-Reid, M. (1998). *The tender years: Toward developmentally sensitive child welfare services for very young children*. New York: Oxford University Press.

16. Wulczyn, F. (1994). Family reunification. *The Future of Children*, 14(1), 95–112.

17. Koh, E. (2007). Predictor of re-entry into foster care. Paper presented at the Conference of the Society for Social Work Research (SSWR), San Francisco, CA, January 11–14, 2007. Shaw, T. (2006). Re-entry into the foster care system after reunification. *Children and Youth Services Review*, 28(11), 1375–1390.

18. Goerge, R. M. (1990). The reunification process in substitute care. *Social Service Review*, 64(3), 422–457. Research on infants and young children entering out-of-home care suggests that about one-quarter of these young children return to their homes within the first 3 months of placement. See: Berrick, J. D., Needell, B., Barth, R.P., & Jonson-Reid, M. (1990). *The tender years: Toward developmentally-sensitive child welfare services for very young children*. New York: Oxford University Press.

19. Note also that Tracy reunified with her infant daughter several months after she was born, and the older children were reunified shortly thereafter.

20. Berrick, J. D., Needell, B., Barth, R. P., & Jonson-Reid, M. (1998). *The tender years: Toward developmentally sensitive child welfare services for very young children*. New York: Oxford University Press; Connell, C. M., Katz, K. H., Saunders, L., & Tebes, J. K. (2006). Leaving foster care: The influence of child and case characteristics on foster care exit rates. *Children and Youth Services Review*, 28, 780–798; Courtney, M. E. (1994). Factors associated with the reunification of foster children with their families. *Social Service Review* 68(1), 81–108; Courtney, M. E., & Wong, Y-L. I. (1996). Comparing the timing of exits from substitute care. *Children and Youth Services Review*, 18(4–5), 307–334; Smith, B. D. (2003). How parental drug use and drug treatment compliance relate to family reunification.

Child Welfare, 82(3), 335–365; Wulczyn, F. (2004). Family reunification. *The Future of Children, 14*(1), 95–114.

21. Berrick, J. D., Needell, B., Barth, R. P., & Jonson-Reid, M. (1998). *The tender years: Toward developmentally sensitive child welfare services for very young children.* New York: Oxford University Press; Courtney, M. E. (1994). Factors associated with the reunification of foster children with their families. *Social Service Review 68*(1), 81–108; Courtney, M. E., & Wong, Y-L. I. (1996). Comparing the timing of exits from substitute care. *Children and Youth Services Review, 18*(4–5), 307–334; Davis, I. P., Landsverk, J., Newton, R., & Ganger, W. (1996). Parental visiting and foster care reunification. *Children and Youth Services Review, 18*(4/5), 363–382; McMurtry, S. L., & Lie, G-Y. (1992). Differential exit rates of minority children in foster care. *Social Work Research and Abstracts, 28*(1), 42–48; Shaw, T. (2006). Re-entry into the foster care system after reunification. *Children and Youth Services Review, 28*(11), 1375–1390; Wells, K., & Guo, S. (1999). Reunification and reentry of foster children. *Children and Youth Services Review, 21*(4), 273–294.

22. The effects of race/ethnicity may be more complicated. Research by Harris and Courtney suggests that children of African-American single parents are least likely to reunify, whereas children in Hispanic two-parent families are most likely to reunify. The study suggests that family structure may interact with race/ethnicity in ways that were previously less well understood. See: Harris, M. S., & Courtney, M. E. (2003). The interaction of race, ethnicity, and family structure with respect to the timing of family reunification. *Children and Youth Services Review, 25*(5–6), 409–429.

23. Barth, R., Guo, S., & Caplick, E. (2007). Child welfare reinvolvement and re-entry following reunification: Implications for practice and for national performance standards. Paper presented at the Conference of the Society for Social Work Research (SSWR), San Francisco, CA, January 11–14, 2007; Courtney, M. E. (1994). Factors associated with the reunification of foster children with their families. *Social Service Review 68*(1): 81–108; Courtney, M. E., & Wong, Y- L.I. (1996). Comparing the timing of exits from substitute care. *Children and Youth Services Review, 18*(4–5), 307–334; Davis, I. P., Landsverk, J., Newton, R., & Ganger, W. (1996). Parental visiting and foster care reunification. *Children and Youth Services Review, 18*(4/5), 363–382; Wells, K. & Guo, S. (1999). Reunification and reentry of foster children. *Children and Youth Services Review, 21*(4), 273–294.

24. Koh, E. (2007). Predictor of re-entry into foster care. Paper presented at the Conference of the Society for Social Work Research (SSWR), San Francisco, CA, January 11–14, 2007; Landsverk, J.,Davis, I., Ganger, W., Newton, R., & Johnson, I. (1996). Impact of child psychosocial functioning on reunification from out-of-home placement. *Children and Youth Services Review, 18*(4–5), 447–462; Wells, S. Ford, K., & Griesgraber, M. (2007). Foster care case types as predictors of case outcomes. Paper presented at the Conference of the Society for Social Work Research (SSWR), San Francisco, CA: January 11–14, 2007.

25. Eamon, M. K. (2002). *The effect of economic resources on reunification of Illinois children in substitute care.* Report No. 0402-C. Urbana, IL: University of

Illinois at Urbana-Champagne, School of Social Work, Children and Family Research Center; Rzepnicki, T. L., Schuerman, J. R., & Johnson, P. R. (1997). Facing uncertainty: Re-uniting high-risk families. In J. D. Berrick, R. P. Barth, & N. Gilbert (Eds.), *Child welfare research review*, Vol. 2. New York: Columbia University Press.

26. See: Courtney, M. E. (1994). Factors associated with the reunification of foster children with their families. *Social Service Review 68*(1): 81–108; Courtney, M. E., & Wong, Y-L. I. (1996). Comparing the timing of exits from substitute care. *Children and Youth Services Review, 18*(4–5), 307–334; Eamon, M. K. (2002). *The effect of economic resources on reunification of Illinois children in substitute care.* Report No. 0402-C. Urbana, IL: University of Illinois at Urbana-Champagne, School of Social Work, Children and Family Research Center. Jonson-Reid, M. (2003). Foster care and future risk of maltreatment. *Children and Youth Services Review 25*(4), 271; Shaw, T. (2006). Re-entry into the foster care system after reunification. *Children and Youth Services Review, 28*(11), 1375–1390. Although parents' income appears to affect reunification, the role of work is less clear. A study conducted by Wells and Guo may indicate that women reliant on TANF as an income source have more difficulties reunifying with their children if they return to work. However, a study by Kortenkamp, Geen, and Stagner suggests that women who were working at the time their child was placed were *more* likely to see their children return home. Kortenkamp, K., Geen, R., & Stagner, M. (2004). The role of welfare and work in predicting foster care reunification rates for children of welfare recipients. *Children and Youth Services Review, 26*(6), 577–590; Wells, K., & Guo, S. (2003). Mothers' welfare and work income and reunification with children in foster care. *Children and Youth Services Review, 25* (3), 203–224.

27. Fuller, T. (2005). Child safety at reunification: A case-control study of maltreatment recurrence following return home fro substitute care. *Children and Youth Services Review, 27*(12), 1293–1306.

28. Courtney, M.E., McMurtry, S., and Zinn, A. (January, 2005). Predictors of reunification in a sample of urban out-of-home care cases. Paper presentation. Society for Social Work Research, Austin, TX.

29. Fraser, M. W., Walton, E., Lewis, R. E., Pecora, P. J., & Walton, W. K. (1996). An experiment in family reunification: Correlates of outcomes at one-year follow-up. *Children and Youth Services Review, 18*(4/5), 335–361.

30. Leathers, S. J. (2002). Parental visiting and family reunification: Could inclusive practice make a difference? *Child Welfare, 81*(4), 595–616; McMurtry, S. L., & Lie, G-Y. (1992). Differential exit rates of minority children in foster care. *Social Work Research and Abstracts, 28*(1), 42–48; Testa, M. F., & Slack, K.S. (2002). The gift of kinship foster care. *Children and Youth Services Review, 24*(1–2), 79–108. Research by Davis and Landsverk also shows that parents who visit with their children at the rate recommended in their case plans were 10 times more likely to reunify with their children than parents who did not visit regularly. Davis, I. P., Landsverk, J. A., Newton, R., & Granger, W. (1996). Parental visiting and foster care reunification. *Children and Youth Services Review, 18*, 363–382. Early research findings on kinship care suggested that children placed with kin were less likely to reunify. Since then, more sophisticated analyses have indicated that

children placed with kin reunify more slowly than children placed with non-kin, but their overall rates of reunification are similar. Barth, R. P., Courtney, M. E., Berrick, J. D., & Albert, V. (1994). *From child abuse to permanency planning: Child welfare services pathways and placements.* New York: Aldine de Gruyter; Testa, M. (1997). Kinship care in Illinois. In J. D. Berrick, R. P. Barth, & N. Gilbert (Eds.), *Child welfare research review*, Vol. II. New York: Columbia University Press.

31. Marsh, J. C., Ryan, J. P., Choi, S., & Testa, M. (2006). Integrated services for families with multiple problems: Obstacles to family reunification. *Children and Youth Services Review, 28*, 1074–1087.

32. See: Festinger, T. (1996). Going home and returning to foster care. *Children and Youth Services Review, 18*(4–5), 383–402; Frame, L., Berrick, J. D., & Brodowski, M. L. (2000). Understanding re-entry to out-of-home care for reunified infants. *Child Welfare, 79*(4), 339–369; Wulczyn, F. (1994). Family reunification. *The Future of Children, 14*(1), 95–112. With approximately 50% of children reunifying, and approximately 30% of these re-entering care, the effective total reunification rate is reduced to about 35%.

33. Smith, B. D. (2003). How parental drug use and drug treatment compliance relate to family reunification. *Child Welfare, 82*(3), 335–365.

34. Frame, L., Berrick, J. D., & Brodowski, M. L. (2000). Understanding re-entry to out-of-home care for reunified infants. *Child Welfare, 79*(4), 339–369.

35. Courtney, M. (1995). Reentry to foster care of children returned to their families. *Social Service Review, 69*, 226–241; Fryer, G. E., & Miyoshi, T. J. (1994). A survival analysis of the revictimization of children: The case of Colorado. *Child Abuse and Neglect, 18*, 1063–1071; Wulczyn, F. (1991). Caseload dynamics and foster care reentry. *Social Service Review, 65*(1), 133–156.

36. Courtney, M. (1995). Reentry to foster care of children returned to their families. *Social Service Review, 69*, 226–241. Miller et al. suggest that family poverty as indicated by AFDC receipt may not be associated with reentry, but that specific correlates of poverty—such as cramped housing, the absence of cognitively stimulating toys and activities, and poorer neighborhoods—may be better predictors of re-entry. See: Miller, K. A., Fisher, P. A., Fetrow, B., & Jordan, K. (2006). Trouble on the journey home: Reunification failures in foster care. *Children and Youth Services Review, 28*, 260–274. Jones also found a relationship between reentry and AFDC receipt, with "no visible income" and with housing inadequacy. See: Joes, L. (1998). The social and family correlates of successful reunification of children in foster care. *Children and Youth Services Review, 20*(4), 305–323.

37. Courtney, M. (1995). Reentry to foster care of children returned to their families. *Social Service Review, 69*, 226–241; Shaw, T. (2006). Re-entry into the foster care system after reunification. *Children and Youth Services Review, 28*(11), 1375–1390.

38. Terling, T. (1999). The efficacy of family reunification practices: Reentry rates and correlates of reentry for abused and neglected children reunited with their families. *Child Abuse and Neglect, 23*(12), 1359–1370. In Terling's study, African-American and Caucasian risks of re-entry were similar.

39. Courtney, M. (1995). Reentry to foster care of children returned to their families. *Social Service Review, 69,* 226–241; Festinger, T. (1994). Going home and returning to foster care. *Children and Youth Services Review, 18*(4/5), 383–402; Fuller, T. L. (2005). Child safety at reunification: A case-control study of maltreatment recurrence following return home from substitute care. *Children and Youth Services Review, 27,* 1293–1306; Jones, L. (1998). The social and family correlates of successful reunification of children in foster care. *Children and Youth Services Review; 20*(4), 305–323; Terling, T. (1999). The efficacy of family reunification practices: Reentry rates and correlates of reentry for abused and neglected children reunited with their families. *Child Abuse and Neglect, 23*(12), 1359–1370. Although Davis et al. (1996) found a significant relationship between parental visiting and reunification, the relationship did not hold for re-entry. See: Davis, I. P., Landsverk, J., Newton, R., & Ganger, W. (1996). Parental visiting and foster care reunification. *Children and Youth Services Review, 18*(4–5), 363–382.

40. Terling, T. (1999). The efficacy of family reunification practices: Reentry rates and correlates of reentry for abused and neglected children reunited with their families. *Child Abuse and Neglect, 23*(12), 1359–1370; Wulczyn, F. (1991). Caseload dynamics and foster care reentry. *Social Service Review, 65,* 133–156. In one recent study, the reentry rate was approximately 25%, however unlike most other studies in the field, there was no association found between more timely reunifications and reentry. See: McDonald, T., Bryson, S., & Poerter, J. (2006). Balancing reunification and reentry goals. *Children and Youth Services Review, 28,* 47–58.

41. The term is used here to differentiate from unstable reunifications where children re-enter foster care.

42. California Department of Social Services. (1983). *California family protection act report.* Sacramento: California Department of Social Services; Jones, M. A. (1985). *A second chance for families, five years later: Follow-up of a program to prevent foster care.* New York: Child Welfare League of America.; Jones, M. A., Neuman, R., & Shyne, A. W. (1976). *A second chance for families: Evaluation of a program to reduce foster care.* New York: Child Welfare League of America; Lahti, J. (1982). A follow-up study of foster children in permanent placements. *Social Service Review,* 556–571; Pike, V. (1976). Permanent planning for foster children: The Oregon project. *Children Today, 40*(6), 22–25; Pike, V., Downs, S., Emlen, A., Downs, G., & Case, D. (1977). *Permanent planning for children in foster care: A handbook for social workers.* Washington, D.C.: U.S. Department of Health, Education and Welfare; Stein, T. J. & Gambrill, E. D. (1977). Facilitating decision making in foster care: The Alameda project. *Social Service Review, 51*(3), 502–513; Stein, T. J., Gambrill, E., & Wiltse, K. T. (1978). *Children in foster homes—achieving continuity in care.* New York: Praeger.

43. Child welfare "waiver demonstration projects" were authorized by Congress under the Personal Responsibility and Work Opportunity Reconciliation Act (the welfare reform law), allowing designated states to experiment with the utilization of federal IV-E foster care funds to improve child welfare services. Most of these projects have been launched with a relatively rigorous research study attached to them. Demonstration

projects have examined subsidized guardianship, flexible funding, services for parents with substance-abuse problems, managed care, postadoption services, and enhanced training for child welfare staff. A handful of studies have examined "intensive services." One such project is currently under way in Arizona, offering intensive services to families who are working to reunify with their children. The project is expected to be completed in 2011. For more information, see: www.acf.hhs.gov/programs/cb/programs_fund/cwwaiver

44. Fein, E., & Staff, I. (1993). Last best chance: Findings from a reunification services program. *Child Welfare, 72*(1), 5–40. Eligibility depended on children being in care fewer than 18 months.

45. Fraser, M. W., Walton, E., Lewis, R. E., Pecora, P. J., & Walton, W. K. (1996). An experiment in family reunification: Correlates of outcomes at one-year follow-up. *Children and Youth Services Review, 18*(4–5), 335–361. A follow-up study was conducted 6 years later, continuing to show generally strong effects: Walton, E., (1998). In home family focused reunification: A six year follow up of a successful experiment. *Social Work Research, 22*(4), 205–214. The sample size for this study was small (n = 57 experimental and n = 53 control), limiting the generalizability of the findings.

46. The proportion of children re-entering care from the experimental group was 27%, while the much lower re-entry rate for children receiving conventional services was 10%.

47. Rzepnicki, T. L., Schuerman, J. R., & Johnson, P. R. (1997). Facing uncertainty: Reuniting high-risk families. In J. D. Berrick, R. Barth, & N. Gilbert (Eds.), *Child Welfare Research Review, Vol. II*. New York: Columbia University Press. Families were eligible for the program if they were relatively new to the child welfare system (i.e., they had no more than three prior substantiated reports of maltreatment), if one child under the age of 13 was involved, and if the child had been in placement for 6 months or less. Researchers examined data for 1,014 families participating in the program. A comparison group was constructed from a computerized database including children with similar personal and case characteristics.

48. The text on p. 241 of Rzepnicki et al.'s article suggests that the difference in reunification rates between the reunification services group and the comparison group was about 20%. The figures, however, show a difference of about 40%. Communication with the lead author indicates that the figure is correct and that the difference between groups was about 40%.

49. Re-entry was calculated only for the program group. The authors estimate that approximately 30% of children in the program group re-entered care within 3 years following reunification.

50. Green, B., Furrer, C., Worcel, S., Burrus, S., & Finigan, M. (2007). How effective are family treatment drug courts? Outcomes from a four-site national study. *Child Maltreatment, 12*(1), 43–59. Importantly, the study did not include random assignment to condition and participants in the family treatment drug courts were voluntary.

51. Given that conventional services are far less expensive than intensive services, the Illinois study does *not* suggest that intensive reunification services be adopted for all children on the caseload.

52. Although the re-entry rate for the treatment group (28%) was similar to the overall re-entry rate we see nationally, their striking reunification rates (almost 100%) result in a net reunification rate (70%) that is very high. Clearly more research is needed into this promising approach. Because the authors found that more functional families were less likely to re-enter care, targeting to these families might reduce the re-entry rate further, or it might suggest a more conservative approach to reunifying families that caseworkers view as particularly risky.

53. Although this study—of the three—was the least methodologically rigorous, the findings are tantalizing and thus call out for more replication.

54. Our efforts to better understand how to deliver effective reunification services also pivot on the experience of African-American children, who are less likely to reunify than Caucasian and Asian-American children, and who are therefore disproportionately represented in the long-term-care caseload. While a significant proportion of this disproportionality can be explained by the greater utilization of kin among African-American families (and the resulting slow reunification rates in kinship care), there persists a gap in reunification rates for African-American compared with Caucasian children placed in non-kin care. In one study, the difference between the proportion of children reunifying from care after 7 years among African American and Caucasian children was 7%. Needell, B. (September 21, 2007). *Child welfare: Ethnic/racial disproportionality and disparity.* Presentation to California Blue Ribbon Commission on Foster Care. San Francisco.

55. Barth, R. P., Wulczyn, F., & Crea, T. (2005). From anticipation to evidence: Research on the Adoption and Safe Families Act. *Virginia Journal of Social Policy and the Law, 12*(3), 371–399.

56. The accumulated research on parent education suggests this is true. Barth, R. P., Landsverk, J., Chamberlain, P., Reid, J., Rolls, J., Hurlburt, M, et al., (2005). Parent training in child welfare services: Planning for a more evidence-based approach to serving biological parents. *Research on Social Work Practice, 15*, 353–371.

57. Visitation is, in fact, a very important component of reunification services and should be conducted thoughtfully in order to enhance parents,' children's, and foster parents' experience. See: Haight, W. L., Black, J. E., Mangelsdorf, S., Giorgio, G., Tata, L., Schoppe, S. J., et al. (2002). Making visits better: The perspectives of parents, foster parents, and child welfare workers. *Child Welfare, 81*(2), 173–202.

58. Whether Tyson's extreme problems were the result of his lengthy and unstable experience in foster care or his lengthy and unstable experience during the first 5 years of life with his mother is unknown. On both counts, the child welfare system did not respond aggressively to meet the needs of this troubled child early on.

59. Barth, R. P. (1997). Effects of age and race on the odds of adoption versus remaining in long-term out-of-home care. *Child Welfare, 76*(2), 285–308; Berrick, J. D., Needell, B., Barth, R. P., & Jonson-Reid, M. (1998). *The tender years: Toward developmentally-sensitive child welfare services for very young children.* New York: Oxford University Press.

60. Gill, M. (1975). The foster care/adoptive family: Adoption for children not legally free. *Child Welfare, 59*(10), 712–720; Gill, M. & Amadio, C.M. (1983). Social work and the law in a foster care/adoption program. *Child Welfare, 62*(5), 455–467; Katz, L. (1990). Effective permanency planning for children in foster care. *Social Work, 35,* 220–226; Katz, L. (1999). Concurrent planning: Benefits and pitfalls. *Child Welfare, 78*(1), 71–87; Lee, R. E., & Hull, R. K. (1983). Legal, casework, and ethical issues in "risk adoption." *Child Welfare, 62*(5), 450–454.

61. Malm, K., Bess, R. Leos-Urbel, J., Geen, R., & Markowitz, T. (2001). *Running to keep in place: The continuing evolution of our nation's child welfare system.* (Occasional Paper Number 54; Assessing the New Federalism). Washington, D.C.: The Urban Institute; Mitchell, L., Barth, R. P., Green, R., Wall, A., Biemer, P., Berrick, J. D., et al. (2005). Child welfare reform in the United States: Findings from the NSCAW Local Agency Survey. *Child Welfare, 84,* 5–14; U.S. Government Accounting Office (May 1997). *Foster Care: State efforts to improve the permanency planning process show some promise.* (GAO/T-HEHS-97-73, May 1997). Washington, D.C.; Westat, Inc. (2001). *Assessing the context of permanency and reunification in the foster care system.* Report for the USDHHS. Retrieved February 26, 2004 from http://aspe.hhs.gov/hsp/fostsercare-reunif01.

62. The term "concurrent doing" comes from Gary Seiser, San Diego County County Counsel. Concurrent planning is not only allowed but required under California law; however, evidence suggests that it is not practiced in most counties. See: D'Andrade, A., Frame, L., & Berrick, J. D. (2006). Concurrent planning in public child welfare agencies: Oxymoron or work in progress? *Children and Youth Services Review, 28*(1), 78–95.

63. Barth, R. P., Courtney, M., Berrick, J. D., & Albert, V. (1994). *From child abuse to permanency planning.* New York: Aldine de Gruyter; Connell, C. M., Katz, K. H., Saunders, L., & Tebes, J. K. (2006). Leaving foster care: The influence of child and case characteristics on foster care exit rates. *Children and Youth Services Review, 28,* 780–798; Goerge, R. M. (1990). The reunification process in substitute care. *Social Service Review, 64*(3), 422–457.

64. Parents ready to reunify in less than 6 months could, of course, do so at any time, as in the current system. The term "eligible" is used to indicate that some parents who have committed egregious harms against their children would be recommended for termination of parental rights (TPR) within 30 days, as current federal law suggests.

65. "Kith care" refers to close friends, godparents, and other individuals close to the family who are perceived *as though* they are family to the child.

66. When Linda Katz developed the concurrent planning model, she introduced a set of characteristics that could be used to assess the likelihood of reunification. These "poor prognosis indicators" were based upon clinical perspectives but not upon research information. More research is needed to better understand the family characteristics and behaviors that put families at risk for losing their children, so that poor prognosis indicators can be used effectively and accurately to target services appropriately.

67. The model is based upon Fein and Staff's research, targeting the candidates least likely to reunify. The approach uses resources liberally,

yet on a narrow target population. See: Fein, E., & Staff, I. (1993). Last best chance: Findings from a reunification services program. *Child Welfare, 72*(1), 5–40.

68. Research to replicate the Utah study would also be important—if targeted families received intensive postreunification services, re-entry rates might decline as well, boosting the net reunification rate.

69. Concentrated Reunification Services (CRS) services should *not* be targeted to all families whose children are in out-of-home care. The evidence suggests that a large proportion of families reunify anyway, with conventional supports that include assistance with transportation, visitation, etc. Given cost-containment concerns, there would be no marginal value to extending CRS services to all families. Although many families identified as *unlikely* to reunify will not benefit from CRS services, some families will (who otherwise would not see their children return home), and others who do not reunify will know that reasonable efforts were indeed extended to them prior to the termination of their parental rights.

70. See: Kim, C. H. (1999). Putting reason back into the reasonable efforts requirements in child abuse and neglect cases. *University of Illinois Law Review,*1999(1), 287–326.

71. The model presumes that the principles of concurrent planning apply to kin-and-kith care as well. That is, frank discussions with birth parents, kin, and kith caregivers at entry to care about the possibility of a permanent placement—including adoption or legal guardianship as a likely outcome— would occur.

72. D'Andrade, A., Frame, L., & Berrick, J. D. (2006). Concurrent planning in public child welfare agencies: Oxymoron or work in progress? *Children and Youth Services Review, 28*(1), 78–95; Frame, L., Berrick, J. D., & Coakley, J. F. (2006). Essential elements of implementing a system of concurrent planning. *Journal of Child and Family Social Work, 11*(4), 357–367. The authors outline seven essential elements, including (1) a pro–concurrent planning philosophy that permeates the child welfare agency; (2) the presence of systems or mechanisms that actively encourage concurrent planning, ensure that it occurs in a timely fashion, and distribute workload; (3) the ability of child welfare workers and supervisors to actively embrace and apply concurrent planning principles in their work; (4) greater integration of child welfare and adoption units and agencies; (5) the availability of an adequate number of concurrent planning families (non-kin and kin), to provide concurrent placements for children; (6) the availability of necessary services to birth parents in a timely fashion; and (7) the active promotion of concurrent planning in the juvenile court. (Courts must also have well-functioning data systems that will allow judges to track children's length of stay in care and keep to the time lines defined by ASFA.)

73. My views on concurrent planning are shaped powerfully by research I conducted with my colleagues at U.C. Berkeley examining six California public child welfare agencies' implementation of concurrent planning. We saw very little evidence of concurrent planning in any of the counties but heard a great deal of lip service to the philosophy undergirding the approach. Other articles outline the pitfalls of the current underresourced approach. They are: D'Andrade, A., & Berrick, J. D. (2006). When policy meets practice: The

untested effects of permanency reforms in child welfare. *Journal of Sociology and Social Welfare. 33*(1), 31–52; D'Andrade, A., Frame, L., & Berrick, J. D. (2006). Concurrent planning in public child welfare agencies: Oxymoron or work in progress? *Children and Youth Services Review, 28*(1), 78–95; Frame, L., Berrick, J. D., & Coakley, J. F. (2006). Essential elements of implementing a system of concurrent planning. *Journal of Child and Family Social Work, 11*(4), 357–367.

74. The term "legal risk" was used by child welfare workers in at least one California county during a study my colleagues and I conducted on concurrent planning. For more information, see: Frame, L., Berrick, J. D., & Coakley, J. F. (2006). Essential elements of implementing a system of concurrent planning. *Journal of Child and Family Social Work, 11*(4), 357–367.

CHAPTER 4

1. Wetzstein, C. (September 10, 2006). 21 states; adoption efforts rewarded. *The Washington Times.*

2. Macomber, J., Zielewski, E. H., Chambers, K., & Geen, R. (2005). *Foster care adoption in the United States: An analysis of interest in adoption and a review of state recruitment strategies.* Washington, D.C.: National Adoption Day Coalition. Other estimates put the number of children waiting for adoption at about 185,000. Testa, M., Salyers, N. S., Shaver, M., & Miller, J. (2004). *Family ties: Supporting permanence for children in safe and stable foster care with relatives and other caregivers.* Urbana, IL: University of Illinois at Urbana-Champagne, School of Social Work.

3. Moses, for example, was an adopted child. See: Kaplan, B. L., & Seitz, M. (1980). *The practical guide to foster family care.* Springfield, IL: Thomas Books.

4. Leavy, M. L. (1954). *The law of adoption.* (2nd ed.). New York, NY: Oceana Publications; Lockridge, R. (1947). *Adopting a child.* New York, NY: Greenberg.

5. Well into the twentieth century, most adoptions were of older children. (Infant mortality rates at the time were exceedingly high, and breast milk was required for an infant's survival; both issues made infant adoptions risky endeavors. Infant formula was not developed until the 1890s.) See: Freundlich, M. (2001). *Adoption and ethics: The impact of adoption on members of the triad.* Washington, D.C.: Child Welfare League of America.

6. Because of exceedingly high infant mortality rates across the world until very recently, less emphasis was placed on infant adoption, since it was unclear which infants would survive even into childhood. According to Mintz, in the mid-1800s "as many as 150 infants' bodies were found in New York City each month." Mintz, S. (2004). *Huck's raft: A history of American childhood.* Cambridge, MA: Harvard University press, pp. 155. For more information on historical adoption practices in the U.S. see: Carp, W. (Ed.) (2005). *Adoption in America.* Ann Arbor, MI: University of Michigan Press.

7. Mintz, S. (2004). *Huck's raft: A history of American childhood.* Boston, MA: Harvard University Press.

8. Lakin, D. S., & Whitfield, L. (1997). Adoption recruitment: Meeting the needs of waiting children. In R. J. Avery (Ed.), *Adoption policy and special needs children*. Westport, CT: Auburn House.

9. Adoption is commonly categorized as *private, public, or international*. "Public adoption" refers to adoption from the foster care system. Independent, or private, adoption usually involves the voluntary placement of an infant or child for adoption from a birth parent.

10. Carp, E. W., & Leon-Guerero, A. (2005). When in doubt, count: World War II as a watershed in the history of adoption. In W. Carp (Ed.), *Adoption in America*. Ann Arbor, MI: University of Michigan Press.

11. Gill, B. (2002). Adoption agencies and the search for the ideal family, 1918–1965. In E. W. Carp, (Ed.), *Adoption in history: New interpretive essays*. Lansing, MI: University of Michigan Press, p. 9.

12. Maas, H. S. (1969). Children in long-term foster care. Child Welfare, 48, 321–333.

13. For a brief history of public adoption see: Lakin, D. S., & Whitfield, L. (1997). Adoption recruitment: Meeting the needs of waiting children. In R. Avery (Ed.), *Adoption policy and special needs children*. Westport, CT: Auburn House.

14. Maza, P. (1984). Adoption tends: 1944–1975. Child welfare research notes #9. U.S. Children's Bureau. Retrieved July 11, 2007: hppt://darkwing.uoregon.edu/~adoption/archive/mazaAT.htm.

15. Flango, V., & Flango, C. (1994). *The flow of adoption information from the states*. Williamsburg, VA: National Center for State Courts.

16. Testa, M. (2004). When children cannot return home: Adoption and guardianship. *The Future of Children 14*(1), 115–129.

17. This statement is true overall, although adoption rates for infants (particularly infants placed in the first month of life) are considerably higher.

18. These figures reflect children entering out-of-home care in California in 2000–2001, placed in non-kin care, and followed over 4 years in California's administrative database, CWS/CMS. Information on gender, ethnicity, and age can be obtained at: http://cssr.berkeley.edu/CWSCMSreports/Cohorts/exits/. The California rates mirror national rates. Adoption has been increasing steadily since ASFA, rising from 16% of all exits in 1999 to 18% of exits in 2001. See: Barth, R. P., Wulczyn, F., & Crea, T. (2005). From anticipation to evidence: Research on the Adoption and Safe Families Act. *Virginia Journal of Law and Social Policy, 12*(3), 371–399. Racial and ethnic differences in adoption rates are substantial. See: Barth, R. P. (1997). Effects of age and race on the odds of adoption versus remaining in long-term out-of-home care. *Child Welfare, 76*(2), 285–308. Odds of adoption for African-American children, in general, are lower in part because of the greater likelihood that they will be placed in kinship foster care, where relatives are less likely to elect adoption as a permanency outcome. Trends may be changing, however. African-American children living in kinship homes in urban areas now represent the fastest-growing group of children to be adopted. See: Wulczyn, F., & Hislop, K. (2003). *Adoption dynamics: Comparative results for sub-populations*. Chicago: Chapin Hall Center for Children.

19. Stein, T. J. (1998). *Child welfare and the law*. Washington, D.C.: Child Welfare League of America. p. 154.

20. Berrick, J. D., Needell, B., Barth, R. P., & Jonson-Reid, M. (1998). *The tender years: Toward developmentally sensitive child welfare services for very young children*. New York: Oxford University Press.

21. See: Barth, R. P. (1997). The costs and benefits of adoption. In R. Avery & D. Mont (Eds.), *Public adoption policy*. New York: Auburn House.

22. Berry, M., Barth, R. P., & Needell, B. (1996). Preparation, support, and satisfaction of adoptive families in agency and independent adoptions. *Child and Adolescent Social Work Journal, 13,* 157–183.; Brooks, D., & Barth, R. P. (1999). Adult transracial and inracial adoptees: Effects of race, gender, adoptive family structure, and placement history on adjustment outcomes. *American Journal of Orthopsychiatry, 69,* 87–99; Smith-McKeever, C. (2006). Adoption satisfaction among African-American families adopting African-American children. *Children and Youth Services Review, 28,* 825–840.

23. Berrick, J. D., Needell, B., Barth, R. P., & Jonson-Reid, M. (1998). *The tender years: Toward developmentally sensitive child welfare services for very young children*. New York: Oxford University Press.

24. For a review, see: Triseliotis, J. (2002). Long-term foster care or adoption? The evidence examined. *Child and Family Social Work, 7,* 23–33.

25. see: Triseliotis, J. (2002). Long-term foster care or adoption? The evidence examined. *Child and Family Social Work, 7,* 23–33.

26. Bohman, M., & Sigvardson, S. (1990). Outcomes in adoption: Lessons from longitudinal studies. In D. M. Brodzinsky & M. D. Schechter (Eds.) *The psychology of adoption*. New York: Oxford University Press.

27. Wulczyn, F., & Hislop, K. B. (2003). Growth in the adoption population. Issue paper on Foster Care and Adoption. Chicago: Chapin Hall Center for Children at the University of Chicago.

28. Barth, R. P., Lee, C. K., Wildfire, J., & Guo, S. (2006). A comparison of the governmental costs of long-term foster care and adoption. *Social Service Review,* 127–158.

29. Spark, K. (1997). Adoption promotion legislation in the 105th Congress. *Congressional Reporting Service Report for Congress, Report 97–491 EPW*. Retrieved July 12, 2007 at: http://digital.library.unt.edu/govdocs/crs/

30. Other initiatives developed since that time, also to encourage greater numbers of adoption, include the 2001 Tax Relief Act (P.L. 107–16), which offers a $10,000 tax credit to families who adopt a special needs child, and President Bush's initiative to feature adoption through a federal website: www.AdoptUSKids.org. Analyses of six states' child welfare data suggest that the number of adoptions have increased since passage of ASFA, but that the time to adopt has not markedly changed. The ASFA legislation was inspired in part by a belief that the length of time from placement to adoption had increased over time; with new adoption incentives, federal policymakers hoped that the time to adoption would decline considerably. To date, this policy goal has not been achieved. See: Wulczyn, F., Chen, L., & Hislop, K. B. (2006). Adoption dynamics and the Adoption and Safe Families Act. *Social Service Review, 80,* 584–608.

31. These incentive payments are given if a state completes more total adoptions in a federal fiscal year than were completed in a specified baseline year, or the year with the highest number of adoptions between federal fiscal year 2002 and 2004.

32. For more information on the reunification exception provision of ASFA see: D'Andrade, A., & Berrick, J. D. (2006). When policy meets practice: The untested effects of permanency reforms in child welfare. *Journal of Sociology and Social Welfare, 33*(1), 31–52.

33. The majority of these conditions were established prior to ASFA. For more information see: Berrick, J. D., Choi, Y., D'Andrade, A., & Frame, L. (in press). Reasonable efforts? Implementation of the reunification exception provisions of ASFA. *Child Welfare.*

34. Reunification exception #13 in California states: Extensive, abusive, chronic history of substance use, and (parent) has resisted court-ordered treatment within last 3 years, or failed case plan compliance for substance abuse treatment twice.

35. Janelle's comments speak to some birth parents' experience of a significant power differential between themselves and officials of the state. This issue is explored in more depth by Jennifer Reich: Reich, J. A. (2005). *Fixing families: Parents, power, and the child welfare system.* New York: Routledge.

36. Mandel, age 5 at the time of the permanency planning hearing, was separated from his younger siblings and placed in his third and final foster home. Because of his age and behavior problems, Mandel was considered "unadoptable" at that time.

37. According to Janelle, another sister was willing to take the children, but the child welfare worker surprised Janelle during the permanency planning hearing, indicating that her sister did not want to care for the children. The truth of the day will never be known. Did the social worker misrepresent the sister's views? Or was the sister unwilling to care for Janelle's children but uncomfortable about telling her? Janelle's sense of loyalty to family tells her that her sister was willing and able and that CPS must have corrupted the truth. She carries with her a palpable sense of betrayal, believing that her children would be home today if the worker had not "lied."

38. Janelle essentially ran away after her permanency planning hearing—from her son and from herself. Years later she had a sort of awakening and simply decided to change. She checked into a residential treatment center and dedicated herself to recovery. Months later, she called her worker and asked what she needed to do to reunify with her son. Within a year, Mandel was home.

39. Janelle submitted the letter to the "postadoption" unit in the child welfare agency, and someone in that unit forwarded the letter to the adoptive parents.

40. The adoptive parents also used the postadoption unit in the child welfare agency as their pass-through for the letter.

41. Had the agency used a concurrent planning approach, the children would have experienced at least one less placement while in care. As it was, all three children were first placed together in a foster home where the two younger children were maltreated. They were moved together to a second foster home,

and Mandel was then moved to his third and final foster home and Richard and Shane were moved to their adoptive placement.

42. In a better-functioning system, substantial efforts would be made to secure a permanent home for 5-year-olds like Mandel.

43. Although the sibling bonds between these children were likely significant, Shane, Richard, and Mandel were unlikely to remain together for their entire childhood in foster care. Placement instability is a common occurrence for many children in foster care. Research on placement moves for children in foster care points to a high degree of mobility over time—and the longer children remain in care and the older they are, the more likely placement changes will occur. Some of the more important papers examining this issue include: Herrenkohl, E. C., Herrenkohl, R. C., & Egolf, B. (2003). The psychosocial consequences of living environment instability on maltreated children. *American Journal of Orthopsychiatry*, 73(4), 367–380; James, S. (2004). Why do foster care placements disrupt? An investigation of reasons for placement change in foster care. *Social Service Review*, 78(4), 601–627; Newton, R. R., Litrownik, A. J., Landsverk, J. A. (2000). Children and youth in foster care: Disentangling the relationship between problem behaviors and number of placements. *Child Abuse and Neglect*, 24(10), 1363–1374; Rubin, D. M., O'Reilly, A. L. R., Luan, X., & Localio, A. R. (2007). The impact of placement stability on behavioral well-being for children in foster care. *Pediatrics, 199*, 336–344. In recent years, much more attention has been paid to the importance of the sibling bond in determining foster care placements (Shlonsky, A., Bellamy, J., Elkins, J., & Ashare, C. J. (2005). The other kin: Setting the course for research, policy, and practice with siblings in foster care. *Children and Youth Services Review, 27*(7), 697–716). Making siblings placements based upon values of "equity" more than on "pragmatism," it is argued, can help workers guide decision making in this area. See: Hollows, A., & Nelson, P. (2006). Equity and pragmatism in judgement-making about the placement of sibling groups. *Child and Family Social Work, 11*, 307–315.

Finally, greater efforts to locate an adoptive home for Mandel could have been made, but social workers do not typically attempt adoption for these older children.

44. For more information, see: Carp, E. W. (2004). *Adoption politics: Bastard nation and ballot initiative 58*. Lawrence, KS: University Press of Kansas.

45. Carp, E. W. (2004). *Adoption politics: Bastard nation and ballot initiative 58*. Lawrence, KS: University Press of Kansas.

46. Carp, E. W. (2004). *Adoption politics: Bastard nation and ballot initiative 58*. Lawrence, KS: University Press of Kansas.

47. Recent estimates suggest that upward of one-third of U.S. adults have considered adopting a child, and over 1 million women have taken steps to initiate the process. See: Geen, R., Malm, K., & Katz, J. (2004). A study to inform the recruitment and retention of general applicant adoptive parents. *Adoption Quarterly, 7*(4), 1–28.

48. As public stigma concerning out-of-wedlock births declined, fewer women placed their children for private adoption.

49. Baran, A., Pannor, R., & Sorosky, A. (1976). Open adoption. *Social Work, 21*(2), 97–100; Baran, A., & Pannor, R. (1993). Perspectives on open adoption.

The Future of Children, 3, 119–124; Pannor, R., & Baran, A. (1984). Open adoption as standard practice. *Child Welfare, 63,* 245–250. Baran and Pannor did not conduct studies to determine the potential impacts of adoption on children and youth but instead theorized based upon their therapeutic work that closed adoptions were harmful to children's identity development.

50. Henney, S. M., McRoy, R. G., Ayers-Lopez, S., & Grotevant, H. D. (2003). The impact of openness on adoption agency practices: A longitudinal perspective. *Adoption Quarterly, 6*(3), 31–51.

51. Grotevant, H. D., & McRoy, R. G. (1998). *Openness in adoption: Exploring family connections.* Thousand Oaks, CA: Sage publications, p. 2.

52. Appell, A. R. (1998). Increasing options to improve permanency: Considerations in drafting an adoption with contact statute. *Children's Legal Rights Journal, 18* (4), 24–51. Concerns about these statutes are raised by Hollinger. See: Hollinger, J. H. (1993). Adoption law. *The Future of Children, 3*(1), 43–61.

53. Bartholet, E. (1999). Family bonds. Adoption, infertility, and the new world of child production. New York: Beacon Press.

54. Wrobel, G. M., Ayers-Lopez, S., Grotevant, H. D., McRoy, R. G., & Friedrick, M. (1996). Openness in adoption and the level of child participation. *Child Development, 67*(5), 2358–2374.

55. For a review, see: Frasch, K. M., Brooks, D., & Barth, R. P. (2000). Openness and contact in foster care adoptions: An eight-year follow-up. *Family relations, 49,* 435–446; Grotevant, H. D., & McRoy, R. G. (1998). *Openness in adoption: Exploring family connections.* Thousand Oaks, CA: Sage. None of the studies have comparison groups, so it is not clear whether the protracted grief that birth parents feel, for example, is any greater in open versus closed adoption.

56. Berry, M., Dylla, D. J., Barth, R. P., & Needell, B. (1998). The role of open adoption in the adjustment of adopted children and their families. *Children and Youth Services Review, 20*(1–2), 151–171.

57. Hughes, B. (1995). Openness and contact in adoption: A child-centered perspective. *British Journal of Social Work, 25*(6), 729–747.

58. Child Welfare League of America. (2000). *Standards of excellence: CWLA Standards of excellence for adoption services.* Washington, D.C.: CWLA. A recent small-scale study also indicated that birth parents can be involved in children's lives many years following placement into foster care and termination of regular contact. New relationships can develop using letters, phone calls, and—in some instances—visits. See: Mapp, S. C., & Steinberg, C. (2007). Birthfamilies as permanency resources for children in long-term foster care. *Child Welfare, 86*(1), 29–51.

59. Frasch, K. M., Brooks, D., & Barth, R. P. (2000). Openness and contact in adoptions by foster families: An eight-year follow up. *Family Relations, 49,* 435–446.

60. Charlton, L., Crank, M., Kansara, K., & Oliver, C. (1998). *Still screaming: Birth parents compulsorily separated from their children.* Manchester, UK.

61. Hughes, B., & Logan, J. (n.d.) *Birth parents: The hidden dimension.* Manchester, UK: Department of Social Policy and Social Work, University of Manchester.

62. Hoffman, D. & Rosenheck, R. (2001). Homeless mothers with severe mental illnesses and their children: Predictors of family reunification. *Psychiatric Rehabilitation Journal, 25*(2), 163–169.

63. Manji, S., Maiter, S., & Palmer, S. (2005). Community and informal social supports for recipients of child protective services. *Children and Youth Services Review, 27*, 291–308; Marcenko, M., & Striepe, M. (1997). A look at family reunification through the eyes of mothers. *Community Alternatives: International Journal of Family Care, 9*(1), 33–48; Smith, N. (2002). Reunifying families affected by maternal substance abuse: Consumer and service provider perspectives on the obstacles and the need for change. *Journal of Social Work Practice in the Addictions, 2*(1), 33–53.

64. Budde, S., & Schene, P. (2004). Informal social support interventions and their role in violence prevention: An agenda for future evaluation. *Journal of Interpersonal Violence, 19*(3), 341–355; Cohen, E., & Canan, L. (2006). Closer to home: Parent mentors in child welfare. *Child Welfare, 85*(5), 867–885; Corcoran, J. (2000). Family interventions with child physical abuse and neglect: A critical review. *Children and Youth Services Review, 22*(7), 563–591; Frame, L. C., Conley, A., & Berrick, J. D. (2006). "The real work is what they do together:" Peer support and child welfare services. *Families in Society, 87*(4), 509–520.

65. Berrick, J. D., Needell, B., Shlonsky, A., Simmel, C., & Pedrucci, C. (1999). *Assessment, support, and training for kinship care and foster care: An empirically based curriculum*. Berkeley, CA: University of California, Berkeley, Center for Social Services Research.

66. Lieber, L. L. & Baker, J. M. (1977). Parents Anonymous—Self-help treatment for child abusing parents: A review and evaluation. *Child Abuse & Neglect, 1*, 133–148.

67. Davidson, L., Chinman, M., Kloos, B., Weingarten, R., Stayner, D. & Tebes, J. K. (1999). Peer support among individuals with severe mental illness: A review of the evidence. *Clinical Psychology: Science and Practice, 6*(2), 165–187.

68. Moos, R., & Moos, B. (2004). Long-term influence of duration and frequency of participation in Alcoholics Anonymous on individuals with alcohol use disorders. *Journal of Consulting and Clinical Psychology, 72*(1), 81–90.

69. Some of the theoretical links between peer support and expected positive outcomes have been summarized by Davidson et al., and by Thoits. See: Davidson, L., Chinman, M., Kloos, B., Weingarten, R., Stayner, D. & Tebes, J. K. (1999). Peer support among individuals with severe mental illness: A review of the evidence. *Clinical Psychology: Science and Practice, 6*(2), 165–187; Thoits, P. A. (1986). Social support as coping assistance. *Journal of Consulting and Clinical Psychology, 54*(4), 416–423.

70. Kennedy-Moore, E., & Watson, J. C. (2001). How and when does emotional expression help? *Review of General Psychology, 5*(3), 187–212.

71. Barth, R. P., & Miller, J. (2000). Building effective post-adoption services: What is the empirical foundation? *Family Relations, 49*(4), 447–455.

72. Birth fathers may also be involved in the lives of their children and have close emotional attachments. For simplicity, and because the child welfare system is dominated by mothers, I refer only to mothers here, but my perspective toward involved fathers would be the same. Although there are books on the individual experiences of birth mothers involved in voluntary adoption, studies on involuntary adoption are few. In one study examining voluntary adoption, the authors suggest that the adopted child remains "psychologically present" to the parent well after the adoption has taken place. See: Fravel, D. L., McRoy, R. G., & Grotevant, H. D. (2000). Birthmother perceptions of the psychologically present adopted child: Adoption openness and boundary ambiguity. *Family Relations, 49*(4), 425–433.

73. Charlton, L., Crank, M., Kansara, K., & Oliver, C. (1998). *Still screaming: Birthparents compulsorily separated from their children*. Manchester, UK: After Adoption; Hughes, B, & Logan, J. (1993). *Birth parents: The hidden dimension*. Manchester, UK: University of Manchester, Department of Social Policy and Social Work; Mason, K., & Selman, P. (1997). Birth parents' experiences of contested adoption. *Adoption and Fostering, 21*(1), 21–28; Ryburn, M. (1992). Contested adoption proceedings. *Adoption and Fostering, 16*(4), 29–38.

74. Mason, K., & Selman, P. (1997). Birth parents' experiences of contested adoption. *Adoption and Fostering. 21*(1), 21–28.

75. Mason, K., & Selman, P. (1997). Birth parents' experiences of contested adoption. *Adoption and Fostering. 21*(1), 21–28.

76. See, for example: Marsh, J. C., Ryan, J. P., Choi, S., & Testa, M. F. (2006). Integrated services for families with multiple problems: Obstacles to family reunification. *Children and Youth Services Review, 28*, 1074–1087.

77. Reich, J. A. (2005). *Fixing families: Parents, power, and the child welfare system*. New York: Routledge.

78. Some women recover from their addiction and change long-standing behaviors many years later. Children can not wait for their parents to change when a recovery is years away, but neither should they lose all contact for a lifetime if parents can effectively engage with their children some years later. The argument in favor of semiopen adoption recognizes the change process that can occur for many parents several years after permanency decisions have been made.

79. Charlton, L., Crank, M., Kansara, K., & Oliver, C. (1998). *Still screaming: Birth parents compulsorily separated from their children*. Manchester, UK.

80. Janelle was under the mistaken impression that if she could explain her circumstances to an individual of authority, the adoption could be reversed and she could regain custody of her children.

81. Although Janelle perceived their responses as helpful, in most cases they certainly were not and they reflect the ignorance of the staff employed in each political sector. While Janelle's circumstances were not within the jurisdiction of the president, for example, neither were they in the jurisdiction of the U.S. Department of Health and Human Services. Only the state legislator who recommended that she contact a member of her county board of supervisors understood the operation of child welfare services.

CHAPTER 5

1. National Commission on Foster Family Care. (1991). *A blueprint for fostering infants, children, and youths in the 1990s.* Washington, D.C.: Child Welfare League of America. In that same decade, the national foster care caseload grew by well over 70%. See: Petit, M. R., & Curtis, P. A. (1997). Child abuse and neglect: A look at the states—The 1997 CWLA stat book. Washington, D.C.: Child Welfare League of America.

2. Burton, L.M., & Dilworth-Anderson, P. (1991). The intergenerational roles of aged black Americans. *Marriage and Family Review, 16*(3–4), 311–330.

3. Gleeson, J., & Craig, L. (1994). Kinship care in child welfare: An analysis of states' policies. *Children and Youth Services Review, 16*(1–2), 7–31.

4. Needell, B., Webster, D., Cuccaro-Alamin, S., Armijo, M., Lee, S., Lery, B., et al. (2005). *Child Welfare Services Reports for California.* Retrieved August 4, 2007, from University of California at Berkeley Center for Social Services Research Web site: http://cssr.berkeley.edu/CWSCMSreports/

5. Wulczyn, F., & Hislop, K. B. (2001) *Multi-state foster care data archive.* Unpublished report. Chicago, IL: Chapin Hall Center for Children.

6. U.S. Department of Health and Human Services, Administration for Children and Families, Administration of Children, Youth and Families, Children's Services Bureau (2006). AFCARS Report #13. Retrieved August 4, 2007, from http://www.acf.dhhs.gov/programs/cb/stats_research/afcars/tar/report13.htm.

7. Child Welfare League of America. (1994). *Kinship care: A natural bridge.* Washington, D.C.: CWLA.

8. Brooks, D., & Barth, R. (1998). Characteristics and outcomes of drug-exposed and non-drug-exposed children in kinship and non-relative foster care. *Children and Youth Services Review, 20*(6), 475–501; Ehrle, J., & Geen, R. (2002). Kin and non-kin foster care: Findings from a National Survey. *Children and Youth Services Review, 24,* 55–78.

9. For a review, see: Geen, R. (Ed.) (2003). *Kinship care: Making the most of a valuable resource.* Washington, D.C.: The Urban Institute.

10. Ehrle, J., & Geen, R. (2002). Kin and non-kin foster care: Findings from a National Survey. *Children and Youth Services Review, 24,* 55–78. Some evidence also suggests that kinship caregivers have fewer economic and social resources, compared to non-kin caregivers. See: Harden, B. J., Clyman, R. B., Kriebel, D. K., & Lyons, M. E. (2004). Kith and kin care: Parental attitudes and resources of foster and relative caregivers. *Children and Youth Services Review, 26,* 657–671.

11. LeProhn, N. (1994). The role of the kinship foster parent: A comparison of the role conceptions of relative and non-relative foster parents. *Children and Youth Services Review, 16*(1–2), 65–81.

12. Berrick, J. D., Barth, R. P., & Needell, B. (1994). A comparison of kinship foster homes and foster family homes: Implications for kinship foster care as family preservation. *Children and Youth Services Review, 16*(1–2), 33–63; Chipungu, S., & Everett, J. (1994). The power of information: Exchange patterns between African-American foster parents and child welfare workers. *Journal of*

Multicultural Social Work, 3(3), 17–33; Gebel, T. (1996). Kinship care and non-relative foster care: A comparison of caregiver attributes and attitudes. *Child Welfare, 75*(1), 5–18. Evidence from one study indicates that child welfare workers provide fewer resources and have less contact with kin out of deference for kinship caregivers' wishes for privacy; other child welfare workers indicate that in a child welfare practice setting that is reactive rather than proactive, kin are less likely to contact child welfare workers and ask for services and support, thus explaining the lower likelihood that contact would occur. See: Berrick, J. D., Needell, B., & Barth, R. P. (1998). Kin as a family and child welfare resource: The child welfare worker's perspective. In R. L. Hegar & M. Scannapieco (Eds.), *Kinship foster care: Policy, practice, and research.* New York: Oxford University Press.

13. For evidence on the intergenerational transmission of maltreatment see: Haapasalo, J., & Aaltonen, T. (1999). Child abuse potential: How persistent? *Journal of Interpersonal Violence, 14*(6), 571–585; Kim, J. (n.d.). Comparative study on intergenerational transmission of child neglect and physical maltreatment. University of South Carolina, College of Social Work; Pears, K. C., & Capaldi, D. M. (2001). Intergenerational transmission of abuse: A two-generational prospective study of an at-risk sample. *Child Abuse and Neglect, 25,* 1439–1461.

14. Dubowitz, H., Feigelman, S., & Zuravin, S. (1993). A profile of kinship care. *Child Welfare, 72*(2), 153–169.

15. Zuravin, S., Benedict, M., & Somerfield, M. (1993). Child maltreatment in family foster care. *American Journal of Orthopsychiatry, 63*(4), 589–596.

16. Berrick's studies found that quality of care was roughly similar in both kin and non-kin settings; however, serious concerns about selection bias in both studies may have biased both kin and non-kin samples to include caregivers generally providing higher quality care. See: Berrick, J. D. (1997). Assessing quality of care in kinship and foster family care. *Family Relations 46*(3), 273–280; Berrick, J. D., Needell, B., Shlonsky, A., Simmel, C., & Pedrucci, C. (1999). *Assessment, support, and training for kinship care and foster care: An empirically based curriculum.* Berkeley, CA: University of California, Berkeley, Center for Social Services Research. Harden et al. also examined a small sample of "traditional" and kinship foster parents. Although kinship foster parents were initially found to have more problematic parenting attitudes – including greater caregiver–child conflict and anger, greater strictness, and less warmth – these findings disappeared when the authors controlled for caregiver age. See: Harden, B. J., Clyman, R. B., Kriebel, D. K., & Lyons, M. E. (2004). Kith and kin care: Parental attitudes and resources of foster and relative caregivers. *Children and Youth Services Review, 26,*657–671.

17. Harden, B. J., Clyman, R. B., Kriebel, D. K., & Lyons, M. E. (2004). Kith and kin care: Parental attitudes and resources of foster and relative caregivers. *Children and Youth Services Review, 26*(7), 657–671.

18. Berrick, J. D., Barth, R. P., & Needell, B. (1994). A comparison of kinship foster homes and foster family homes: Implications for kinship foster care as family preservation. *Children and Youth Services Review, 16*(1–2), 33–64; Tripp de Robertis, M., Litrownik, A. J. (2004). The experience of foster care: Relationships

between foster parent disciplinary approaches and aggression in a sample of young foster children. *Child Maltreatment, 9*(1), 92–102.

19. Keller, T. E., Wetherbee, K., LeProhn, N. S., Payne, V., Sim K., Lamont, E. R. (2001). Competences and problem behaviors of children in family foster care: Variations by kinship placement status and race. *Children and Youth Services Review, 23*(12), 915–940; Iglehart, A. P. (1994). Kinship foster care: Placement, service, and outcome issues. *Children and Youth Services Review, 16*(1–2), 107–122; Timmer, S. G., Sedlar, G., & Urquiza, A. J. (2004). Challenging children in kin versus nonkin foster care: Perceived costs and benefits to caregivers. *Child Maltreatment, 9*(3), 251–262.

20. Shore, N., Sim, K. E., LeProhn, N. S., & Keller, T. E. (2002). Foster parent and teacher assessments of youth in kinship and non-kinship foster care placements: Are behaviors perceived differently across settings? *Children and Youth Services Review, 24*(1–2), 109–134.

21. Singer, L. T., Mimes S., Short, E., Arendt, R., Farkas, K., Lewis, B., et al., (2004). Cognitive outcomes of preschool children with prenatal cocaine exposure. *Journal of the American Medical Association, 291*(20), 2448–2456.

22. Taussig, H. N., & Clyman, R. B. (in press). Impact of kinship care on adolescent well-being. *Pediatrics.* This study did not compare long-term outcomes for children placed with kin versus non-kin. Instead, this study examined only children in kin care, showing the effects of duration on children's outcomes.

23. Benedict, M. I., Zuravin, S., & Stallings, R. Y. (1996). Adult functioning of children who lived in kin versus nonrelative family foster homes. *Child Welfare, 75*(5), 529–549; Carpenter, S. C., & Clyman, R. B. (2004). The long-term emotional and physical well-being of women who have lived in kinship care. *Children and Youth Services Review, 26,* 673–686; Carpenter, S., Clyman, R., Davidson, A., & Steiner, J. (2001). The association of foster care or kinship care with adolescent sexual behavior and first pregnancy. *Pediatrics, 108*(3), 1–6.

24. The first researchers to examine state differences in kinship care policies were Gleeson and Craig [see: Gleeson, J., & Craig, L. (1994). Kinship care in child welfare: An analysis of states' policies. *Children and Youth Services Review, 16*(1–2), 7–31]. Since that time, the Urban Institute has conducted three waves of a study examining state policies toward kin. See: Janz, A., Geen, R., Bess, R., Andrews, C., & Russell, V. (2002). *The continuing evolution of state kinship care policies.* Washington, D.C.: The Urban Institute.

25. The generic word, "welfare," is used here. Previous to the Personal Responsibility and Work Opportunity Reconciliation Act (PRWORA – or welfare reform) law, this cash assistance program was called AFDC—Aid to Families with Dependent Children. After 1996, the program was renamed TANF—Temporary Assistance for Needy Families.

26. Although the bill passed in 1997, the U.S. Department of Health and Human Services did not release the Adoption and Safe Families Act (ASFA) "final rules" until January 2000. These rules indicated how the department would implement the provisions of ASFA. Their ruling relating to kin was much anticipated and changed state kinship policy considerably in many jurisdictions.

27. Importantly, licensing standards are set at the state level and vary considerably. Licensing standards have been constructed in most states to reflect basic child safety measures. Caregivers must pass criminal background and child abuse registry checks. Other standards are less relevant to child safety. These include minimum square footage in the household, number of bedrooms, age requirements for caregivers, income requirements, and training requirements. In some states, additional standards apply, such as adequate transportation, a high school (or GED equivalent) education, and length of marriage for couples. In less than half of the states, standards for kin and non-kin are identical. In the other states, certain licensing standards are waived for kin on a case-by-case basis, depending on individual circumstances. For a review, see: Geen, R. (Ed.) (2003) *Kinship care: Making the most of a valuable resource*. Washington, D.C. Urban Institute Press. The effect of licensing standards on kinship foster care was rather dramatic in some states. California saw a significant decline in its use of kinship care as many caregivers—who in previous years would have qualified as kinship foster parents—were not made eligible for foster care payments. The proportion of all out-of-home care dedicated to kin declined, but the quality of care likely improved overall.

28. Brown, S., Cohon, D., & Wheeler, R. (2004). Kinship care: How relevant is the foster care model for kinship care? *Children and Youth Services Review*, 24(1–2), 53–77.

29. Berrick, J. D., Barth, R. P., & Needell, B. (1994). A comparison of kinship foster homes and foster family homes: Implications for kinship foster care as family preservation. *Children and Youth Services Review, 16*(1–2), 33–64.

30. Barth, R., Courtney, M., Berrick, J. D., & Albert, V. (1994). *From child abuse to permanency planning*. New York: Aldine de Gruyter; Chipungu, S., Everett, J., Verduik, M., & Jones, J. (1998). *Children placed in foster care with relatives: A multi-state study*. Washington, D.C.: U.S. Department of Health and Human Services.

31. Berrick, J. D., Barth, R. P., & Needell, B. (1994). A comparison of kinship foster homes and foster family homes: Implications for kinship foster care as family preservation. *Children and Youth Services Review, 16*(1–2), 33–63; Shlonsky, A., Webster, D., & Needell, B. (2003). The ties that bind: A cross-sectional analysis of siblings in foster care. *Journal of Social Science Research, 29*(3), 27–52.

32. Berrick, J. D. (1998). When children cannot remain at home: Foster family care and kinship care. *The Future of Children, 8*(1), 72–87; Courtney, M., & Needell, B. (1997). Outcomes of kinship foster care: Lessons from California. In J. D. Berrick, R. P. Barth, & N. Gilbert (Eds.), *Child Welfare Research Review* (Vol. II). New York: Columbia University Press.

33. Berrick, J. D., & Needell, B. (1999). Recent trends in kinship care: Public policy, payments, and outcomes for children. In P. A. Curtis & G. Dale (Eds.), *The foster care crisis: Translating research into practice and policy*. Lincoln, NB: University of Nebraska Press.

34. Berrick, J. D. (Spring, 1998). When children cannot remain home: Temporary foster care and kinship care. *Future of Children, 8*(1), 72–87.

35. One study in Texas found a placement disruption rate of about 50%. The principal reason for disruption was the kinship caregivers' inability to set appropriate boundaries between children and their birth parents.

Terling-Watt, T. (2001). Permanency in kinship care: An exploration of disruption rates and factors associated with placement disruption. *Children and Youth Services Review, 23*(2), 111–126.

36. Testa, M. (2001). Kinship care and permanency. *Journal of Social Service Research. 28*(1), 25–43.

37. Courtney, M., & Needell, B. (1997). Outcomes of kinship foster care: Lessons from California. In J. D. Berrick, R. P. Barth, & N. Gilbert. (Eds.), *Child Welfare Research Review* (Vol. II). New York: Columbia University Press; Smith, C. J., Rudolph, C., & Swords, P. (2002). Kinship care: Issues in permanency planning. *Children and Youth Services Review, 24*(3), 175–188. Because children placed in kin care are more likely to be African American, their long durations in care in part explain the large overrepresentation of African-American children in out-of-home care.

38. Berrick, J. D., Barth, R. P., & Needell, B. (1994). A comparison of kinship foster homes and foster family homes: Implications for kinship foster care as family preservation. *Children and Youth Services Review, 16*(1–2), 33–63; Burnette, D. (1997). Grandparents raising grandchildren in the inner city. *Families in Society: The Journal of Contemporary Human Services, 3*, 489–501.

39. Testa, M. F. (2002). Subsidized guardianship: Testing an idea whose time has finally come. *Social Work Research, 26*(3), 145–158.

40. Magruder, J. (1994). Characteristics of relative and non-relative adoptions by California public adoption agencies. *Children and Youth Services Review, 16*(1–2), 123–132.

41. Parents also retain the right to consent to an adoption. For more information, see: National Conference of State Legislatures. (2000). *A place to call home*. Denver, CO: NCSL.

42. The Adoption and Safe Families Act clarified the definition of guardianship to be used across states. It reads: "A judicially created relationship between a child and caretaker which is tended to be permanent and self sustaining as evidenced by the transfer to the caretaker of the following parental rights with respect to the child: protection, education, care and control of the person, custody of the person, and decision-making. The term 'legal guardian' means the caretaker in such a relationship." ASFA, P.L. 105–89, (42 USC 675).

43. National Conference of State Legislatures. (2000). *A place to call home*. Denver, CO: NCSL.

44. Weissman, I. (1949). *Guardianship: A way of fulfilling public responsibility for children*. Washington, D.C.: Children's Bureau Publication #330.

45. Taylor, H. B. (1966). Guardianship or "permanent placement" of children. *California Law Review, 54*, 741–747.

46. Alaska, however, offered only a guardianship option to non-kin.

47. Information on legal guardianship state policies comes from Miller and colleagues. In that study, although researchers attempted to obtain information from all 50 states, they were able to collect information from only 9. Although limited, these data suggest the variability in state policies relating to guardianship in the early 1990s. See: Miller, P. S., Sawsa, K. F., & Watkins, K. C. (1994). An exploratory study of nonrelated legal guardianship as a form of

permanency planning for abused and neglected children. *Social Work in the Inland Empire, 1,* 35–61.

48. This is the case in California, but California's history with legal guardianship is unique. Prior to 1978, evidence suggests that some social service agencies may have used guardianships and guardianship funding inappropriately and that home studies were not routinely conducted. In the notorious 1978 "Jonestown" incident, wherein 900 followers of the cult leader, Jim Jones, participated in a mass suicide, it was later discovered that some number of the children were legal wards who had been placed under guardianship from foster care. The incident and resulting investigations led that state to maintain a policy of joint custody for children in foster care with supervision provided by social workers every 6 months. For more information see: Shlonsky, A. R. (2002) *Relative permanence: An evaluation of KinGAP, California's subsidized guardianship program for kinship caregivers.* Unpublished dissertation. Berkeley, CA: University of California at Berkeley.

49. Welfare, previously known as AFDC and now commonly known as TANF, is available to children whose parents are absent. If the adult caregiver is income eligible, the adult will be considered as part of the assistance unit and he or she will be included in the monthly grant. If the adult is income ineligible, a partial, child-only grant can still be made available for the child.

50. National Conference of State Legislatures (2000). *A place to call home.* Denver, CO: NCSL.

51. Cornerstone Consulting Group, Inc. (2001). *Guardianship: Another place called home.* Houston: Cornerstone Consulting.

52. Testa, M., & Cook, R. (2003). *Subsidized guardianship: An experiment in family permanence.* Paper prepared for the Joint Center for Poverty Research. Washington, D.C.

53. The two youngest (ages 1 and 2) were placed with Grace in a residential drug treatment program.

54. For more information see: Shlonsky, A. R. (2002). *Relative permanence: An evaluation of KinGAP, California's subsidized guardianship program for kinship caregivers.* Unpublished dissertation. Berkeley, CA: University of California at Berkeley. Children must have lived with their caregiver for at least 12 months, the home must be assessed as safe and stable, reunification and adoption must first have been ruled out as an option, and the relative must be willing to assume guardianship.

55. Grace's experience is not atypical. Recall Tracy's experience (Chapter 3), wherein her children also shuttled back and forth from her home to her relatives,' even though the children were in foster care. Similarly, Amanda came and went at will (Chapter 1), staying for days and weeks at a time at her mother-in-law's home when the grandmother was caring for her three children. The children were equally likely to leave their grandmother's home and live with their mother for several weeks at a time. These private arrangements are very hard to detect by researchers because of the social desirability bias that emerges when sensitive questions about family living arrangements are addressed. But in one small-scale study of 39 caregivers of drug-exposed infants (11 of whom were kin), Rodning and associates found that over half of

the children placed with kin in their sample were being surreptitiously cared for by their biological mothers. Rodning, C., Beckwith, L., & Howard, J. (1991). Quality of attachment and home environments in children prenatally exposed to PCP and cocaine. *Development and Psychopathology, 3,* 351–366.

56. Grace later clarified that the KinGap checks continue to come to her, then she redirects the funds to her daughter.

57. This assumes, of course, that LaDonna does not work. If she were working, she would provide for her family financially through her wages with, possibly, some combination of public assistance.

58. Under TANF, Grace would have received funding for six children (three of her own plus her three grandchildren) at a monthly rate of approximately $1200. (She also received SSI for herself, given some health complications.) Instead, she received approximately $1,500 per month for the three grandchildren, plus an additional $700 (TANF), plus SSI. (Personal communication, Vince Tulan, California Department of Social Services.)

59. Williams, C. (1991). Expanding the options in the quest for permanence. In J. E. Everett, S. S. Chipungu, & B. R. Leashore (Eds.), *Child welfare: An Africentric perspective.* New Brunswick, NJ: Rutgers University Press.

60. Simmons, B., & Barth, R.P. (1995). Legal guardianship and child welfare in California: An empirically based curriculum. Berkeley, CA: University of California.

61. Testa, M. (2002) Subsidized guardianship: Testing an idea whose time has finally come. *Social Work Research, 26*(3), 145–158.

62. Testa, M. (2002). Subsidized guardianship: Testing an idea whose time has finally come. *Social Work Research, 26*(3), 145–158. The Illinois waiver demonstration involved 26,592 children assigned to experimental or control conditions from January 1997 to June 1999. Data were tracked until June 30, 2000.

63. Mandell, M. B., Harrington, D., & Orlin, M. (2001). *The effect of subsidized guardianship on exits from kinship care: Results from Maryland's guardianship assistance demonstration project.* Paper presented at the Association for Public Policy and Analysis and Management, Washington, D.C. This study fits into a larger, developing literature showing that family patterns are influenced by the amount of income available to the primary caregiver. See: Brandon, P. D., & Fisher, G. A. (2001). The dissolution of joint living arrangements among single parents and children: Does welfare make a difference? *Social Science Quarterly, 82*(1), 1–19.

64. Shlonsky, A. R. (2002). *Relative permanence: An evaluation of KinGAP, California's subsidized guardianship program for kinship caregivers.* Unpublished dissertation. Berkeley, CA: University of California at Berkeley.

65. Testa, M. F., & Cook, R. (2001). *The comparative safety, attachment, and well-being of children in kinship adoption, guardian, and foster homes.* Paper presented at the Association for Public Policy and Analysis and Management, Washington, D.C.

66. For more information on the argument in favor of federal funding for legal guardianship see: Testa, M., Salyers, N. S., Shaver, M., & Miller, J. (2004). *Family ties: Supporting permanence for children in safe and stable foster care with*

relatives and other caregivers. Urbana–Champagne, IL: University of Illinois at Urbana–Champaign, School of Social Work.

67. Otherwise referred to as the *primordial perspective* by Testa. See: Testa, M. (2001). Kinship care and permanency. *Journal of Social Service Research*, 28(1), 25–43. Testa borrows from Coleman (1990) in his discussion of the primordial perspective and its relevance to kinship guardianship. See: Coleman, J. *Foundations of social theory*. Cambridge, MA: Harvard University Press.

68. Joseph Crumbly captures the unique and challenging circumstances many families face in kinship arrangements, including powerful emotions – issues relating to loyalty, anger, embarrassment, and resentment – along with the tensions that can result from a shared history, conflicts over parenting, unclear roles and responsibilities, and many other issues. See: Crumbley, J., & Little, R. (1997). *Relatives raising children: An Overview of kinship care*. Washington, DC: Child Welfare League of America.

69. This perspective holds sway in non-kin guardianship, at least in California, where guardianship is ordered, but the child welfare case remains open and social worker contact is maintained on a semiannual basis.

70. Testa, M. (2001). Kinship care and permanency. *Journal of Social Service Research*, 28(1), 25–43.

71. Giddens, A. (1992). *The transformation of intimacy*. Stanford, CA: Stanford University Press, as cited in Testa, M. (2001). Kinship care and permanency. *Journal of Social Service Research*, 28(1), 25–43.

72. Stacey, J. (1991). Brave new families: Stories of domestic upheaval in late twentieth century America. New York: Basic Books.

73. Coontz, S. (1992). The way we really are: Coming to terms with America's changing families. New York: Basic Books.

CHAPTER 6

1. U.S. Department of Health and Human Services, Administration for Children and Families, Administration of Children, Youth and Families, Children's Services Bureau. (2006). *AFCARS Report #13*. Retrieved August 4, 2007, from http://www.acf.dhhs.gov/programs/cb/stats_research/afcars/tar/report13.htm.

2. U.S. Department of Health and Human Services, Administration for Children and Families, Administration on Children, Youth and Families, Children's Bureau. (2003). *The AFCARS report*. Washington, D.C.: U.S. Government Printing Office. The foster parent shortage also appears to be uneven. That is, in some communities, the supply of foster parents may be ample for children with certain characteristics (young children, for example), but it may be difficult to locate caregivers willing to serve large sibling groups, adolescents, and/or sexually active children or children with severe medical or behavioral problems. Agencies are also challenged to develop a cadre of willing and available foster parents who may become licensed yet wait for a child to be placed; agencies are reluctant to make foster caregivers wait for children and therefore are hesitant to develop a larger supply of caregivers than might be

necessary on any given day. Recruitment also must be ongoing, as some foster parents adopt the children in their care, resulting in their exit from the ranks of foster parents. Cox, M. E., Orme, J. G., & Rhodes, K. W. (2002). Willingness to foster special needs children and foster family utilization. *Children and Youth Services Review*, 24(5), 293–317.

3. Baring-Gould, M., Essick, D., Kleinkauf, C., & Miller, M. (1983). Why do foster homes close? *Arete*, 8(2), 49–63; Chamberlain, P., Moreland, S., & Reid, K. (1992). Enhanced services and stipends for foster parents: Effects on retention rates and outcomes for children. *Child Welfare*, 71, 387–401; Ryan, P. (1985). Analysis of foster parents who leave fostering. *Impact*, 1, 3. More recent work by Rhodes et al., suggests that up to 50% of families initiating preservice training do not complete the training and do not become foster parents. Families with higher incomes were more likely to complete the training; families with more psychosocial problems were less likely to complete the training, as were African-American and single-parent families. See: Rhodes, K. W., Orme, J. G., Cox, M. E., and Buehler, C. (2003). Foster family resources, psychosocial functioning, and retention. *Social Work Research*, 27(3), 135–150.

4. Rhodes, K. W., Orme, J. G., & Buehler, C. (2001). A comparison of family foster parents who quit, consider quitting, and plan to continue fostering. *Social Service Review*, 75, 85–114.

5. Campbell, C., & Downs, S. W. (1987). The impact of economic incentives on foster parents. *Social Service Review*, 61(4), 599–609; Hegar, R., & Scannapieco, M. (1995). From family duty to family policy: The evolution of kinship care. *Child Welfare*, 74(1), 201–215.

6. See the 2002 and 2005 AFCARS reports:
http://www.acf.dhhs.gov/programs/cb/stats_research/afcars/tar/report12.htm.
http://www.acf.dhhs.gov/programs/cb/stats_research/afcars/tar/report13.htm.
Some of the overall decline in the utilization of kin is largely due to the reduction in California and Illinois, two of the largest states contributing substantially to the total U.S. out-of-home care population. Some states (e.g., Utah) may still have room to expand their use of kin (see: Stewart, K. (July 29, 2007). Place more foster kids with kin. *The Salt Lake Tribune*. http://www.sltrib.com/news/ci_6491668xx); but with very small caseloads overall, an increase in kin utilization in that state or similar states is unlikely to make a large contribution to the total proportion of children placed with kin.

7. The 16% to 19% figures come from: AFCARS: U.S. Department of Health and Human Services, Administration for Children and Families, Administration of Children, Youth and Families, Children's Services Bureau (2002). http://www.acf.dhhs.gov/programs/cb/stats_research/afcars/tar/report12.htm. Generally, states try to limit group care placements, although the range in utilization between states can be significant. Data from the Government Green Book show enormous variability in states' use of group care and residential treatment from a low of about 4% in Hawaii to a high of about 30% in Tennessee. U.S. House Ways and Means Committee. (2002). *Government Green Book*. Washington, D.C.: U.S. Government Printing Office.

8. Costs in North Carolina, for example, hover around $4,000 per month (Barth, R. P., Lee, C. K., Wildfire, J., & Guo, S. (2006). A comparison of the governmental costs of long-term foster care and adoption. *Social Service Review, 80*(1), 127–158), whereas costs in California average closer to $5,200 per month (California Alliance of Child and Family Services. (2000). Group homes. Retrieved on July 1, 2006, from www.cacfs.org/advocacy/docs/grouphomefactsheet.doc).

9. Murray, C. (October, 29, 1993). The coming white underclass. *Wall Street Journal*. Murray's article was focused largely on the former public aid program for single-parent families, Aid to Families with Dependent Children (AFDC). In his proposal to abolish AFDC, Murray recognized that some children might be maltreated by mothers who had no other means of support. For these children, Murray argued, "government should spend lavishly on orphanages." The op-ed sparked a flurry of controversy, with some politicians embracing the notion and other figures denouncing the proposal. See: Gingrich offers defense of plan on orphanages. (December 5, 1994). *The New York Times*; The orphanages. (December 12, 1994). *Newsweek*, 28–32; Weisman, M. L. (July 1994). When parents are not in the best interest of the child. *Atlantic Monthly*, 43–66.

10. Since the entries to out-of-home care are dominated by very young children, under age 6, group care is also highly inappropriate for this age group.

11. Chapman, M. V., Wall, A., Barth, R. P., & the NSCAW Research Group. (2004). Children's voices: The perceptions of children in foster care. *American Journal of Orthopsychiatry 74*(3), 293–304.

12. The state of Illinois has been at the forefront in commissioning studies soliciting the perspectives of children in care. Several studies were conducted in the 1990s by Wilson and associates [discussed further in: Wilson, L., & Conroy, J. (1999). Satisfaction of children in out-of-home care. *Child Welfare*, 78(1), 53–68]. More recently, researchers at the Children and Family Research Center at the School of Social Work at the University of Illinois at Urbana–Champaign have conducted studies of Illinois children in care. See: Hartnett, M. A., & Bruhn, C. (2006 and 2005). *The Illinois Child Well-being study*. Urbana–Champaign, IL: University of Illinois.

13. For a review, see: Fox, A., & Berrick, J. D. (2006). A response to "No one ever asked us:" A review of children's experiences in out-of-home care. *Journal of Child and Adolescent Social Work*.

14. For example, see: Hartnett, M. A., & Bruhn, C. (2005). *The Illinois child well-being study*. Urbana–Champaign, IL: University of Illinois.

15. Blome, W. W. (1997). What happened for foster kids: Educational experiences of a random sample of foster care youth and a matched group of non-foster care youth. *Child and Adolescent Social Work Journal, 14*(1), 41–53.

16. General Accounting Office (1995). *Child welfare: Complex needs strain capacity to provide services*. GAO/HEHS-95-208. Washington, D.C.: General Accounting Office.

17. Farmer, E. M. Z., Burns, B. B, Chapman, M. V., Phillips, S. D., Angold, A., & Costello, E. J. (2001). Use of mental health services by youth in contact with social services. *Social Service Review, 75*(4), 605–624.

18. The national standard set by the federal government is 0.57% of children in care both reported and substantiated for maltreatment. In 2001, a total of 38 states had data available to submit to the federal government. Of these, rates of substantiated maltreatment in out-of-home care ranged from 0.02% to 1.62% [DePanfilis, D., & Girbin, H. (2005). Investigating child maltreatment in out-of-home care: Barriers to effective decision making. *Children and Youth Services Review, 27*(4), 353–374]; 17 states were in "substantial conformity" with the national standard. [U.S. House Ways and Means Committee (2002). *Government green book*. Washington, D.C. Government Printing Office.] It is unclear whether many states and jurisdictions necessarily report on child maltreatment in foster care to their child abuse hotline, thus calling into question the validity of the numbers reported. Other studies utilizing official management information systems report maltreatment rates in care of less than 3%. See: Poertner, J., Bussey, M., & Fluke, J. (1999). How safe are out-of-home placements? *Children and Youth Services Review, 21*(7), 549–563.

19. U.S. Department of Health & Human Services. (2006). *Summary of the results of the 2001 and 2002 Child and Family Service Reviews*. http://www.acf. hhs.gov/programs/cb/cwmonitoring/results/2002cfsrresults.htm

20. Zimmerman, R. (1982). *Foster care in retrospect*. New Orleans: Tulane University.

21. Fanshel, D., Finch, S. J., & Grundy, J. F. (1990). *Foster children in a life course perspective*. New York: Columbia University Press.

22. Courtney, M. E., Piliavin, I., Grogan-Kayler, A., & Newmith, A. (2001). Foster youth transitions to adulthood: A longitudinal view of youth leaving care. *Child Welfare, 80*(6), 685–718. Courtney et al.'s study examined a cohort of youth who exited out-of-home care in Wisconsin in 1995 and 1996. The sample included youth ages 17 or older who had been in care at least 18 months. A sample of 149 youth was drawn, 95% of whom were interviewed prior to exiting care (n = 141) and 80% (n = 113) of whom were interviewed about a year after discharge.

23. Numerous studies point to the elevated behavioral and emotional problems of foster children and youth compared to the general population. Heflinger, C. A., Simpkins, C. G., & Combs-Orme, T. (2000). Using the CBCL to determine the clinical status of children in state custody. *Children and Youth Services Review, 22*(1), 55–73; Rosenfeld, A. A., Pilowsky, D. J., Fine, P., Thorpe, M., Fein, E., Simms, M. D., et al. (1997). Foster care: An update. *Journal of the American Academy of Child and Adolescent Psychiatry, 36*(4), 448–457.

24. Barnes, G. M., & Farrell, M. P. (1992). Parental support and control as predictors of adolescent drinking, delinquency, and related problem behaviors. *Journal of Marriage and the Family, 54*, 763–776; Maccoby, E. E., & Martin J. A. (1983). Socialization in the context of the family: Parent-child interaction. In P. H. Mussen (Ed.), *Handbook of child psychology* (Vol. 4, pp. 1–101); Scaramella L. V., Conger, R. D., & Simons, R. L. (1999). Parental protective influences and gender-specific increases in adolescent internalizing and externalizing problems. *Journal of Research on Adolescence, 9*, 111–141.

25. O'Keefe, M. (1994). Adjustment of children from maritally violent homes. *Families in Society: The Journal of Contemporary Human Services, 75*, 403–415;

Shagle, S. C., & Barber, B. K. (1993). Effects of family, marital and parent–child conflict on adolescent self-derogation and suicidal ideation. *Journal of Marriage and the Family, 55,* 964–974.

26. Dishion, T. J., Patterson, G. R., Stoolmiller, M., & Skinner, M. L. (1991). Family, school, and behavioral antecedents to early involvement with antisocial peers. *Developmental Psychology, 27,* 172–180; Harold, G. T., & Conger, R. D. (1997). Marital conflict and adolescent distress: The role of adolescent awareness. *Child Development, 68,* 333–350; Lamborn, S. D., Mounts, N. S., Steinberg, L., & Dornbusch, S. M. (1991). Patterns of competence and adjustment among adolescents from authoritative, authoritarian, indulgent, and neglectful families. *Child Development, 62,* 1049–1065.

27. Barber, B. K., Olsen, J. E., & Shagle, S. C. (1994). Associations between parental psychological and behavioral control and youth internalized and externalized behaviors. *Child Development, 65,* 1120–1136; Baumrind, D. (1991). Effective parenting during the early adolescent transition. In P. A. Cowan & E. M. Heterington (Eds.), *Family transitions.* Hillsdale, NJ: Erlbaum; Herman, M. R., Dornbusch, S. M., Herron, M. C., & Herting, J. R. (1997). The influence of family regulations, connection, and psychological autonomy on six measures of adolescent functioning. *Journal of Adolescent Research, 12,* 34–67; Scaramella L. V., Conger, R. D., & Simons, R. L. (1999). Parental protective influences and gender-specific increases in adolescent internalizing and externalizing problems. *Journal of Research on Adolescence, 9,* 111–141.

28. Among two-parent families.

29. Children raised in low-income families are more likely to exhibit problem behaviors than children raised in higher-income families; mother's education appears also to play a role in reducing problematic behaviors in children. Although the evidence is less clear, some studies suggest that children raised in single-parent families may exhibit more problematic behaviors, and children of African-American and Hispanic parents may show more behavioral problems. Because single-parent status and ethnicity are so closely tied to income in the United States, however, it is difficult to disentangle the unique contributions of these variables to child outcomes. See: Chase-Lansdale, P. L., & Brooks-Gunn, J. (1995). *Escape from poverty: What makes a difference for children?* New York: Cambridge University Press; Duncan, G. J., & Brooks-Gunn J. (Eds.), *Consequences of growing up poor.* New York: Russell Sage Foundation.

30. Orme, J. G., & Buehler, C. (2001). Foster family characteristics and behavioral and emotional problems of foster children: A narrative review. *Family Relations, 50*(1), 3–15. Their review is extremely helpful as it is the only one available in the field assessing quality dimensions across studies. The authors readily admit that many studies are significantly flawed, using small sample sizes from unrepresentative populations. Further, several studies suffered from relatively low response rates. These biases make interpretation of the findings somewhat difficult. As Barth has suggested, respondents in these studies may represent the most committed, highest-quality caregivers; those most willing to submit to study. If so, the study findings may exaggerate the positive characteristics, painting an even more damning picture of the overall

quality of care. See: Barth, R. P. (2001). Policy implications of foster family characteristics. *Family Relations*, *50*, 16–19.

31. Orme, J. G., & Buehler, C. (2001). Foster family characteristics and behavioral and emotional problems of foster children: A narrative review. *Family Relations*, *50*(1), 12.

32. Orme, J. G., Buehler, C., Rhodes, K. W., Cox, M. E., McSurdy, M., & Cuddeback, G. (2006). Parental and familial characteristics used in the selection of foster families. *Children and Youth Services Review*, *28*, 396–421.

33. Unpublished data provided by Jennifer Ehrle Maccombe, Urban Institute, from the National Survey of America's Families (June 13, 2006).

34. Barth, R. P., Green, R., Wall, A., Webb, M. B., Gibbons, C., & Craig, C.D. (in press). Characteristics of out-of-home caregiving environments provided under child welfare services. *Child Welfare*.

35. It is probably inappropriate to refer to foster parenting as a profession, since it has no agreed upon professional standards to which it must adhere. There are no educational qualifications, and no particular skills are required of applicants. Instead, it is generally viewed as a voluntary service activity requiring minimal qualifications. This characterization, however, could change.

36. Barth, R. P. (2001). Policy implications of foster family characteristics. *Family Relations*, *50*, 17.

37. In some states (e.g., Minnesota) at least two bedrooms are required; in other states, "adequate space" is assessed on a case-by-case basis or based upon other standards.

38. These regulations may vary considerably by state. Some states may have more extensive requirements about cleaning chemicals and prescription drugs being in secured locked cabinets; most have requirements concerning smoke detectors; some require fences around bodies of water (i.e., pools, ponds, etc.).

39. Some states set the younger age limit at 18 and other states require caregivers to be 21 years of age or older; some states set an upper age limit (e.g., North Carolina sets an upper age limit of 65). Most states allow married parents or single parents to serve as caregivers. In some states, gay or lesbian couples are also allowed to provide care, but in others this remains an area of great controversy. Licensing standards for states can be obtained from state Web sites such as the following:
http://www.dss.state.la.us/departments/ocs/Foster_Parents.html#What AreTheBasic
http://www1.dshs.wa.gov/ca/fosterparents/be_FosterLicense.asp
http://www.dhhs.state.nc.us/dss/licensing/fosterhomes.htm

40. Prospective foster parents are cautioned that they will not be paid to care for children through foster care. The basic rate is provided to pay for the child's basic care needs and is not to be considered a payment or salary to caregivers.

41. All adults over the age of 18 must be free of criminal convictions and may not have had a previous substantiated report for child maltreatment.

42. Foster parent applicants must show that they are free from tuberculosis or other highly communicable diseases; other health conditions may be allowed. However, sound mental health is usually assessed in very general terms by a licensed social worker through an in-depth interview.

43. Examining data from the National Survey of Current and Former Foster Parents, Rhodes et al. found that the average length of time from application to licensure was 9 months. See: Rhodes, K. W., Orme, J. G., & Buehler, C. (2001). A comparison of family foster parents who quit, consider quitting, and plan to continue fostering. *Social Service Review, 75*, 84–114.

44. A number of studies were conducted in the 1960s and 1970s focused on foster care quality. Several of these are reviewed in: Rowe, D. C. (1976). Notes on policy and practice: Attitudes, social class, and the quality of foster care. *Social Service Review, 50*, 506–513. References to Fanshel and Cautley follow: Fanshel, D. (1966). *Foster parenthood: A role analysis.* Minneapolis, MN: University of Minnesota Press; Cautley, P., Aldridge, M., & Finifter, B. (1966). *Successful foster homes: An exploratory study of their characteristics.* Madison, WI: Department of Public Welfare.

45. Dando, I., & Minty, B. (1987). What makes good foster parents? *British Journal of Social Work, 17*(4), 383–400. Dando and Minty included 80 foster mothers from a northern metropolitan area of England in the mid-1980s. Researchers conducted in-person interviews with foster parents; "fostering officers" rated each foster parent as either "excellent," "generally good," or "barely adequate."

46. Research by Walsh and Walsh also identified a number of factors that characterized foster parents capable of caring for especially challenging children. These included foster parents' comfort with their several roles, enjoying children, strong emotional coherence, ability to handle anger, and a physically affectionate family style. Walsh, J. A. & Walsh, R. A. (1990). *Quality care for tough kids.* Washington, D.C.: Child Welfare League of America.

47. Buehler, C., Rhodes, K. W., Orme, J. G., & Cuddeback, G. (2006). The potential for successful family foster care: Contextualizing competency domains for foster parents. *Child Welfare, 85*(3), 523–557.

48. One foster mother's account of her experiences caring for children is noteworthy: Harrison, K. (2003). *Another place at the table.* New York: Jeremy P. Tarcher/Putnam.

49. Baring-Gould, M., Essick, D., Kleinkauf, C., & Miller, M. (1983). Why do foster homes close? *Arete, 8*(2), 49–63; Berrick, J. D., Needell, B., Shlonsky, A., Simmel, C., & Pedrucci, C. (1998). *Assessment, support, and training for kinship care and foster care.* Berkeley, CA: University of California at Berkeley; Brown, J., & Calder, P. (1999). Concept-mapping the challenges faced by foster parents. *Children and Youth Services Review, 21*(6), 481–495; Denby, R., Rindfleisch, N., & Bean, G. (1999). Predictors of foster parents' satisfaction and intent to continue to foster. *Child Abuse and Neglect, 23*, 287–303; Rhodes, K. W., Orme, J. G., & Buehler, C. (2001). A comparison of family foster parents who quit, consider quitting, and plan to continue fostering. *Social Service Review, 75*, 85–114; Rindfleisch, N., Bean, G., & Denby, R. (1998). Why foster parents continue and cease to foster. *Journal of Sociology and Social Welfare, 25*(1), 5–24; Triseliotis, J., Borland, M., & Hill, M. (1998). Foster carers who cease to foster. *Adoption and Fostering, 22*(2), 54–61.

50. Buehler, C., Cox, M. E., & Cuddeback, G. (2003). Foster parent's perceptions of factors that promote or inhibit successful fostering. *Qualitative Social Work*, 2(1), 61–83.

51. Baring-Gould, M., Essick, D., Kleinkauf, C., & Miller, M. (1983). Why do foster homes close? *Arete*, 8(2), 49–63; Rhodes, K. W., Orme, J. G., & Buehler, C. (2001). A comparison of family foster parents who quit, consider quitting, and plan to continue fostering. *Social Service Review*, 75, 85–114; Triseliotis, J., Borland, M., & Hill, M. (1998). Foster carers who cease to foster. *Adoption and Fostering*, 22(2), 54–61.

52. These problems, in addition to a concern that they are not respected as valued team members, are echoed in several studies. See: James Bell et al. (1993). The national survey of current and former foster parents. U.S. Department of Health and Human Services Administration for Children and Families; General Accounting Office. (1989). *Foster parents: Recruiting and preservice training practices need evaluation*. GAO-HRD-89–86. Washington, D.C.: General Accounting Office.

53. U.S. Department of Health and Human Services. (1993). Administration for Children and Families, Administration on Children, Youth and Families. *The national survey of current and former foster parents*. Rockville, MD: Author. The study included 1,400 current and former foster parents randomly selected from nine states. It is important to note that this study was conducted just before the nation witnessed an explosive growth in the foster care caseload. Small-scale studies conducted since that time suggest that the demographic characteristics of foster parents have not changed dramatically, although they may vary by community. The majority of foster parents still hail from low-income, two-parent families. See: Cox, M. E., Orme, J. G., Rhodes, K. W. (2003). Willingness to foster children with emotional or behavioral problems. *Journal of Social Service Research*, 29(4), 23–51.

54. Kortenkamp, K., & Ehrle, J. (January 2002). *The well-being of children involved with the child welfare system: A national overview*. New Federalism Series B., No. B-43, Washington, D.C.: Urban Institute, p. 2.

55. Unpublished estimates from the National Survey of America's Families, provided by Jennifer Ehrle Maccombe, Urban Institute. Another study of kin and non-kin foster parents from the Baltimore area indicated that approximately 20% of non-kin foster parents had annual incomes below $20,000 (over 60% of kin caregivers had these low incomes). See: Harden, B. J., Clyman, R. B., Kriebel, D. K., & Lyons, M. E. (2004). Kith and kin care: Parental attitudes and resources of foster and relative caregivers. *Children and Youth Services Review*, 26, 657–671.

56. Barth, R. P., Green, R., Wall, A., Webb, M. B., Gibbons, C., & Craig, C. D. (in press). Characteristics of out-of-home caregiving environments provided under child welfare services. *Child Welfare*.

57. U.S. Department of Health and Human Services, Administration for Children, Youth, and Families. (2001). *NSCAW: One year in foster care wave 1 data analysis report*. Washington, D.C.: Author. Some additional information on foster parents can be derived from the U.S. Census. Analyses conducted by William O'Hare of the Annie E. Casey Foundation suggests that foster children live in

larger households than children in typical American families, their foster parents are more likely to be high school dropouts and not to have completed a 4-year college degree than the typical American parent; their foster parents are more likely to be poor or living on a low income. O'Hare, W. (December 2007). *Review of data on foster children collected by the U.S. Census Bureau*. Presentation to the John Burton Foundation, San Francisco.

58. For a review of the relationship between family income and child outcomes in the general population, see: Duncan, G. J., & Brooks-Gunn J. (Eds.). *Consequences of growing up poor*. New York: Russell Sage Foundation. Among the foster care population, Fein and associates' study showed a positive relationship between foster parent income and children's outcomes, as did Gaudin and Sutphen's research. See: Fein, E., Maluccio, A. N., Hamilton, J. V., & Ward, D. E. (1983). After foster care: Outcomes of permanency planning. *Child Welfare, 62*(6), 485–558; Gaudin, J. M., & Sutphen, R. (1993). Foster care vs. extended family care for children of incarcerated mothers. *Journal of Offender Rehabilitation, 19*(3–4), 129–147.

59. The average foster care rate is derived from the *Government Green Book* (2004) for the year 2000 for a 2-year-old child. Based upon these data, the average national monthly foster care payment is $387. It bears noting that these rates differ substantially by state from a low of $216 in Missouri to a high of $670 in Connecticut. These figures also do not take into account special needs increments that might be available by state or locality, clothing allowances, or other specialized payments social services agencies might arrange with caregivers. Information pertaining to the U.S. Department of Agriculture (USDA) is derived from estimates of rearing a 0- to 2-year-old child in a before-tax, low-income family with income less than $43,200 annually. Estimates of the discrepancy between foster care rates and USDA estimates of the cost of rearing children have widened in recent years. In 1997, foster care rates were about 27% below USDA estimates; today they have fallen by another 10%. Lino, M. (2006). *Expenditures on children by families, 2005*. U.S. Department of Agriculture, Center for Nutrition Policy and Promotion. Miscellaneous Publication No. 1528–2005. Washington, D.C.

60. At the end of 2007, Governor Schwartznegger signed a bill increasing the base rate for foster parents in California by 5%. The California State Foster Parent Association filed a lawsuit shortly thereafter claiming that the state was not in compliance with federal law by paying caregivers too little to provide for children's basic needs. The lawsuit had not yet been resolved at the time of this printing. In January, 2008, facing a $14–$16 billion state budget shortfall, the Governor proposed a 10% cut to foster care subsidies starting July 1, 2008.

61. U.S. House and Ways Committee. (2004). *Government Green Book*. Washington, D.C.: U.S. Government Printing Office.

62. Farber, J., DePanfilis, D., & Jorgenson, K. (2007). *Hitting the M.A.R.C.: Establishing foster care Minimum Adequate Rates for Children*. Baltimore, MD: University of Maryland School of Social Work.

63. Joseph Doyle and H. Elizabeth Peters have written a provocative paper on the relationship between foster care subsidies and the supply of foster parents. In their paper, they suggest that the supply of foster care providers is

responsive to payment subsidies and that supply could be expanded in many states by increasing rates. They suggest, however, that at a certain point (approximately $300 per month in 1987 dollars), the effect disappears and payment rates beyond this amount in any given state would do little to attract additional caregivers. In 2007, the $300 per month figure computed to approximately $500 per month. Importantly, they suggest that while higher subsidies beyond $300/month ($500/month in today's dollars) might not attract additional caregivers, the higher subsidy might improve the quality of care for children. The authors do a good job of defining the "demand" side of their equation, but unfortunately they do not have data on the "supply" side. In other words, there is no database that would describe the number of foster parents available in any given state, the number of foster home "beds" unoccupied, or the number of foster children per foster home in any state; their conclusions, therefore, must be interpreted with extreme caution. See: Doyle, J. J. Jr., & Peters, H. E. (2007). The market for foster care: An empirical study of the impact of foster care subsidies. *Review of Economics of the Household, 5*(4), 329–351. To calculate today's dollar value from the $300/1987 dollars see: U.S. Department of Labor: Bureau of Labor Statistics.

64. According to Lino, the average monthly cost to care for a child under the age of 2 in a low-income family is $608. Lino, M. (2006). *Expenditures on children by families, 2005*. U.S. Department of Agriculture, Center for Nutrition Policy and Promotion. Miscellaneous Publication No. 1528–2005. Washington, D.C.

65. Hurl, L.F., & Tucker, D.J. (1995). Constructing an ecology of foster care: An analysis of the entry and exit patterns of foster homes. *Journal of Sociology and Social Welfare, 22*(3), 89–119; Zelizer, Z. A. (1985). *Pricing the priceless child: The changing social value of children*. New York: Basic Books.

66. Titmuss, R. (1971). The gift relationship: From human blood to social policy. New York: Pantheon Books

67. Lemay R. (1991). Against the professionalization of foster care: An essay. *The Social Worker, 59*, 101–104.

68. Tucker, D. J., & Hurl, L. F. (1992). An ecological study of the dynamics of foster home entries. *Social Service Review, 66*, 617–641. Foster parents often must expend additional dollars for the foster children in their care, well above their foster care board rate. See: Kriener, K., & Kazmerzak, D. (1994). *Foster family satisfaction survey report*. Des Moines, IA: Iowa Department of Human Services.

69. Other arguments include the assumption that foster children should be considered much like birth children. By introducing economic gain into the equation, the fundamental nature of caregiving is reconstituted. See Tucker, D. J., & Hurl, L.F. (1992). An ecological study of the dynamics of foster home entries. *Social Service Review, 66*, 617–641.

70. The term "emotional labor" is used by Tucker and associates in referring to the works of Hochschild, 1983; James, 1989; Lynch, 1989; and Nelson, 1990. See: Tucker, D. J., Hurl, L. F., & Ford, H. (1994). Applying organizational ecology to the family: The case of who persists in providing foster care. *Journal of Marriage and the Family, 56*(4), 1008; Hochschild, A.R (1983). *The managed heart*. Berkeley, CA: University of California Press; James, N. (1989). Emotional labour: Skill and

work in the social regulation of feelings. *The Sociological Review, 37,* 15–42; Lynch, K. (1989). Solitary labor: Its nature and marginalization. *Sociological Review, 37,* 1–13; Nelson, M. K. (1990). Mothering others' children: The experience of family day-care providers. *Signs, 15,* 586–605.

71. Woodward, C. (June 21, 2006). Washington foster parents want to form union. Wired News. Retrieved June 29, 2006 from: http://wireservice.wired.com/wired/story.asp?section=Breaking&story. Efforts to unionize in Washington State are motivated not only by a need for a higher subsidy. Foster parents in that state are seeking higher standards for education and training, retirement benefits, and health insurance.

72. Based on the assumption that care for foster children is at least a 12-hour daily activity, 7days a week (not acknowledging the work that might be required during the nighttime hours) = 12 hours per day x 30.4 days per month = 365 hours per month/$500 = $0.73 per hour.

73. Hegar, R., & Scannapieco, M. (1995). From family duty to family policy: The evolution of kinship care. *Child Welfare, 74*(1), 201–215.

74. Bellm, D., & Whitebook, M. (2005). *Compensation and comparable worth: What lies ahead for California's preschool teachers? Building California's Preschool For All workforce.* Berkeley, CA: Center for the Study of Child Care Employment.

75. In addition to health insurance, foster parents usually are not provided liability insurance. This may be a substantial deterrent for some prospective foster parents and/or may contribute to low retention rates as foster parents must absorb the costs that may be associated with children's disruptive behaviors, including damage to their or others' property. See: General Accounting Office. (1989). *Foster parents: Recruiting and preservice training practices need evaluation.* GAO-HRD-89–86. Washington, D.C.: General Accounting Office.

76. This situation thus favors two-parent families over single–parent families unless the single parent has benefited employment, including full-time child care.

77. According to editor John Diaz of the *San Francisco Chronicle,* California pays more to house dogs in a kennel than it does for foster care. He states: "Food, clothes, shoes, milk, toys, transportation, dental bills, birthday presents—it costs a lot to raise a child in California. The average middle-income parent must agree, considering how much he or she spends: $11,551 per year. Compare that price tag to the state of California's average spending on children in county foster-family homes: $6,057. That rate isn't even fit for dogs, and the state knows it: it spends $7,440 per year to house a dog in a kennel." Diaz, J. (May 23, 2007). Pay more for our children. *San Francisco Chronicle.* http://www.sfgate.com/cgi-bin/article.cgi?f=/c/a/2007/05/23/EDGKOP3ENP1.DTL

78. Various studies show that foster parents who remain in the field report being better trained than foster parents who discontinue care. See: Rhodes, K. W., Orme, J. G., & Buehler, C. (2001). A comparison of family foster parents who quit, consider quitting, and plan to continue fostering. *Social Service Review, 75,* 85–114; Ryan, P. (1985). Analysis of foster parents who leave fostering. *Impact, 1,* 3; Urquhart, R. (1989). Separation and loss: Assessing the impacts on foster parent retention. *Child and Adolescent Social Work, 6,* 193–209.

79. See: Burry, C. L. (1999). Evaluation of a training program for foster parents of infants with prenatal substance effects. *Child Welfare, 78,* 197–214; Minnis, H., Pelosi, A. J., Knapp, M., & Dunn, J. (2000). Mental health and foster care training. *Archives of Disease in Childhood, 84,* 302–306. In some states, training is still minimal, and in many, kin do not receive training at all. Barth, R. P. (2001). Policy implications of foster family characteristics. *Family Relations, 50,* 16–19.

80. Puddy, R. W., & Jackson, Y. (2003). The development of parenting skills in foster parent training. *Children and Youth Services Review, 25,* 987–1013. This study examined the widely used "MAP" training for foster parents.

81. Linares, L. O., Montalto,D., Li, M. M., & Oza, V. S. (2006). A promising parenting intervention in foster care. *Journal of Consulting and Clinical Psychology, 74*(1), 32–41.

82. Arad, B. D. (2001). Prenatal features and quality of life in the decision to remove children at risk from home. *Child Abuse and Neglect, 25,* 47–64; Hochstadt, N., Jaudes, P., Zimo, D., & Schachter. J. (1987). The medical and psychological needs of children entering foster care. *Child Abuse and Neglect, 2,* 53–62; McIntyre, A., & Keesler, T. (1986). Psychological disorders among foster children. *Journal of Clinical Child Psychology, 15,* 297–303; Pilowsky, D. (1995). Psychopathology among children placed in family foster care. *Psychiatric Services, 46*(9), 906–910; Rutter, M. (2000). Children in substitute care: Some conceptual considerations and research implications. *Children and Youth Services Review, 22,* 685–703; Zima, B. T., Bussing, R., Freeman, S., Yang, X., Belin, T. R., & Forness, S. R. (2000). Behavior problems, academic skill delays and school failure among school-aged children in foster care: Their relationship to placement characteristics. *Journal of Child and Family Studies, 9,* 87–103.

83. Lawrence, C. R., Carlson, E. A., & Egeland, B. (2006). The impact of foster care on development. *Development and Pychopathology, 18,* 57–76.

84. Brown, J., & Calder, P. (1999). Concept-mapping the challenges faced by foster parents. *Children and Youth Services Review, 21*(6), 481–495; Denby, R., Rindfleisch, N., & Bean, G. (1999). Predictors of foster parents' satisfaction and intent to continue to foster. *Child Abuse and Neglect, 23*(3), 287–303.

85. See: Berrick, J. D., Needell, B., Shlonsky, A., Simmel, C., & Pedrucci, C. (1999). *Assessment, support, and training for kinship care and foster care: An empirically based curriculum.* Berkeley, CA: University of California, Berkeley, Center for Social Services Research.

86. Studies of foster youth consistently suggest that they would appreciate more frequent visits by licensing workers and social workers to their foster parents' homes to assess quality. Preferably, these visits would be unannounced. California Youth Connection (2007). *Summary of foster care speak outs.* San Francisco, CA.

87. In 2006, Senator Nell Soto proposed SB 1335 in California, a bill to reinstitute annual licensing visits. Owing to budgetary concerns, the bill was vetoed by the governor.

88. County and nonprofit agencies are sometimes reluctant to revoke foster parents' licenses unless an egregious offense occurs. Worries about defamation lawsuits or similar hazards make county agencies cautious about the revocation

process; often it is easier to simply stop using a home rather than actually revoke a license.

89. For more information see the Annie E. Casey Web site: http://www.aecf.org/initiatives/familytofamily/

90. Barbara Needell, personal communication.(12/6/2007). Based upon data retrieved from the U.C. Berkeley CWS/CMS data archive. http://cssr.berkeley.edu/cwscmsreports/Pointintime/fostercare/childwel/prevsFrameset.asp?whichForm=&data=data&pyear=ju12006

91. Pasztor, E. M., & Wynne, S. F. (1995). *Foster parent retention and recruitment: The state of the art in practice and policy.* Washington, D.C.: Child Welfare League of America.

92. Ernst, J. S. 2000. Mapping child maltreatment: Looking at neighborhoods in a suburban county. *Child Welfare* 79(5): 555–72.

93. Coulton, C., Jill, J., Korbin, E., & Su, M. (1999). Neighborhoods and child maltreatment: A multi-level study. *Child Abuse and Neglect 23*(11), 1019–1099; Coulton, C., Jill, J., Korbin, E, Su, M., & Chow, J. (1995). Community level factors and child maltreatment rates. *Child Development 66*(5), 1262–76; Drake, B. & Pandey, S. (1996). Understanding the relationship between neighborhood poverty and specific types of child maltreatment. *Child Abuse and Neglect 20*(11), 1003–1018; Young, G., & Gately, T. (1988). Neighborhood impoverishment and child maltreatment: An analysis from the ecological perspective. *Journal of Family Issues 9*(2), 240–254.

94. Furstenberg, F. F. Jr., & Hughes, M. E. (1997). The influence of neighborhoods on children's development: A theoretical perspective and a research agenda. In Brooks-Gunn, J., Duncan, G. J., & Aber, J. L. (Eds.) *Policy implications in studying neighborhoods* (Vol. 2). New York: Russell Sage Foundation.

95. Brooks-Gunn, J., Duncan, G. J., & Aber, J. L. (Eds.) (1997). *Policy implications in studying neighborhoods* (Vol. 2). New York: Russell Sage Foundation.

96. Kohen, D.E., Leventhal, T., Dahinten, V.S., & McIntosh, C.N. (2008). Neighborhood disadvantage: Pathways of effects for young children. *Child Development, 79*(1), 156–169.

97. The approach is controversial in the sense that it is likely to draw upon caregivers with fewer resources and less social capital than what might be advantageous to troubled foster children. For more information see: Berrick, J. D. (2006). Neighborhood based foster care: A critical examination of location-based placement criteria. *Social Service Review, 80*(4), 569–583.

98. Furstenberg, F. F. Jr., Cook, T. D., Eccles, J., Elder, G. H. Jr., & Sameroff, A. J. (1998). *Managing to make it: Urban families in high risk neighborhoods.* Chicago: University of Chicago Press.

99. Chandra, A., Abma, J., Maza, P., & Bachrach, C. (1999). Adoption, adoption seeking and relinquishment for adoption in the U.S. *National Center for Health Statistics,* advance data no. 306; Macomber, J.E., Zielewski, E., Chambers, K., & Geen, R. (2005). *An analysis of interest in adoption and a review of state recruitment strategies.* Washington, D.C.:The Urban Institute; Wilson, J.B., et al., (2005). *Listening to parents: Overcoming barriers to the adoption of children from foster care.*

Boston, MA: Harvard University faculty research working paper series. John F. Kennedy School of Government.

100. National Survey of Current and former foster parents. U.S. Department of Health and Human Services. Contract # 105–89–1602.

101. Many foster parents restrict their care to children who possess certain characteristics. Some caregivers specialize in caring for infants, for example. Shortages among foster parents appear to be particularly acute for teenagers and children with special needs. See: Cox, M. E., Orme, J. G., & Rhodes, K. W. (2002). Willingness to foster special needs children and foster family utilization. *Children and Youth Services Review*, 24(5), 293–317.

102. Research conducted by Tucker and associates indicates that although foster parents may not be drawn to the field initially based upon pay—although he looked at higher payment rates that were only marginally different than traditional payments—retention in the field is probably tied to levels of payment. They show that once the hardships of foster care are revealed, higher payment rates may help to counterbalance some of the burdens associated with care. Tucker, D. J., Hurl, L. F., & Ford, H. (1994). Applying organizational ecology to the family: The case of who persists in providing foster care. *Journal of Marriage and the Family*, 56(4), 1005–1018. Earlier work conducted by the same authors suggested that payment rates had no effect on foster home openings – but again, the differences in pay rates between traditional caregivers and his higher-paid caregivers were not substantial. See: Tucker, D. J., & Hurl, L. F. (1992). An ecological study of the dynamics of foster home entries. *Social Service Review*, 66, 617–641. Early work by Chambers and colleagues included provision of a $75-per-month additional stipend for some randomly assigned foster parents as compared with foster parents with no additional compensation. They also found retention rates to be much higher for the higher-paid group, in addition to lower child behavior problems (a third group of foster parents received higher pay along with additional support) and higher satisfaction among caregivers and social workers. Chamberlain, P., Moreland, S., & Reid, K. (1992). Enhanced services and stipends for foster parents: Effects on retention rates and outcomes for children. *Child Welfare*, 71, 387–401.

103. Testa, M. F., & Rolock, N. (1999). Professional foster care: A future worth pursuing? *Child Welfare*, 78(1), 108–124. The study included five groups: professional foster parents, regular foster parents, relative foster parents, "urban foster parents" (a special group of caregivers who received a typical monthly foster care payment plus a tax-free housing subsidy and security deposit), and "sibling foster parents" (another specialized group of caregivers who received a typical foster care payment, a tax-free housing subsidy, and a security deposit that was somewhat higher than the deposit "urban foster parents" received). Professional foster parents and relative foster parents had overall outcomes that were similar. While professional foster parents had positive outcomes on most measures, children in these settings were less likely to achieve alternative permanency if they did not go home. One of the significant problems associated with higher payments for caregivers is the

disincentive to elect adoption or guardianship and therefore forgo the higher payment rate.

104. According to the *Oxford English Dictionary*, a profession is distinguished by "advanced knowledge or training in some branch of learning," or "any occupation as a means of earning a living." It does not necessarily connote an advanced degree, nor does it specify the level of payment required.

105. Chamberlain, P. (2000). What works in treatment foster care. In M. P. Kluger, G. Alexander, & P. A. Curtis (Eds.), *What works in child welfare*. Washington, D.C.: Child Welfare League of America.

106. Adoption subsidies are usually pegged at the average foster care rate in a given state.

107. One study suggests that adoption might be practiced more often if payment subsidies were increased. See: Hansen, M. E., Hansen, B. A. (2006). The economics of adoption of children from foster care. *Child Welfare, 85*(3), 559–583.

108. Scott examines the differences between natural and rational systems. Scott's work as it applies to foster care is examined by Hurl and Tucker. See: Scott, W. R. (1991). *Organizations: Rational, natural and open systems* (3rd ed.). Englewood Cliffs, NJ: Prentice-Hall; Hurl, L. F., & Tucker, D. J. (1995). Constructing an ecology of foster care: An analysis of the entry and exit patterns of foster homes. *Journal of Sociology and Social Welfare, 22*(3), 89–119.

109. The term is used by Hurl and Tucker (1995), but it is borrowed from other authors. See: England, P., & Farkas, G. (1985). *Households, employment, gender: A social economic and demographic view*. New York: Adline; Hochschild, A. R. (1979). Emotion work, feeling rules and social structure. *American Journal of Sociology, 85*, 551–575.

110. Some might argue that increased pay is likely to draw caregivers with ill intentions and mercenary motivations; these caregivers will need even more monitoring than what might be customary. But why would one assume that caregivers—professionally trained and well educated—would pose more risks to children than caregivers living in poverty who enter into foster care as one avenue to make ends meet? At least higher pay might invite more individuals to apply for caregiving positions, allowing social service agencies greater opportunities to select the most appropriate caregivers and thus screen for pure motives and high quality from the outset.

111. Hurl and Tucker refer to this as the "threshold of payment" perspective, suggesting that foster care agencies might need to raise payment rates substantially to attract individuals who might otherwise enjoy greater financial rewards in other professional venues. See: Hurl, L. F., & Tucker, D. J. (1995). Constructing an ecology of foster care: An analysis of the entry and exit patterns of foster homes. *Journal of Sociology and Social Welfare, 22*(3), 89–119.

112. Also referred to as Fisher's Multidimesional Treatment Foster Care for Preschoolers (MTFC-P). The program draws on the model of the Multidimensional Treatment Foster Care program designed for juvenile delinquents. For evidence on this program's effectiveness, see: Chamberlain, P., & Reid, J. B. (1998). Comparison of two community alternatives to incarceration

for chronic juvenile offenders. *Journal of Consulting and Clinical Psychology*, *66*, 624–633.

113. Fisher, P. A., & Kim, H. A. (2007). Intervention effects on foster preschoolers' attachment-related behaviors from a randomized trial. *Prevention Science, 8*(2), 161–170.

114. Fisher, P. A., Gunnar, M. R., Dozier, M., Bruce, J., & Pears, K. C. (2006). Effects of therapeutic interventions for foster children on behavioral problems, caregiver attachment, and stress regulatory neural systems. *Annals of the New York Academy of Science, 1094*(1), 215–225.

115. The study involved random assignment to experimental and control conditions. Fisher, P. A., Burraston, B., & Pears, K. (2005). The early intervention foster care program: Permanent placement outcomes from a randomized trial. *Child Maltreatment, 10*(1), 61–71.

116. Dozier, M., Peloso, E., Lindhiem, O., Gordon, M. K., Manni, M., Sepulveda, S., et al. (2006). Developing evidence-based interventions for foster children: An example of a randomized clinical trial with infants and toddlers. *Journal of Social Issues, 62*(4), 767–785.

117. Information pertaining to the television show can be found at: http://abc.go.com/primetime/supernanny.

118. Christophersen, E. R. (2005). Super Nanny. *Pediatrics, 115*, 1768–1769.

119. Lelchuk, I. (August 20, 2006). Mom, Dad, stop your crying—you can hire a parenting coach. *San Francisco Chronicle*.

120. Some of these issues and others are discussed in more detail in: Berrick, J. D., Needell, B., Shlonsky, A., Simmel, C., & Pedrucci, C. (1998). *Assessment, support, and training for kinship care and foster care*. Berkeley, CA: University of California at Berkeley.

121. Infants, of course, cannot be interviewed, but infants and young children should nonetheless be observed during periods of wakefulness to determine their growth, achievement of developmental milestones, and emotional affect.

122. When children are placed in foster care, judges make important decisions about them unless this authority is delegated to social workers or foster parents. Some courts are reluctant to give foster parents decision-making authority regarding children's educational needs; if foster parents were better prepared for the task, this reluctance might dissipate.

123. ASFA replaces the term "long-term foster care" with the new term "planned permanent living arrangement."

124. Barth argues that ASFA may shift "the locus of services for troubled children who have been abused and neglected from foster care to being at home and being adopted." Barth, R.P. (2001). Policy implications of foster family characteristics. *Family Relations, 50*, 16–19.

CHAPTER 7

1. Stein, T. J. (2006). *Child welfare and the law* (3rd ed.). Washington, D.C.: Child Welfare League of America.

2. Tony Maluccio has been one of the most vocal advocates for family reunification. See: Maluccio A. N, Pine B. A, & Walsh R. (1994). Protecting

children by preserving their families. *Children and Youth Services Review, 16,* 295–307; Maluccio, A. N., Abramczyk, L. W., & Thomlison, B. (1996). Family reunification of children in out-of-home care: Research perspectives. *Children and Youth Services Review, 18,* 287–305.

3. See Wald, M. S., Carlsmith, J. M., & Leiderman, P. H. (1988). *Protecting abused and neglected children.* Stanford, CA: Stanford University Press; Fanshel D, Shinn E. B. (1978). *Children in foster care: A longitudinal investigation.* New York: Columbia University Press; Runyan, D., & Gould, C. (1985). Foster care for child maltreatment: Impact on delinquent behavior. *Pediatrics, 75*(3), 562–568. For a review of a number of these older studies, see: McDonald, T., Allen, R., Westerfelt, A., & Piliavin, I. (1993). *Assessing the long-term effects of foster care: A research synthesis.* (Special report 57–63). Madison, WI: Institute for Research on Poverty. One study examining a cohort of young children placed in Connecticut's child welfare system, who were offered conventional foster care services, suggests that the majority of children improved in at least one domain of functioning using the Vineland Adaptive Behavior Scale (VABS); the study did not include a comparison group. Horwitz, S. M., Balestracci, K. M. B., & Simms, M. D. (2001). Foster care placement improves children's functioning. *Archives of Pediatrics and Adolescent Medicine, 155,* 1255–1260.

4. Taussig, H., Clyman, R., & Landsverk, J. (2001). Children who return home from foster care: A 6-year prospective study of behavioral health outcomes. *Pediatrics, 108*(1), 1–7. See: http://pediatrics.aappublications.org/cgi/content/full/108/1/e10

5. At the point of the second interview, children who had returned home had been with their parents for an average of about 4 years.

6. Litrownik, A.J., Newton, R., Mitchell, B.E., & Richardson, K.K. (2003). Long-term follow-up of young children placed in foster care: Subsequent placements and exposure to family violence. *Journal of Family Violence, 18*(1), 19–28.

7. Davidson-Arad, B. (2005). Fifteen-month follow-up of children at risk: Comparison of the quality of life of children removed from home and children remaining at home. *Children and Youth Review, 27,* 1–20. The study is particularly limited not only for its small sample size but also because the social workers completing the assessment forms were not blind to condition. The extent to which the sample can be generalized to an American population is also in question.

8. Lawrence, C. R., Carlson, E. A., & Egeland, B. (2006). The impact of foster care on development. *Development and Psychopathology, 18,* 57–76. The study is limited not only by its small sample size but also by the range of children's ages in the sample, varying lengths of stay in care, and varying ages of entry to foster care.

9. Jonson-Reid, M., & Barth, R. P. (2000). From maltreatment report to juvenile incarceration: The role of child welfare services. *Child Abuse and Neglect, 24*(4), 505–520. Effects were strongest for African-American and Hispanic youth.

10. Doyle, J. J. Jr. (2007). Child protection and child outcomes: Measuring the effects of foster care. *American Economic Review, 97*(5), 1583–1610.

11. One should hardly jump to the conclusion—as did *USA Today*—that "Kids in troubled homes still better off than in foster care, study finds. Less likely to become delinquent or pregnant." Koch, W. (July 3, 2007). *USA Today.*

12. For a review see: Fox, A., & Berrick, J. D. (2007). A response to *No one ever asked us:* A review of children's experiences in out-of-home care. *Child and Adolescent Social Work Journal.* 24(1), 23–51.

13. Advocates of "Shared Family Care" might argue that children need not be separated from parents; that children can remain with their parents in family contexts, with foster parents serving as caregivers for the whole family. While the idea has merit and has been implemented on a small scale in some communities, large-scale adoption of the model has not worked. In part, recruitment of foster parents willing to take on this significant challenge has been highly problematic. For more information on shared family care, see: Simmel, C., & Price, A. (2002). The shared family care demonstration project: Challenges of implementing and evaluating a community-based project. *Children and Youth Services Review.* 24(6–7), 455–470. Other options might include residential treatment where children reside with their parents, although this has not been tested with non-substance-abusing families.

14. Testa, M. (2004). When children cannot return home: Adoption and guardianship. *The Future of Children,* 14,(1), 115–129.

15. Team Decision Making (TDM) supported by the Family to Family initiative of the Annie E. Casey Foundation is often used with positive effects to identify relatives who may be engaged in family support. Family Findings techniques also harness new technologies to locate relatives who might otherwise be missed as individuals available to support family needs. See, for example: Binkley, C. (August 23, 2007). Foster kids' last resort: Finding the lost relative. *Washington Post.*

16. Malm, K., & Geen, R. (2003). *When child welfare agencies rely on voluntary kinship placements.* No. A-61. Washington, D.C.: Urban Institute. Malm and Geen estimate that there are approximately 300,000 children living in voluntary kinship arrangements.

17. See: Gibbs, D., Kasten, J., Bir, A., Hoover, S., Duncan, D., & Mitchell, J.B. (2004). *Children in Temporary Assistance for Needy Families (TANF) child-only cases with relative caregivers.* RTI Project No. 07147.018. Research Triangle Park, NC: Research Triangle International.

18. According to Jantz et al., seven states make extensive use of voluntary kinship placements. They include: Florida, Kentucky, Ohio, South Carolina, Utah, and Virginia. See: Jantz, A., Geen, R., Bess, R., Andrews, C., & Russell, V. (2002). *The continuing evolution of state kinship care policies.* Washington, D.C.: The Urban Institute. *Assessing the New Federalism* Discussion Paper 02–11.

19. Urban Institute. (2001). *Kinship care: When parents can't parent.* Retrieved November 20, 2007 from: http://www.urban.orgurl.cfm?ID+900378&renderfor print=1. According to Urban Institute researchers, about 20% of children residing in kinship foster care face three or more documented risk factors in their kinship home environments. This compares unfavorably with the 8% of children in the general population facing such a high degree of disadvantage.

Among children in voluntary kinship placements, 30% face three or more risk factors in their caregiving environment. For more information see: Ehrle, J., Geen, R., & Clark, J. (2001). *Children cared for by relatives: Who are they and how are they faring?* Washington, D.C.: Urban Institute.

20. Geen, R. (2003). *Kinship care: Making the most of a valuable resource.* Washington, D.C.: Urban Institute.

21. Hispanic children appear to be equally represented in kin and non-kin settings, according to the National Survey of Child and Adolescent Well-Being. See: U.S. Department of Health and Human Services, Administration for Children, Youth, and Families. (November, 2001). *National survey of child and adolescent well-being: One year in foster care report.* Washington, D.C.: Author.

22. Fuller writes about early childhood education rather than child welfare, but his characterization of institutional liberals and decentralized progressives is apt for this discussion as well. See: Fuller, B. (2007). *Standardized childhood.* Palo Alto, CA: Stanford University Press.

23. National Research Council and Institute of Medicine. (2000). *From neurons to neighborhoods: The science of early childhood development.* Committee on Integrating the Science of Early Childhood Development. Jack P. Shonkoff and Deborah A. Phillips, Eds. Board on Children, Youth, and Families, Commission on Behavioral and Social Sciences and Education. Washington, DC: National Academy Press.

24. Children suffering from marginal cases of child maltreatment should not be taken in to foster care anyway. As Doyle's research suggests, these children are probably better off with their birth families; other living arrangements with kin might also prove beneficial for these children.

25. The system we design should make sense to the average person and should fit within a framework of what reasonable parents might want for their children. If any of us were asked to separate from our children, we would want to help determine where they would live and with whom; family and close friends would likely top our list.

26. Some small proportion of children and youth can not reside with relatives or with foster parents; high-quality group care and/or residential treatment should be available to serve their needs. The key is to develop high-quality services that match the unique behavioral, mental health, and health needs of some children. Wulczyn et al. discuss this point in greater detail in: Wulczyn, F., Barth, R. P., Yuan, Y-Y. T., Harden, B. J., & Landsverk, J. (2006). *Beyond common sense: Child welfare, child well-being, and the evidence for policy reform.* New York, NY: Aldine de Gruyter.

27. Nasuti, P. J., & Pecora, P. P. (1993). Risk assessment scales in child protection: A test of the internal consistency and interrater reliability of one statewide system. *Social Work Research and Abstracts, 29*(2), 28–33; Rossi, P., Schuerman, J., & Budde, S. (1996). *Understanding child maltreatment decisions and those who make them.* Chicago: Chapin Hall Center for Children; Cash, S. J. (2001). Risk assessment in child welfare: The art and science. *Children and Youth Services Review, 23*(11), 811–830. The Doyle study noted earlier also alludes to significant differences in decision making about child removal by worker, although that is not the central focus of his paper.

28. The General Accounting Office published a report in July 2007 chronicling a number of issues relating to the overrepresentation of African-American children in out-of-home care. The report is based upon a survey of state administrators. [See: General Accounting Office (2007). *African American children in foster care*. Washington, D.C.: Author.] The best document to critically examine the issue using multiple data sources shows the significant complexity of this important issue. See: Derezotes, D. M., Poertner, J., & Testa, M. F. (Eds.), *Race matters in child welfare*. Washington, D.C.: Child Welfare League of America.

29. Doyle, J. J. Jr. (2007). Child protection and child outcomes: Measuring the effects of foster care. *American Economic Review, 97*(5), 1583–1610.

30. For a more extensive discussion of this issue see: Baird, C. (2006). The effect of risk assessments and their relationship to maltreatment recurrence across races. In D. M. Derezotes, J. Poertner, & M. F. Testa (Eds.), *Race matters in child welfare*. Washington, D.C.: Child Welfare League of America.

31. The same can be said for calls to reduce the overall foster care caseload. Some argue that 500,000 children in care is "too many" and that the caseload should be reduced. But until we know whether some or most of the children currently in care should not be there (i.e., marginal cases), we can not argue about the size of the foster care population. By developing standardized strategies for measuring safety and applying these to children and families, we may find that foster care caseloads rise rather than fall as we discover more children who need protective care.

32. Actuarially based risk-assessment scales are used increasingly in child welfare agencies to aid decision making about children's risk of future harm. For a discussion relating to risk assessment, see: Shlonsky, A., & Gambrill, E. (2001). The assessment and management of risk in child welfare services. *Children and Youth Services Review, 23*(1), 1–2, and the special issue Assessing and managing risk in child protective services (2001). *Children and Youth Services Review*.

APPENDIX

1. The voices of children and youth are increasingly captured by child welfare researchers [for reviews, see: Chapman, M., Wall, A., & Barth, R. (2004). Children's voices: The perceptions of children in foster care: *American Journal of Orthopsychiatry, 74*(3), 293–304; Fox, A., & Berrick, J. D. (2006). A response to *No one ever asked us:* A review of children's experiences in out-of-home care. *Child and Adolescent Social Work Journal*], although the methodological challenges associated with gleaning youths' perspectives on their experience are formidable [see: Berrick, J. D., Frasch, K., & Fox, A. (2000). Assessing children's experiences of out-of-home care: Methodological challenges and opportunities. *Social Work Research, 24*(2), 119–127]. A few studies include birth parents' perspectives on their child welfare system, but these are still remarkably few, and most were conducted outside the United States. See: Dumbrill, G. C. (2006). Parental experience of child protection intervention: A qualitative study. *Child Abuse and Neglect, 30*(1), 27–37; Freundlich, M., Avery, R. J., Munson, S., &

Gerstenzang, S. (2006). The meaning of permanency in child welfare: Multiple stakeholder perspectives. *Children and Youth Services Review, 28*, 741–760; Kapp, S. A., & Vela, R. H. (2004). The unheard client: Assessing the satisfaction of parents of children in foster care. *Child and Family Social Work, 9*, 197–206; Palmer, S., Maiter, S., & Manji. S. (2006). Effective intervention in child protective services: Learning from parents. *Children and Youth Services Review, 28*, 812–824; Spratt, T., & Callan, J. (2004). Parents' views on social work interventions in child welfare. *British Journal of Social Work, 34*, 199–224.

2. Diorio, W. D. (1992). Parental perceptions of the authority of public child welfare caseworkers. *Families in Society, 73*, 222–235.

3. Becker, H. S. (1970). *Sociological work: Method and substance*. Chicago: Aldine; Jarrett, R. L. (1992). A family case study. In J. F. Gilgun, K. Daly, and G. Handel (Eds.), *Qualitative methods in family research*. Thousand Oaks, CA: Sage; Yin, R. K. (1989). *Case study research: Designs and methods*. Newbury Park, CA: Sage.

4. Bulmer, M. (1986). The value of qualitative methods. In M. Bulmer, K. G. Banting, S. S. Blume, M. Carley, & C. Weiss (Eds.), *Social science and social policy*. Boston: Allen & Unwin.

5. Jorgensen, D. L. (1989). Participant observation: A methodology for human studies. Newbury Park, CA: Sage.

6. Funding for this study was made possible through a Stuart Foundation grant.

7. Berrick, J. D. (1995). *Faces of poverty: Portraits of women and children on welfare*. New York: Oxford University Press.

8. Berrick, J. D., Frasch, K., & Fox, A. (2000). Assessing children's experiences of out-of-home care: Methodological challenges and opportunities. *Social Work Research, 24*(2), 119–127.

9. Burgess, R. G. (1984). *In the field: An introduction to field research*. Boston: Allen & Unwin.

10. Emerson, R. M. (1981). Observational field work. *Annual Review of Sociology, 7*, 351–378.

11. Jarrett, R. L. (1992). A family case study. In J. F. Gilgun, K. Daly, & G. Handel (Eds.), *Qualitative methods in family research*. Thousand Oaks, CA: Sage.

12. Miles, M., & Huberman, A. (1984, pp. 230–231). *Qualitative data analysis: A sourcebook of new methods*. Beverly Hills, CA: Sage Publications.

influences, 15
injustice, 34, 85, 115
institution, 67, 83, 112, 114, 115
isolation, 40, 63-65
interventions, 9, 10, 13, 18, 20, 12-22, 24, 56
Intimate Partner Violence, *see Domestic Violence*
investigation, 12, 17, 33, 34, 54,78, 88

jail, 6, 7, 16, 18, 32
juvenile delinquency, 23,

kinship care, 7, 10, 33, 37, 44, 45, 48, 53, 59, 63, 65, 67-82

labor market, 22
lifelong relationship, 53
long-term care, 34, 44, 53, 55, 56, 59, 65, 70, 71, 78-80, 107
low-income, 13, 18, 39, 40, 65

maltreatment, 6, 8-10, 12-14, 17-28, 64, 68, 79, 80, 85, 86, 88, 89, 96, 97, 99, 105, 110, 116, 117
mandated, 17, 68, 98
Massachusetts Adoption Act, 54
mediated adoption, 62, 63, 66
medical assistance/care, 15, 18, 72
medication, 44, 59, 66
mental health, 4, 38, 39, 44, 52, 62-65, 85, 89-91, 102
mental illness, 40
mental institution, 32
modeling, 21, 32, 49, 64, 93, 103
morphine, 58, 59
motivation, 42, 81, 91, 95

National Incidence Study, 13
neglect, 3, 12, 13, 19, 25, 33, 39, 44, 64, 84, 86, 98, 116
network, 14, 21, 50, 63, 114
Nurse Family Partnership Program, 22, 23
nurture, 8, 17, 27, 49

open adoption, 61-63
out-of-home care, 20, 31, 33, 39, 44, 54,71, 83-87, 98, 99, 106, 109, 117

parent education classes, 18, 23, 31, 37, 38, 43

parenting, 4, 14, 15, 21-24, 27, 38, 40, 43, 52, 60, 89-91, 93, 97, 100,101, 104
parental capacity, 18
parental incapacity, 13
parental rights, 44, 46, 53, 58, 63, 71, 72, 103, 107
primary prevention, 19
prison, *see jail*
private funding, 19
professionals, 15-17, 22, 59, 61, 63
Promoting Safe and Stable Families Amendments, 27
prostitution, 6
protocol, 49, 98
psychological, 14, 20, 44, 63, 97
public assistance, 9, 23
permanency, 3, 8, 10, 11, 27, 39, 42-50, 52, 54, 55, 56, 58-60, 67, 71.72, 78,79,81, 82, 101-103, 117
physical abuse, *see child abuse*
placement, 14, 19, 20, 21, 25, 26, 30, 37, 40, 44-46, 48, 50, 54, 67, 69-71, 74-76, 79, 82, 84, 85, 92, 98, 101-106, 108, 110, 111, 115
police, 33, 87
policy, 3, 4, 11, 45, 55, 57, 61, 69,71, 80, 84, 106
policymakers, 38, 69. 84
Positive Toxigenic Screen, 5, 16, 33, 34
poverty, 4, 11, 17, 18, 68, 99, 100, 114
powerless, 66, 85
prevention, 8-10, 12-14, 19, 21, 22, 25-28, 30, 84, 107, 116, 117

quality of care, 69, 74, 83, 84, 88, 92, 96-98

race, 54, 115
reasonable efforts, 10, 30, 31, 40, 43, 45, 48, 49, 57, 60
recommendation, 59
recovery, 60, 63, 74-76, 92
re-entry, 40-42, 47, 55, 58, 79, 80
reform, 3-5, 69, 84, 98, 99, 102, 106, 108, 112
rehabilitation, 32, 36
relapse, 57, 59, 74, 87
religion, 54
removal, 16, 18, 20, 33, 34, 39, 43, 51, 115, 116
research, 8, 10, 20-22, 26, 28, 38, 41, 43, 47, 51, 54, 62, 68, 70, 79, 84, 89-91, 94, 99, 101-103, 108-111, 116, 117